Kripalu®
Kitchen

A Natural Foods Cookbook
& Nutritional Guide

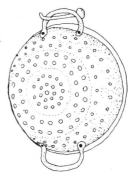

Kripalu® Kitchen

A Natural Foods Cookbook & Nutritional Guide

by
JoAnn Levitt (Parimala)
Linda Smith (Chitra)
Christine Warren (Sukanya)

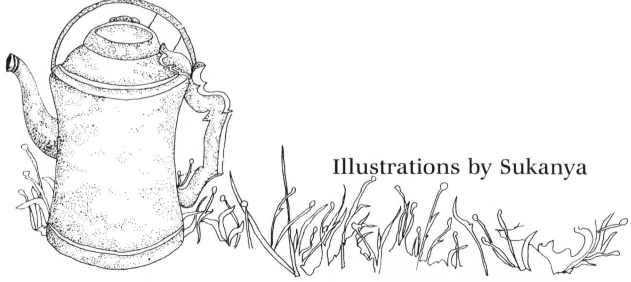

Illustrations by Sukanya

Kripalu Publications

Acknowledgments

Honing down our retreat-sized recipes (serving upwards of 200 people) to proportions suitable for the average reader was a service of many long, wonderful and fulfilling hours. We offer our gratitude and thanks to the following cooks, chefs, and faithful testers and re-testers of innumerable recipes for *Kripalu Kitchen:*

Chitra, whose centered energy kept it all flowing in the kitchen . . . Parimala, the sparkle at the ovens . . . Hira, who forgave us cheerfully even when we lost the tofu recipes . . . Nisha, who wouldn't give up on the banana bread . . . Shubhagini, whose sweet nature was her secret ingredient . . . Gautami, who gave everyone samples . . . Sunishta, who patiently tested without becoming ruffled . . . Sukanya, purveyor of unlimited pancakes . . . and in the Sumneytown Kripalu Kitchen, Narendra, Balaram and Saguna, for double-checking recipes and sharing their own remarkable specialties (from pizza to rye bread).

. . . and to all the residents of Kripalu Yoga Retreat, who for many months sampled, tested, and offered praise and honest input on the stream of recipe tests emerging from the kitchen (and who are probably sorry it has all ended.)

The work of many, may *Kripalu Kitchen* reach many more with health and pleasant repasts.

Library of Congress Number 80-68122
ISBN: 0-940258-01-3

First printing 1980.
Second printing 1981.
Third printing 1983.
Fourth printing 1987.
Fifth printing 1990.
Sixth printing 1992.

To Yogi Amrit Desai, our spiritual guide, who teaches us whole-heartedness in all we do. May these pages prove "tasteful". May all who pore through these chapters receive the benefit of your love and soulful nourishment, as through your teachings we have been nourished. We offer you these fruits of our labor in gratitude and joyful service.

Contents

A Personal Preface by Chitra, Kripalu Kitchen Coordinator 1
The inside story from one who had a hand in it all.

Origins: An Introduction 3
How this book took birth, and why.

PART I • NURTURING OUR HEALTHY SELVES

One • Eating For Health 8
A comprehensive understanding of health and vitality and the role of proper diet. Prana: the life-force within, and foundation for healthful living. Guidelines for healthy eating. Converting Recipes chart: turning your pantry into a place of vitality.

Two • Why Vegetarian? 14
Vegetarianism: social, political, nutritional, and spiritual bases. World hunger and protein possibilities. What happens when you eat meat? Eggs, fish, and other creatures.

Three • A Vegetarian Diet 18
Types of foods and their nutritional componenets. Fats, oils, carbohydrates, and their roles in balanced eating. Health-giving condiments. Vitamin and Mineral Chart: natural food sources and physical effects.

Four • Food Combining 28
Food combinations and their effects on digestion, energy levels and nutrition. The digestive process within us. Basic rules for good food combining. Quick-Reference Chart on food combining.

Five • The Joy of Conscious Eating 34
Eating attitudes and digestion. Learning to eat consciously: guidelines for practice. Affirmation to the body: a grace for mealtimes.

Six • Fasting and Purification 38
Understanding body toxicity and dietary habits. The purification diet: a body cleansing to practice at home. The 9-Day Cleansing Diet: an outlined experience. Suggested juices for fasting and their effects on the body.

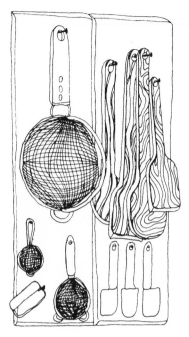

A Personal Preface
by Chitra, Kripalu Kitchen Coordinator

 teacher by trade, and a spiritual seeker by nature, in 1976 I moved to Kripalu Yoga Retreat to deepen my understanding of myself and to learn how to better love and be of service to others. I visualized myself spending hours in meditation and performing complex yogic postures with grace and ease. My diet, I imagined, would be light, and prepared (by someone else) with love and in-depth nutritional understanding.

Blithely I embarked on my career as a spiritual aspirant, having conveniently forgotten that for everyone who receives, someone is giving, that meals are not magically cooked, and that pots and pans need washing. I knew very little about nutrition; to me, being vegetarian simply meant not eating meat, and a healthful diet just meant being vegetarian. My education in nutrition began suddenly and in earnest when, to my great surprise, I was invited to join the Retreat kitchen staff, which at that time was serving 75 residents year round and up to 300 guests during large retreats. I distinctly recalled my mother having told me that as a child I successfully and consistently managed to burn boiling water. However, I agreed to give it a try, and silently offered a prayer of thanks that Retreat residents are so fond of peanut butter and jelly. If I could just figure out how to make the bread in 30-loaf batches!

For the next few years I buried myself in books on nutrition, health and cooking. What I found was a mass of contradictions and dietary theories so diverse and complex as to make me want to run to the nearest grocery store for the safety of frozen pizza and canned string beans.

During the following months, I learned a lot about diet, a lot about cooking, and most of all about myself. After all, it's one thing to feel love and joy sitting in contemplative silence or walking through the beauty of our Blue Mountains, but quite another level of experience to smile through burnt potatoes with 300 guests and residents hungrily waiting to eat them; or to feel sisterly love for my fellow cook who, having just spilled our last 5-gallon can of oil, unsuccessfully tried to stifle an affectionate giggle as I fell on my tail while trying to help clean it up. Such is the life of a kitchen staff member.

I have learned that there is nothing quite like finding out at 12:20 that the soup has fermented when lunch is at 12:30 for developing creative thinking. And little can top the requests from residents and guests, covering every mental, physical and emotional dietary need possible, for developing understanding, compassion and flexibility. Working in the kitchen, I have laughed more than I ever had in my previous 26 years of life. I have also cried more, loved more deeply and grown more into the kind of person that I want to be. And if that weren't enough, much to the relief of my fellow residents, I have even learned how to cook!

The peanut butter and jelly days have slowly given way to sauteed tofu and curried vegetables. As I have come to understand more the process of healthful eating, the sugar on our shelves has been replaced with honey and blackstrap molasses, and the refined oil with expeller-pressed corn and safflower oils.

I have pored over food combining charts and taken protein complementing diagrams to bed with me until, finally, the complexity of it all has given way to a basic understanding and then deeper, to personal experience and, finally, to creative expression. I hope to share that experience and understanding with you in this book.

I can now unblushingly and openly admit that I love to work with food, to plan menus, and to cook. But it was not always so. To become a good cook, I have had to learn sensitivity, understanding and un-wavering fearlessness. My motto is, "There are no failures in the kitchen." We just need to readjust our expectation of what the final result should look and taste like, give it a new name, decorate it up a bit and serve it with a flair. Our "failures" are often our most popular successes. Our guests are forever asking for the recipe of "whatever-we've-got-leftover-in-the-refrigerator-soup" and the carob pudding pie that was made out of the proverbial soggy-in-the-middle and crispy-on-the-edges cake. Through the metaphor of cooking, life teaches me about love, expectation, and acceptance.

Love and laughter are important ingredients in whatever we make, and hold equal positions with skill, knowledge, and creativity. "Failure" isn't as fearful now as it once was, nor does it happen as often. Cooking has become our way of learning about ourselves and of loving our family and guests, helping us all to grow step by step, mouthful by mouthful to healthier, happier beings.

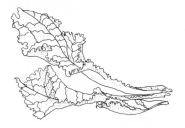

Origins
An Introduction

ripalu Kitchen. The essence of a lifestyle of caring, sharing, and personal unfoldment, this book reflects, in microcosm, the elements of patience, humor, high standards and personal excellence that characterize our lifestyle at Kripalu Yoga Retreat. A growing yoga center of (currently) 150 residents and numerous year-round guests, Kripalu Retreat is nestled in the gentle slopes of Pennsylvania's Blue Mountains. The Retreat is the fertile ground in which the wisdom, knowledge and good cooking in this book first germinated and then sprouted into a vast amount of know-how and healthful good eating. It is our special privilege to be able to share within these pages much of the harvest of our ten years' forays into nutrition and healthful, delicious cookery.

How did this book come to be? You may well ask. Most people recognize that they have a voice of inner wisdom within themselves, an inner guide or helper. But did you know there was an "inner cookbook" as well? Well, we didn't know, but we've been learning, and we thought you might want to be informed.

Once upon a time, after having answered the 999th question: "How do you make yeasted breads?" or was it, "What's in the chickpea dish besides chickpeas?", or perhaps, "How do you make such good ice cream at home?", we began to feel the inner murmurings of our cookbook. We had the sense that something else, some other presence, wanted to be expressed. Then at night during sleepytime or first thing in the morning we would hear whispers and hints: "Don't forget the lady who wants to learn the art of sprouting…" and "Two students in Washington D.C. asked for seed cheese recipes…"

The coaxing grew from within. Seeing the smiling faces after a Sunday dinner, it was hard to suppress the voice that declared, "How much longer are you going to keep Narendra's pizza a secret to the world?" Nudges would come when we least expected, or when we were the most preoccupied, as in the middle of a big feast day, making rice pulau for 500 people: "Where else can a would-be vegetarian cook learn so much about both nutrition *and* good eating?"

Who else cooks like us? Not very many people. For nearly ten years now we've had the opportunity to prepare food in a variety of ways for a variety of people with a variety of needs, all of which has led us to develop a variety of approaches. Throughout this period our knowledge of nutrition, technical skills and cooking experience has grown at a remarkable rate. This is precisely what we wanted to share with you -- the wealth of experience we've grown heir to. One thing remains forever constant in our changing lives here: the fact that meal times are times of brotherhood and enjoyment. And the reason we love to cook (and do it so well) is undeniably because we enjoy our repasts together. Our approach to both the preparing and partaking of food reflects and preserves the heart of the yogic tradition and its most important guidelines for healthy and happy living. One of the fundamental guidelines is to live fully in the moment, taking each moment as it comes. And what better way to "be here now", than in quiet moments, at a noontime meal, with nourishing fare taken in gratitude?

If you were to build yourself a home in a beautiful wooded glade, you would not begin (we hope) by collecting boards, nails and roofing materials and then erecting your home using the first blueprint to come down the road. So it is with the art of healthful eating. Our bodies are truly our "homes", for we inhabit them and dwell within their walls for all the years of our lives. And healthy, happy bodies, like sturdily and artfully constructed buildings, begin with knowledge, experience and understanding of the basic principles of body-building. Hence, Part I of *Kripalu Kitchen* is entitled, "Nourishing Our Healthy Selves", and introduces and explains the basic principles of health, diet, and vegetarian cooking which are foundational to the wonderful meals served at Kripalu Retreat. Read and absorb. Find yourself a cozy chair in your kitchen, or perhaps a grassy spot beneath your favorite shade tree, and give yourself (if you haven't already) the gift of understanding what makes your body work. Learn what you can do, diet-wise, to effect a healthier, more energetic and radiant physical self. Add intuition, experimentation with our recipes in Part II, "Food For The Soul", and the simple enjoyment of eating, and you will certainly evolve into a true Cook: one who doesn't merely toss a meal together, but who nourishes -- with wisdom and caring -- body, mind and spirit.

ust as our meals are characterized by variety, liveliness and simplicity, the Kripalu kitchen reflects these same qualities. A personality in its own right, the kitchen lovingly seems to acknowledge and reflect our mood changes and bursts of activity -- anything from the quiet stillness of early morning breakfast preparation (beginning at 4:30 am) to a pre-banquet frenzy of many cooks stirring farina in huge braziers, attempting to duplicate the recipe for shiro, an Indian dessert.

A day in the life of Kripalu Kitchen? It begins with a breakfast kitchen crew, greeting the morning and its warm smells and sights. Nisha is here, her chestnut hair twisted into a graceful knot, and long skirt swishing around the kitchen as she prepares the lunch for residents holding jobs in the local towns. Grated Jack cheese, basil, thyme, spinach noodles and sliced tomatoes are transformed magically under her skillful hands into a work of culinary love and appeal. Hira's twinkley eyes and freckles flash a morning smile, as she twists cinnamon and honey into yeasted whole wheat dough for breakfast muffins. At the sink, Mira and Pandavi contentedly sing together as they wash romaine, spinach, cress, cucumber, and radish for salad, working steadily through the bushel of vegetables at their feet. Individually concentrated in each task, yet one in spirit and purpose, the breakfast cooks move in their own rhythms of work, of laughter and talk, of still concentration, of song and discussion -- as breakfast is born through their efforts.

Three resident carpenters, leaving early for a lumber trip, poke their noses in the door for an early breakfast. Hira gives them a plateful of hot-from-the-oven muffins, the sticky honey sauce running onto the plate, and directs them to the spiced yogurt drink and sweet Blue Mountain tea brewing on one of the several stoves. Huge bowls of fresh apples, bananas, pears and grapefruits are placed on the serving line alongside the muffins, yogurt drink and tea. At the lunch-taker's window, Dipika stations herself with salad, vegetable-tofu casserole, and homemade sesame-rye crackers to serve residents going off to work a nutritious and yummy lunch, as well as her cheery smile.

Flute music gently drifts around the kitchen as the meal is whisked out to a line of hungry residents, and breakfast is served.

It's now 6:40 am, and those in the kitchen lean on counter and stove, grinning at one another over mugs of hot tea and sticky-bun fingers, savoring together the goodness of their morning service. Providing whole, healthy food which nourishes and gives radiant health to others, as well as tasting wonderful, is a satisfying experience. Before the crew breaks, they stand for a few moments in a circle, joining hands, and give thanks for the morning's sharing and creating. And in that moment, as we chant the mantra "Om" together, the joy of cooking and creating in Kripalu Kitchen provides the link of caring that runs through each one of us.*

In many ways the center of life in this spiritual community, Kripalu Kitchen reflects utility, beauty, and an atmosphere of warmth and bustle. Music is often heard in the background: soft classical, chanting, or the strains of a sitar piece. Several pictures and portraits on the walls evoke a mood of peaceful contemplation; in contrast, the kitchen mail bins in one corner are stuffed with messages, requests for extra sandwiches and reminders for "dish crew" replacements.

The kitchen itself is large and bright, with a main work area, a dish room, and an adjacent storage and work space. The main kitchen is separated into different work areas according to function. Near the huge bake ovens a mixing and bake area is set up; space near the Hobart bread kneader and the sinks is arranged for vegetable preparation and washing. There are steamers and stoves in the cooking area and a separate space for blending food and creating desserts, smoothies and salad dressings.

Efficiency and organization do not detract from the sense of "hominess" however. One entire wall houses a myriad of slotted spoons, vegetable knives, strainers, peelers and what-have-you's, while huge pots, woks and braziers are perched overhead. Flowered and denim aprons frame the dishroom doorway, through which hungry dishwashers emerge every so often to sample whatever's baking in the ovens. In the baking area, a huge bread kneader-cum-seed and grain grinder sits in dignified repose. And everywhere grains, seeds, flours and herbs, in jars or bottles or cans, give an old-country feeling to the scene. This, then, is Kripalu Kitchen, where meals are prepared and served with warmth, creativity, and home-spun love.

---

*Om is a traditional Sanskrit mantra, or sound, which embodies all sounds in the universe. Om is chanted to begin or end many Retreat activities on a note of oneness with each other and all things.

Part 1: Nourishing Our Healthy Selves

1·
Eating for
Health

Sukanya

The key to healthful nutrition lies in our awareness -- awareness of what it is that constitutes a balanced diet, the nutrients that foods provide, and more importantly *how* those particular foods are going to affect us and our life energy. Most of us in our daily lives prepare, serve and eat meals with only a very limited awareness of what effects foods have on us. Not only the food, but also its manner of preparation, the atmosphere or environment in which we eat, and the attitude we have toward our meal -- all of these are very real factors influencing our health and nutrition.

Reflecting upon the meaning of health in our lives at the Retreat, we have arrived at these important conclusions:

1) Health is our natural birthright.

2) Health equals wholeness: a harmonious functioning and interdependence of body, mind and spirit. In other words, when we are truly healthy there is a congruence between what we think, feel and do.

3) Not merely an absence of disease, health implies the presence of "at-ease-ness", nourishing ourselves in a robust manner with proper exercise, sun, air, rest, activity and, of course, a healthy and natural diet.

4) We are the ones who make ourselves healthy or diseased, and we are the only ones who can create wellness, health and harmony within our own lives.

These are important considerations, especially as they apply to our diet. When we eat for convenience or relegate low priority to adequate meal planning and nutrition, we lose the sense of ourselves as our own creation; that is, that through what we eat we are constantly rebuilding our cells, organs and body systems as well as contributing to our state of mind and emotions. Overlooking the simple cause and effect laws which apply when, for instance, we devour pizza, soda, pastries and snacks, we then question our headache, constipation, acne or acid stomach. Although these are blatant examples, there are many more subtle interactions taking place between the foods we eat and our state of health. Each of us may vary in constitution and needs, yet there is much we can learn about ourselves through diet.

Arriving at a keener understanding of the relationship between what we eat and who we are is possible only through heightened awareness, observation and experiment. At Kripalu Retreat we are a community of 150 who have carried out dietary observation and experimentation for nearly ten years; we have experimented with fasting and purification diets as well as dairy vs. non-dairy based vegetarian eating. Our conclusions concur with much of modern nutritional and scientific analysis. We have observed that imbalance and disease are often created in our bodies through improper diet. Everyday we have clear choices as to how we will nourish ourselves. In the past, many of us often chose a diet high in concentrated starches and sugars and heavily laden with protein, and the result was uneven health with more extended periods of "dis-ease" and discomfort. I myself remember even in the "early" vegetarian days at the Retreat how we tended to overload our systems with dates, yogurt, molasses, peanut butter and several slices of bread, even at breakfast. Generally, at such times I had to rest halfway through the day, and experienced a clogged nose, dull mind, constipation, flatulence and difficulty arising early in the morning.

Now, through adjustments in diet, not only Retreat residents,but also guests and health center participants experience increased vitality, fewer colds, brighter, healthier complexions and a balancing of their

their weight when following our vegetarian diet. Some residents have discovered through personal experimentation that particular foods such as dairy products and sweeteners or oil taken in excess tend to slow down their digestion considerably and create undesirable effects, such as stiffness, irritability, or a tendency to colds, headaches or the flu. Thus cutting back on excessive oil, sweetener and dairy products has brought about marked changes in physical well-being for those who have felt the need for change. Naturally, balance and common sense in making dietary choices are always of prime importance to us. Although diet is not the only factor in health, it certainly has been proven to play a major role in contributing to health or disease. Try experimenting with your own diet and you may make some interesting discoveries. The key lies in your ongoing awareness and observation of how you and the foods you eat interact.

We consider live foods, natural foods, foods which look, taste and exude the feeling of health and vitality to be essential in promoting radiant health and well-being. To understand our food choices, it is helpful to digress for a minute so that we may acquaint you with the yogic principle of *prana,* which is important to us in our practice of an optimum diet.

The thread of life common to the plant and animal kingdoms which provides our major energy for growth and survival is known to yogis as prana or life-force. Prana helps regulate our life functions and cooperates with us in producing optimum health. Every living organism is not only derived from prana but also continues its growth and sustenance through the activities of prana. And when we die, prana is the last to go.

The key constituent regulating our body's functioning, prana is a form of energy which varies in function according to each system of our body: prana helps maintain the nerves, heart, circulation, digestion, and all activities necessary for life's functioning. Alive in the workings of each cell, prana is considered the governor of our involuntary system and communicates to us in a variety of ways. Very simple messages tell us prana is at work, such as the experience of hunger pangs, or the need to go to the bathroom or to sneeze or yawn. And far more complex activities also come under prana's control: the healing of broken bones, the coordination of many life processes happening at once, the intricate process of building cells, maintaining a healthy system and destroying old, decaying matter -- all this is within prana's province. Whenever there is a need or imbalance within the body, prana is quickly at work, communicating with us when necessary, so that on a conscious level, we can do whatever is needed to allow our bodies to return to homeostasis, or a state of balance.

As prana is a form of energy at work in our bodies, we need to replenish its activities; thus we take in food which contributes its own prana or life-giving energy to us. This is then transformed in our bodies from gross physical matter into more subtle energies, producing movement, heat, thought, and activity. As vegetarians opting for the most "pranic" foods, we choose those which have been least tampered with, grown in organic* soils and which provide us optimal food value and nutrients; natural or "live" foods such

---

*We use the term "organic" when referring to the choice of vegetable or plant foods grown in properly balanced soils having rich sources of "organic" as opposed to inorganic materials (natural composting, humus, etc.) The common usage refers to plant or vegetable foods uncontaminated by fungicides, pesticides, wax or other types of additives.

Converting Recipes

Suggested healthy ingredients to substitute for low-nutrition ingredients in cooking. Note: For descriptions and explanation of the healthy ingredients listed here, see Chapter 3, pp. 19 to 27.

If recipe calls for:	Substitute:
refined oils, margarine, lard	unrefined oils, butter
white flour	whole grain flours (wheat, oat, rye, rice, millet, buckwheat, soy, barley, corn)
white pasta	artichoke or whole wheat pasta
salt	herbs, kelp (in partial or full substitution, as you desire)
packaged cereals	whole grain cereals (oatmeal, 3-grain or 7-grain cereals, rice, oat or wheat flakes)
commercial jelly	fruit butters made without sugar
table sugar and brown sugar	honey, molasses, barley malt, maple syrup
jello and gelatin (made from meat by-product)	agar-agar
corn starch	arrowroot flour
meat bouillon cubes for seasoning	tamari, miso
pancake syrup (with sugar)	fruit butters, maple syrup, honey
canned foods (vegetables, fruits)	fresh produce
chocolate (caffeinated, blocks digestive process)	carob powder
meat stock	vegetable stock
iceberg lettuce	dark green leafy lettuces
bottled salad dressings	homemade dressings

as fresh vegetables, whole grains, nuts, seeds, legumes, and fruits are our main choices.

Taking in processed, devitalized food, food with an abundance of oils, concentrated sweeteners or other additives, though providing nourishment in the grossest way, does not provide complete and hearty nutrition. These foods rob us of our own body's nutrients which aid in digestion, and deposit harmful agents in our blood stream and tissues, as well as contributing to fatigue, irritability and restlessness. This is mainly due to the fact that the prana in these foods is low or negligible, owing to the effects of processing or additives. "Live" foods, on the other hand, are glowing examples of prana in motion, since they continue to grow and partake of the life-force. Gradually, through the years, we have made it a point to reduce all processed or unnatural foods and include instead only the freshest and simplest of food products. Included here are some of the dietary guidelines we follow. In Chapter 6, you'll also become acquainted with more specific practices we use in our approach to what we call "conscious eating."

GUIDELINES FOR HEALTHY EATING

1) Eat fresh, preferably organic, wholesome foods as much as possible.

2) Avoid all devitalized, processed and refined foods, including white flour products, sugar, pre-packaged or prepared foods.

3) Avoid meat, fish and eggs (See Chapter 2, "Why Vegetarian?").

4) Avoid stimulants and depressants, such as alcohol, caffeine or tobacco.

5) Eat food in simple combinations, avoiding the mixture of diversified proteins, carbohydrates, and fats in one meal as much as possible (See Chapter 4, "Food Combining").

6) Eat only when hungry and only enough to satisfy your hunger. Complete your meal *before* you feel a sensation of "fullness."

7) Enjoy your food thoroughly, eat slowly and consciously, when feeling inwardly attuned and relaxed, and chew thoroughly.

The preparation of food is a life-giving act, a gift which you hold in your hands. As you become more sensitive and attuned, not only to the foods you prepare, but also to yourself as creator and provider, your gifts will become ever finer tools of love and health. This is a book dedicated to life in all its vibrancy. In it, you are invited to explore what it means to eat for health, for joy and for life.

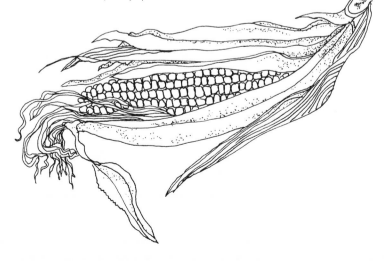

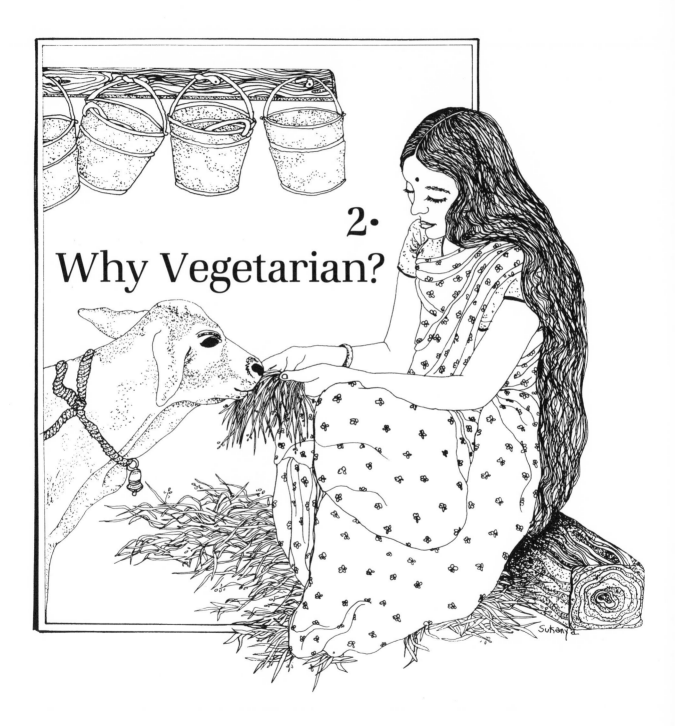

2.
Why Vegetarian?

Consuming a diet of grains, vegetables, dairy products, fruits, nuts and legumes, we are lacto-vegetarians at Kripalu Retreat, and this is the diet upon which the recipes in this book are based. There are many different degrees of vegetarianism; variations throughout the world are made intentionally in some cases, and for expediency in others.

Generally, vegetarian diets exclude meats and fish, and then vary as to their inclusion of dairy products and eggs. At one extreme are the "fruitarians" who prefer only fruit and nuts; then the vegans, whose diet excludes all foods of animal origin but includes grains, nuts, vegetables, seeds, etc. Lacto-vegetarians add dairy products to this regime and lacto-ovo-vegetarians also consume eggs. In most cases, a diet which includes a variety of different food forms provides the greatest possibility for fulfilling one's nutritional needs.

WHY VEGETARIANISM?

Living at Kripalu Retreat, we are often posed the question by outsiders, "Why do you choose a vegetarian diet?" Each time the question comes up, there are new insights uncovered. In a sense, vegetarianism is a way of life for us as much as our yogic practices, or the ideals we strive to follow in leading a more sensitive, "prana-oriented" lifestyle. Vegetarianism is an expression of how we relate to ourselves and our community, valuing the life energies we have been given.

One of the principles of yogic living is called *ahimsa* or nonviolence, an important attitude which we attempt to integrate into our lives. Ahimsa includes both physical and mental non-violence to one's self, one's neighbor, and to all of life. Thus we choose not to kill or harm animals unnecessarily and have opted for vegetarianism. At the same time, because we believe the ingestion of animal foods to be harmful to our health, the choice to eat a vegetarian diet also represents non-violence or non-harmfulness to our own bodies.

There are other reasons for turning to a vegetarian diet. Among these is a socially-conscious orientation, in which we view the world as one community. Choice of diet individually, locally, and nationally affects the entire balance of world food supply. Every day, 2/3 of the world goes to sleep hungry. An answer to the world food shortage can be derived through reconsidering, on an individual basis, the choices we make in diet, particularly in terms of meeting protein needs.

Consider these basic facts:

1) Representing 6% of the world's population, the U.S. consumes 30% of the world's available meat supply and 40% of its natural resources.

2) We feed cattle approximately 16-19 pounds of protein in fodder to derive only 1 pound of meat protein. The same beans and grains used in fodder could be directly applied for human consumption. Thus, as explained by Frances Moore Lappe, in her book, *Diet for a Small Planet,* roughly only 6% of total protein consumed by beef cattle is returned for human consumption as meat. With hogs, chickens, eggs and milk the percentages increase only slightly from 12 to 23%.

3) And finally, as noted by William Shurtleff, in *The Book of Tofu*,[2] soybeans alone produce over 33% more protein per acre of land than any other known crop and twenty times as much usable protein as

could be raised on an acre given over to grazing beef cattle or growing their fodder.

> The 47 million tons of soybeans harvested in 1973 is enough to provide every person in the U.S. with 165 pounds of pure, high-quality protein. If all of this protein were used directly as food (which most of it is not), it would be sufficient to fulfill the average adult protein requirement of every American for about three years. And if the protein obtainable from one year's harvest of America's soybeans were distributed equally among all people on the planet, it would fulfill about 25% of their yearly protein requirements." [3]

Amazing facts to ponder! As more of us become conscious of the food shortage and particularly the roles of animal versus vegetable protein, we can make an impact upon farmers, producers and agriculturalists through our food consumption patterns, freeing up more grain and vegetable protein to feed hungry nations.

Thus charity begins at home, in a real sense. It's time to put away the sausage, eggs and bacon and substitute crunchy granola, fruits and hot soy milk, providing your family with delicious, economic, nutritionally high-quality meals, that free up animal life and help feed one more starving person on a long term basis.

In addition to subscribing to these views, we have chosen vegetarianism mainly because of its fundamental relationship to our health and well-being. A vegetarian diet is physiologically highly suitable for human beings. Vegetables derive their energy from earth, water and sunshine. They are high in vitamins and minerals, and as a primary form of food, can be eaten and digested easily. Meat is converted from plant life, on the other hand, and its molecules are complex and hard to digest. While meat is high in protein, it is also high in fat. For every 5% of protein, a slice of beef contains from 12 to 18% fat.

For meat-eaters, it is difficult at times to find wholesome cuts of meat, and the question of sanitation and proper storage is still relevant, particularly when shipping long distances. In addition, many health problems are caused by the toxicity arising from the high uric acid and saturated fat content of meat. Excess uric acid is deposited and accumulated in various organs, causing such diseases as gout and rheumatism. Saturated fats cause blood pressure problems, hardening of the arteries and heart disease. [4]

And finally, because of the increasing use of sprays and pesticides in agriculture, animals fed upon products which have been sprayed tend to retain greater proportions of these toxins within their own tissues, thus contributing to a higher level of meat toxicity:

> As early as 1962 it was found that the levels of DDT in the bodies of those who ate meat was more than double that of those who didn't...Meat, fish and poultry contain 2½ times more DDT and similar pesticides than do dairy products. In addition, meat products contain thirteen times as much pesticides as the average content of grains and vegetables. [5]

Thus, there are proven health hazards in a meat-eating diet which tend to accumulate slowly in the body. This does not guarantee that eating a vegetarian diet is pure and toxin-free; however, a smaller incidence of pollutants is introduced into the body through vegetarian food. It is also true that vegetable fiber has the ability to absorb a variety of environmental pollutants and carry them out of the body. [6]

Also omitted from many vegetarian diets, eggs are considered to contain the life-force in potential; thus eating them is destructive to that potential. This is part of the principle of ahimsa, as was explained earlier. Another more current reason for not eating eggs has to do with the conditions in which livestock are frequently raised -- with hormones, additives and many antibiotics fed to increase their growth. Thus eggs may be potentially toxic in much the same way that livestock, meat, chicken, etc. carry these chemical residues.

Consumption of meat products, then, creates as many difficulties as it solves in terms of fulfilling protein needs. The amount of toxins deposited in the system, the excess fat content, and harmful additives contribute to many potentially hazardous health conditions.

For us, at Kripalu Retreat, recognizing and avoiding toxic agents is of great importance to our health. Thus, we attempt through a healthful lifestyle and attentiveness to a vegetarian diet, to balance and purify our bodies, allowing ourselves to manifest our fullest expression of health.

As human beings, we are a microcosm of the world community. The natural balance of resources, and experience of peace and harmony will ultimately be established on a world-wide basis when we have achieved and integrated these same ideals individually. Eating a vegetarian diet is one very concrete means we have for promoting health, "at-ease-ness" and a disease-free body. As we learn to eat properly and take care of ourselves, we eventually extend the boundaries of our caring to a global level.

3·
A Vegetarian
Diet

Sukanya

In choosing a nutritionally balanced vegetarian diet, our objective is to develop a diet with balance and completeness in terms of the six major nutritional sources: carbohydrates, fats, proteins, vitamins, minerals, and enzymes. Since each of our bodies is unique, no formula can be drawn up which suits everyone's needs. Experimentation and awareness, therefore, are fundamental. Our bodies, then, can be seen as laboratories, and we ourselves as the scientists, continuing through different dietary experiences to observe, test, change, review and evolve according to our needs. As we become more and more attuned to prana, our life-energy, through proper eating and living habits, food choices become almost instinctive. Until that time, however, it is helpful to learn the general nutritional principles and to adapt them to our own individual needs. The following information may prove helpful in evaluating your own diet and nutritional status.

MAJOR NUTRITIONAL SOURCES

CARBOHYDRATES

Carbohydrates are the body's fuel. Energy is released through the process of metabolism, when carbon is oxidized to carbon dioxide and hydrogen to water. We use the energy derived from this process for every movement in our body, from the tiniest molecular transformation to the most complex mental or physical feat. Thus carbohydrates are our principle energy source. In a healthful diet, carbohydrates are primarily derived from whole grains, breads, cereals, fruits and unrefined sugars such as honey and molasses.

Refined sugars such as sucrose (table sugar) speed through the digestive system and into the bloodstream, causing a dramatic rise in blood sugar level. This in turn signals the pancreas to secrete insulin to restore the blood sugar to lower levels. If it drops too low, the body enters a period of stress, causing adrenalin to be secreted, which additionally increases the need for sugar, resulting in a cycle of high and low energy swings. Products such as honey, molasses or maple syrup enter the bloodstream more slowly, creating less imbalance in the body and emotions. In addition, these sweeteners retain a balance of vitamins and minerals, such that their assimilation does not require leaching from other tissues of the body, as is the case with refined sugars.

It is recommended, in addition, that you consume only unrefined, unheated honey or maple syrup since in the process of refining, these natural sugars are heated and changed in molecular structure, reducing their nutritional content and digestability.

FATS

Fats are composed of carbon, hydrogen and oxygen. Occurring naturally in many foods, fats have a higher proportion of oxidizable elements and thus have twice the energy value of carbohydrates. Many vitamins such as A,D, and E are fat soluble and need a sufficient quantity of unrefined fat in the diet to be used for assimilation. A very small quantity of fat has been shown to be necessary in the diet; however, the amount varies from person to person. For vegetarians, no more than 1 or 2 tablespoons a day of good-quality added fat or oil is generally necessary, while an over-abundance leads to overweight, clogged tissues and a tendency toward arteriosclerosis, cholecystitis and other diseases. For many of us, a diet with adequate amounts of raw nuts and seeds and plenty of cooked whole grains will provide all the daily requirements of fat intake. Because most of us feel the need to use oil for flavor and texture in food preparation, an unrefined expeller-pressed oil or cold-pressed oil as well as unprocessed butter is recommended.

Unrefined oils are far superior to refined oil products which have been chemically altered so that they can be left out on the kitchen counter or shelf for weeks, and no form of life will grow in them. They are tasteless, odorless and indigestable by the body. Natural oils, on the other hand, need to be kept refrigerated, as they will go rancid at room temperature. They have distinct flavors according to the source from which they're derived. We enjoy using safflower oil for baking and salad dressings, and corn oil in dressings and entrees. Sesame and olive oil, when obtained cold-pressed, are excellent, and also more expensive. Soy oil has a much stronger taste but can be used occasionally with a nice effect. If you've been used to refined oils, as I had been, it will be a new experience for you to consider the rich flavors of unrefined oils in your cooking. Our recipes are written for good quality oils and take their flavors into consideration as significant ingredients.

PROTEINS

Proteins have often been referred to as the "building blocks of the body". Our cellular structure is made up of links of amino acids found in proteins. Though a vital part of our daily diet, when taken in excess, protein foods are burned up by the body as fuel and stored as fat. Because the molecular structure of protein molecules is more complex than that of carbohydrates or fats, proteins do not "burn clean" and leave toxic residues in the system that eventually clog organs and tissues.

How much protein is enough? This is a question that is not easily answered. Each of our bodies has different needs and at the same time is constantly changing, so the amount of protein needed today will be different from that needed yesterday or tomorrow. In general, 1 gram of protein for every 40 calories needed to maintain body weight each day is recommended. The average adult daily requirement ranges from 45 to 75 grams. Some studies show that only 30-45 grams are necessary daily.

Good sources of proteins are dairy products, soy products, nutritional yeast, sprouts, whole grains, nuts, seeds, legumes and vegetables themselves. Surprising as it may seem, it is actually difficult not to overeat protein on a vegetarian diet rather than being in danger of getting too little, since so many vegetarian foods are good protein sources.

Combining certain foods is helpful for obtaining maximum protein potential. All proteins are made up of amino acids. Amino acids are necessary for our bodies' use; of these, only eight cannot be manufactured by the body. These are called essential amino acids, because we need to acquire them daily in our diet. Foods which contain all eight of these essential amino acids in proper proportions are called complete proteins; those which are missing one or more of the amino acids are called incomplete proteins. By combining together foods which are high in opposing amino acids, a proper balance can be established, resulting in a greater quantity of usable protein. See the Complementary Protein chart (page 21) for examples.

Complementary Proteins

Food Combinations which provide high-protein, with some suggested dishes. To achieve the proper complete protein balance of amino acids as discussed in this chapter, use the foods given in the ratios suggested (ratios refer to uncooked amounts). The dishes suggested here utilize this amino-acid, high-protein ratio and are all found in this cookbook (see index).

DAIRY (1 PART) AND GRAINS (2-3 PARTS)

Narendra's Knockout Pizza

Macaroni & Cheese

Pizza Bulgar, with any baked carrot dish and milk

Crunchy Granola with milk or soymilk

Homemade Ice Cream with any whole wheat cookie

Happy Apple Muffins and Yogurt or Milk drink

Raisin and Rice Pudding

RICE (2-3 PARTS) AND SESAME PRODUCTS (1 PART)

Brown rice with toasted sesame seeds

Rice Pulau with Garden Salad and any tahini-based dressing

GRAINS (2-3 PARTS) AND LEGUMES (1 PART)

Country-style Cornbread and Hira's Multi-bean soup

Tacos and Taco Bean Filling

Brown rice and Feast of Wok veggies, with tofu chunks

Mala-Bean Dip and Whole Wheat Sesame Crackers

Peanut Butter Cookies

SEEDS (1-2 PARTS) AND LEGUMES (1 PART)

Chickpea Patties with Tahini Sauce

Peanut Butter-Tahini Spread with toasted sunflower seeds mixed in

DAIRY (2 PARTS) AND LEGUMES (1 PART)

Soyburgers topped with melted cheese

High-Protein drink

Banana-Peanut Froth

NOTE: All soy products, all dairy products, avocadoes, and brown rice contain complete high-proteins with all the essential amino acids. When eaten in combination with grains, legumes, seeds, etc. as suggested above, they also complete the amino acid balance in the combined food, greatly increasing the protein yield of the meal.

Apart from combining foods for high-quality protein, there are many independently complete proteins in a vegetarian diet. Soy foods are an excellent example. Containing all of the essential amino acids, they are low in fat, carbohydrate and cholesterol, making them an excellent diet food. Non-mucus forming, they can be used to make a milk replacement for cow's milk in any recipe. Those with allergies to dairy foods often find soy an easy-to-digest, nutritious and enjoyable alternative. We have found soy products, particularly soybeans, soy cheese, tofu, soymilk and ice cream, extremely versatile and palatable high-quality protein sources in our diet.

VITAMINS AND MINERALS

Vitamins and minerals are used as catalysts for many important chemical reactions in the body and contribute to all aspects of metabolism and growth. They are found abundantly in all fresh fruits and vegetables and sprouts as well as in whole grains and legumes. Fresh vegetable and fruit juices are an especially delectable and nutritious source. (See Chapter 6 on Purification for more detail.) On the following page is a table of the most common vitamins and minerals, with a description of their use in the body as well as a list of foods in which they are found in greatest abundance.

I am often asked in nutritional workshops about the value of using packaged vitamins. My response is that the healthy body can obtain all the vitamins and minerals it needs from pure foods grown in good soil. However, most of us do not have completely healthy bodies, nor have we necessarily derived optimum nutrition from the type of foods we have chosen to eat. In most cases, I prefer recommending the use of natural food sources to derive balanced nutrition. However, in more extreme circumstances, organic vitamin supplements can also be helpful.

ENZYMES

The body uses enzymes, tiny protein substances, for the breakdown of all foods and their transformation into usable substances. In fact, for nearly all reactions within the cells, some special enzyme is needed. Foods such as yogurt or tempeh[2], wheatgrass, rejuvelac[3], sprouts and miso are particularly excellent sources of enzymes. Thirty percent of the dry weight in our colon is made up of bacteria and other micro-organisms. The kind of foods that we eat determines whether we nourish helpful or harmful bacteria in our system. Enzyme foods nourish and help to propogate those bacteria which are most helpful to us in carrying on life activities, while discouraging the growth of their harmful counterparts.

We use our condiment table to supply our family with many extra vitamins, minerals and enzymes. The following list contains a description of many of the regular items we use to supplement our diet, which are referred to throughout this book. Especially note nutritional yeast; we use a special good-tasting variety which gives a pleasant flavor. In using the recipes given in this book, it is important not to use usual bitter-tasting nutritional or brewer's yeast, or the taste of the food will be changed.

HIGH-NUTRITION FOOD SUPPLEMENTS

APPLE CIDER VINEGAR

Particularly high in potassium and Vitamin C, apple cider vinegar is known for its versatility in toning, cleansing and rejuvenating many parts of our bodily system. When taken ½-hour before meals in a cup of warm water and honey, it stimulates and improves digestion. We keep it on the condiment table to be used on sprouts, salad and vegetables. In the summer it's a thirst-quenching drink: add a tablespoon each of vinegar and honey to a cup of cold water and you have an old-time farmers' drink called "switchel".

BLACKSTRAP MOLASSES

Less sweet and somewhat stronger in taste than lighter molasses, blackstrap molasses is high in calcium, iron and potassium and is an excellent source of B-complex vitamins. High in many trace vitamins and minerals, molasses is also helpful in regulating the bowels, particularly when taken in hot water with a tablespoon of lemon juice upon arising. We mix our blackstrap with a lighter molasses and serve it with yogurt, fruit dishes, beverages and cereals as well as in baked products, muffins and pies. It's less expensive than honey and has a stronger sweetening power.

BRAN

Bran is the outer coating of the wheat berry, the edible kernel of the wheat plant. It's high in protein, phosphorous, potassium, B-vitamins and iron. Because of its high roughage make-up, bran is a valuable help in proper elimination. Add it to baked goods or sprinkle on salads or yogurt; a good balance in baking is approximately one tablespoon of bran per cup of flour. One to two teaspoons is good for salad, yogurt or your entree. Bran is an excellent and inexpensive source of good nutrition.

CAYENNE

Cayenne is similar in taste to hot pepper and is usually purchased as a red powder. Non-irritating to the system, it is a stimulant which gives tone to the circulation, increases appetite, stimulates the secretion of saliva, and aids in digestion. It is also useful in building a strong heart. Use it as a spice in dressings, chilis, soups, and curry dishes. We find cayenne to be a particularly valuable condiment in the winter time as it warms us up from the inside out on cold, snowy days; it also has the ability to break up mucus in the system. It's a nice addition to a cup of hot lemon water when a cold starts to set in. Retreat residents are fond of adding it to orange juice for an energy lift, and for help in purifying the body.

CLOVES

Clove is an antiseptic and germicide for the system. When chewed or taken as a tea, it can help to relieve nausea; also, oil of clove helps relieve the pain of a toothache. We place a bowl of cloves on our condiment table, Indian style, primarily as breath fresheners; they're soothing and leave the mouth feeling clean and fresh.

FENNEL SEEDS

Used in much the same way as cloves, fennel seeds are an aid to digestion, relieving flatulence, and when chewed, leave the breath sweet. This is also an Indian custom.

GOMASIO

A nutritious alternative to plain salt, gomasio is prepared by toasting sesame seeds and blending or grinding them with sea salt. We avoid commercial salts, since they lack the nutrients due to refinement and also may have sugar added to make them pour smoothly. A tasty condiment for soups and salads,

Vitamins and Minerals:
Effects and Natural Sources

Vitamins	Effects on the Body	Natural Sources
A	helps fight infection, used in tissue repair, aids night vision.	milk, apricots, spinach, carrots, green and yellow fruits and vegetables.
B-complex	maintenance of muscle tone, aids metabolism. Essential for energy production in cells.	nutritional yeast, whole grains, blackstrap molasses
B-12	aids blood cell formation, promotes healthy nervous system, aids metabolism.	dairy products, some nutritional yeast has B-12 added (check labels), tempeh
C	aids digestion, bone and tooth formation, red blood cell formation and aids blood vessel repair; helps fight infection, and insulates the system against shock.	citrus fruit, peppers, broccoli, dark leafy greens
D	maintains healthy nervous system, aids bone formation and blood clotting.	dairy products, sunflower seeds, sunlight (to assimilate Vitamin D after sun exposure, do not wash off for 2 hrs. following exposure. The oils on the skin are needed to "collect" the sun's Vitamin D and then reabsorb it into the skin afterwards.)
E	maintains healthy nerves and muscles, reduces blood cholesterol, strengthens capillary walls, aids fertility.	dark green vegetables, wheat germ, vegetable oils, tomatoes, peanuts, oatmeal
F	normalizes blood pressure, lowers cholesterol, helps blood coagulate.	wheat germ, sunflower seeds, vegetable oils

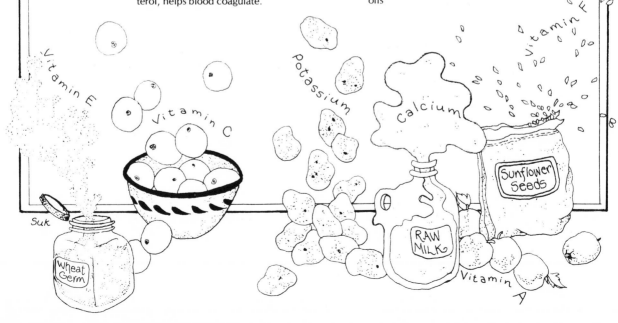

Vitamins and Minerals:
Effects and Natural Sources

Minerals	Effects on the Body	Natural Sources
Calcium	used in forming teeth and bones; nerve tranquilizer; aids muscle growth and blood clot formation.	dairy products, molasses, dark leafy grains, almonds, sunflower seeds
Copper	aids red blood cell formation, body healing processes, bone formation, and hair and skin color	molasses, legumes, raisins
Iodine	aids metabolism, physical and mental development, and energy level, thyroid function.	kelp, iodized salt
Magnesium	aids metabolism, and the acid-alkaline balance in the body.	green vegetables, honey, bran, kelp, nuts
Phosphorous	aids cell growth and metabolism, aids bone and tooth formation and kidney functioning.	grains, dairy products, carob, wheat germ
Potassium	helps regulate growth; acts as a nerve tranquilizer; regulates heart beat.	bananas, potatoes, sunflower seeds, figs, dates, raisins, blackstrap molasses, peanuts, peaches, tomatoes, apricots
Sodium	helps maintain cellular fluid level, muscle contraction.	dairy products, salt
Zinc	aids reproductive and sex organ growth and development, aids proper metabolism, and wound and burn healing.	sunflower seeds, soybeans, nutritional yeast, spinach
Iron	aids in resisting stress and disease and hemoglobin production	wheat germ, blackstrap molasses, raisins, eggplant, endive

gomasio contains sesame seeds, which themselves are a very concentrated form of protein, and are high also in calcium, iron, phosphorous and niacin.

KELP

Kelp is a powdered seaweed product. It yields a liberal supply of iodine, which is beneficial to the thyroid gland. It contains up to 22 amino acids, 12 different vitamins and 40 minerals. Kelp stimulates glandular secretion and helps to maintain a balanced acid-alkaline base in the body. We like to keep a shaker of powdered kelp on our salad table and also enjoy its added flavor sprinkled on crackers and added to soups.

LEMON JUICE

Found at all meals on our condiment table, lemon juice is purifying to the entire system. It is a stimulant to the liver and intestines, helping to cleanse and tone the digestive system. Many of us enjoy a glass of warm lemon water and either honey or molasses first thing in the morning, to purify the liver and the system in general. We also like it on salad. Sprinkle lemon juice on cut fruits to prevent discoloration if you have to prepare them in advance.

MISO

Miso is a fermented soybean mash. It's high in protein and minerals and easy to digest. Containing acidophilus bacteria (as in yogurt), it aids in maintaining healthy intestinal flora. We like to use it in dips and dressings and as a soup base. Miso comes in a variety of strengths. Brown rice miso is one of the lightest and mildest and can be used as a spread on bread or crackers.

NUTRITIONAL YEAST (BREWER'S YEAST)

This is a staple in our diet. An excellent source of protein and B-vitamins, nutritional yeast is easily digested and contains all of the essential amino acids. The kind we use is Saccavomyces cerevisiae, a food yeast grown in a molasses solution. We love its cheesy taste and use it liberally on salads, vegetables, and in soups. It is an excellent source of thiamin, niacin and riboflavin. Be careful when you go to purchase nutritional yeast, as it has been our experience that many brands have bitter, unpleasant flavors which will change the taste of your recipes considerably. (Our own good-tasting yeast is available through our shop. ½ lb. costs $1.59. Write us to order.)

TAMARI

Tamari (soy sauce) is a fermented soybean mash similar to miso. It's lighter in taste and liquid in consistency. It's one of our most frequently used seasonings. We keep a container on our condiment table for those who like its salty taste, and we use it in cooking many vegetable and soup dishes.

WHEAT GERM

Wheat germ is part of the outer layer of the wheat kernel. It is rich in B-vitamins, Vitamin E, and minerals. It has a high fiber content and is a good quality protein. Because of its high oil content, wheat germ can quickly go rancid. It should be stored in a cool, dry place and eaten as fresh as possible. We like to use it as a topping for desserts, salads, and yogurt or as an addition to many cereals, breads and grain dishes.

4.
Food
Combining

"A loaf of bread, a piece of cheese, a jug of wine and thou..." The perfect combination for happiness and fulfillment, right? Well, truthfully, it may be a combination for intestinal gas. For most of us, in choosing what we eat, are more often governed by habit and desire, than by the true needs of our body. For example, our body may feel the need for nourishment, perhaps specifically for protein; however it is our personal desires that lead us to believe the only way to satisfy that need is through a cheese sandwich and a bottle of wine. The result is that the body's original message is altered by our associations with food choices of the past. The more we confuse these messages that the body offers us, the more we become the authors of our own "dis-at-easeness" and physical imbalance. However, it takes some practice (and physical purification) to be able to respond to the body's true needs...something we're all learning ongoingly. The key, here as elsewhere, is trial and error, an attitude of openness and heightened awareness about the effects of our own eating habits.

Proper food combining, a much-disputed topic in nutritional circles, is nevertheless fundamental to sensible eating, and has scientific support in terms of the digestive process as well as the validation of our own practical experience. Here, as in other instances, we provide you the building materials and foundation for food combining; whatever "structure" you might build in terms of diet is best derived through integrating your own needs, experience and dietary awareness with this information. The first step is always a return to awareness and observation: how have certain food combinations affected you?

Consider, for example, what happens to you after eating a concentrated starch and protein combination such as lasagna, or ravioli. Do you perhaps feel tired or lethargic or experience that "too-full" feeling? These foods take longer to be digested and demand more energy to be processed than simpler foods. As a result, most of our energy is concentrated in the digestive system for several hours after eating them. A piece of fruit or fresh salad, in contrast, is digested quickly. After eating them, you may often feel energetic and refreshed. The way you feel after eating indicates your body's message to you about the kinds of food you have chosen to ingest and their combination. And of course the quantity of food you eat is equally if not more important than the quality of combinations.

In order to better understand some of the body's messages, it is helpful to know more about the digestive process. The process of digestion begins with the senses. As we see and smell the food we are about to eat, our body organs biochemically prepare to receive the nourishment. As the food enters the mouth, enzymes in the saliva begin breaking down starches; traveling down the esophagus into the stomach, the food is further broken down by enzymes secreted there and in the intestines.

The digestive process extends over 20 feet of body tissue and is intricately timed to allow every type of food to be broken down and utilized to maximum potential for the body's energy and health. When we eat moderately and simply, the body is able to perform its digestive function efficiently. Problems begin, however, when we eat processed foods, too many foods, or foods in improper combination. These substances cause undue strain on the digestive organs and leave toxic residues in the body. Eating a multiplicity of foods at once slows the digestive process and may cause discomfort, flatulence, fatigue, or irritability. Although many of us have experienced these symptoms from time to time, because of lack of awareness we have failed to associate them with the appropriate cause. Now is the time to increase your own awareness.

Consider the example of a cheese sandwich. First of all, the body beings the digestion of starch in the alkaline medium of the mouth. If we eat a starch such as bread with an acid food, such as a tomato, the enviornment of the mouth becomes acid rather than alkaline and the starch enzyme, ptyalin, is inhibited from working effectively. Suppose that the bread and tomato are joined by a nice thick piece of cheese. Cheese is a concentrated protein, and needs an acid environment in which to begin its digestion in the stomach. When we eat cheese the stomach secretes hydrochloric acid and enzymes to break it down into amino acid chains. Meanwhile, the bread, needing a more alkaline environment, is totally inhibited by the large quantitles of hyrodchloric acid. Had we eaten the bread alone, the body would not have secreted much acid, and the enzymes secreted in the mouth for starch digestion would have continued to be active in the stomach. Let's follow our cheese sandwich a little further. If we have chewed it well, the enzymes all along the digestive tract will have been able to attack small particles of the food. If we have eaten it quickly, swallowing large pieces, the enzymes will only be able to attack and break down the periphery of the food, leaving the middle undigested. As the food is churned in the stomach, it will not be digested thoroughly. Reaching the entranceway of the duodenum, it may be squirted back for further processing. If allowed to pass out of the stomach into the small intestine, the food matter will be welcomed with digestive enzymes from the liver, gall bladder and pancreas. This is where the final breakdown of the foods occurs.

The more foods that we have eaten in combination, the more we have overeaten, and the less thoroughly that we have chewed the food, the more work there is to do -- by all of the organs along the digestive tract. This is precisely what gives rise to feelings of gastric upset, constipation, colitis, lethargy, and a whole host of disturbances related to digestion and assimilation. The message from our body is that we're overtaxing our system; it's time to slow down and take a good look at our diet.

GUIDELINES FOR FOOD COMBINING

Although each person's body and digestive process is unique, there are basic guidelines for food combination that help our systems work with maximum ease and efficiency. Use these as aids to formulate your own dietary planning, as well as a basis for further observation and fact-gathering about your eating habits.

1. Fruits can be classified into three categories: acid, subacid, and sweet. Fruits in these categories are best eaten separately, although sub-acid and sweet fruits can be combined with minimal strain on the system. Acid fruits include oranges, grapefruits, or other citrus; sub-acid are pears or apples, and sweet fruits include bananas, dates, etc.

2. When combined together, proteins and starches remain longer in the digestive system than they do if eaten separately, often times giving rise to putrefaction and gas. They require different acid-alkaline mediums for digestion and inhibit each others' enzyme action.

3. Fats and proteins are a poor food combination. Fats create a depressing effect on the digestive system by lowering the amount of pepsin and hydrochloric acid that is secreted. So, if a protein and a fat are eaten together, the protein foods stay in the system for an over-extended period of time, again giving rise to putrefaction and gas.

4. Sugars are digested only in the small intestine. When eaten alone, sugar goes quickly through the system. When taken with a starch or a protein, the sugar is held up in the stomach, causing fermentation. Sugar also has a depressing effect on the flow of gastric juices.

5. Concentrated proteins, when eaten together, cause internal disturbance, as the timing of digestive secretions is different for each type of protein. Although the strongest acid-enzyme secretion is emitted in the last hour of the digestion of milk, it is needed at other times for cheese, nuts, and other protein foods. When eaten in combination, the enzyme secretions cannot be timed as effectively for all of the foods.

6. Acid foods such as oranges, grapefruits, or pineapples, are best not eaten in combination with starches or proteins. They create a depressing effect on the enzyme secretions for both starches and proteins. The acid inactivates both ptyalin (used in starch digestion) and pepsin (used in protein digestion).

7. Melons should be eaten alone, as they decompose very quickly.

8. The drinking of liquids dilutes and inhibits the flow of digestive juices. Liquids are best taken ½ to 1 hour before, or one or two hours after eating a meal.

9. Avocados combine best with fruit, tomatoes, green vegetables or sprouts.

10. Green leafy vegetables aid in fat and protein digestion.

11. Good food combinations include:

   a. proteins and vegetables
   b. starches and vegetables
   c. sweet and sub-acid fruits
   d. any simple food taken alone

One additional note for your awareness: although we propose the above food-combining rules to you, they are meant as *guidelines,* not as hard and fast rules. You will encounter among our recipes some foods, such as the inevitable "cheese sandwich", which contradict these combining rules. This does not mean that because we have these principles, we completely avoid such foods; it means only that we try eating as simply as possible and are aware that the more complex the food combination, the more difficult its digestion for us. There is no dogma attached, just good common sense and the dictates of your personal experience. See which guidelines make the most sense for your own system. And above all, enjoy your meals thoroughly!

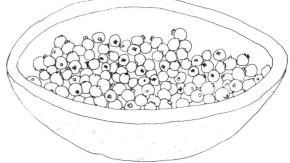

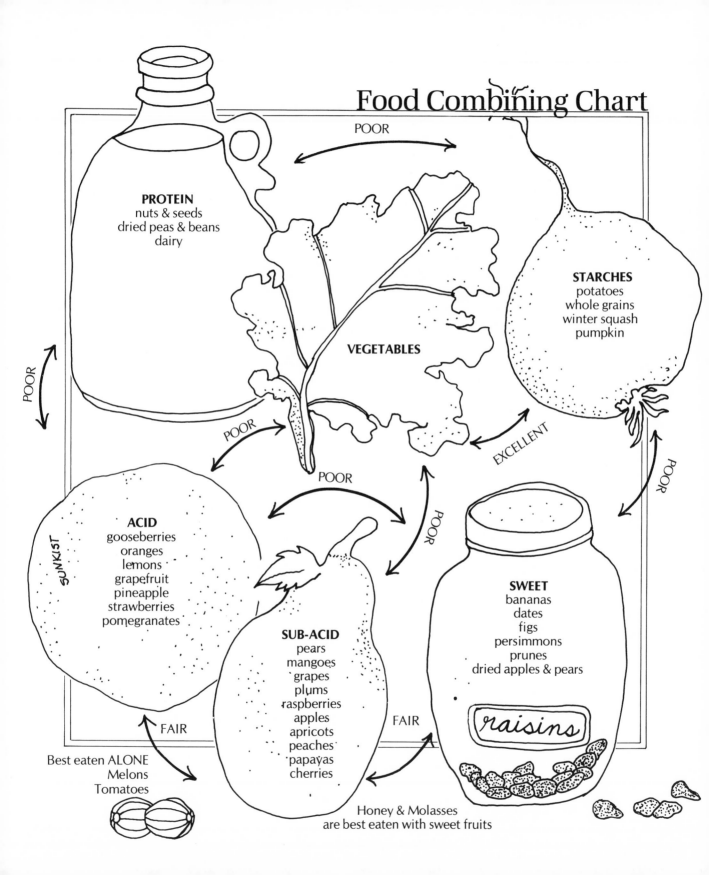

Food Combining Chart

POOR

PROTEIN
nuts & seeds
dried peas & beans
dairy

STARCHES
potatoes
whole grains
winter squash
pumpkin

POOR

VEGETABLES

POOR

POOR

POOR

EXCELLENT

POOR

POOR

SUNKIST

ACID
gooseberries
oranges
lemons
grapefruit
pineapple
strawberries
pomegranates

SUB-ACID
pears
mangoes
grapes
plums
raspberries
apples
apricots
peaches
papayas
cherries

SWEET
bananas
dates
figs
persimmons
prunes
dried apples & pears

raisins

FAIR

FAIR

Best eaten ALONE
Melons
Tomatoes

Honey & Molasses
are best eaten with sweet fruits

5·
The Joy
of Conscious Eating

Thus far, we've discussed what to eat, in what combination to eat it, and how different foods affect us on all levels of our being. Equally important and often a greater challenge to us is the question: *how* do we eat? How much and in what manner must we eat to ultimately derive the greatest nourishment and satisfaction?

This is not an easy question to answer, as each of us has varying physical, mental and emotional needs, and even our individual requirements vary from day to day. Because we have acquired improper habits, often eating inadequately or excessively, it is difficult to listen to our body's inner wisdom or prana and assume its messages will be clear. However, there are simple steps to take in order to begin eating more wisely, and as mentioned before, the key lies in developing keener awareness and responsibility for our eating patterns. With conscious eating as the tool, moderation in diet is often the outcome.

Just what is conscious eating? Very simply, it's an approach to eating in which you: 1) take your food in silence, 2) concentrate all your senses and awareness on the process of eating, 3) eat slowly and chew thoroughly, and 4) adapt an attitude of thankfulness and reverence toward the food you receive.

At the Retreat, meals are a time of enjoyment as well as attentive consciousness. Our breakfasts and lunches (the noon meal is our main meal) are taken together in silence, allowing us to concentrate our full attention on eating. Free from the distractions of reading, talking or listening to music or T.V., at silent mealtimes we nonverbally share together in a quiet meditative experience. It's a welcome time for tuning in to the experience of eating itself -- savoring the foods and sensations while eating, rejuvenating and relaxing ourselves before going on to our next round of activities. At supper, a lighter meal consisting of salads or fruits, there is sharing or talking among the residents in a more informal way, and yet, so often the experience of silent eating quietly carries over even at this "talking permitted" meal time. Once you've experienced stillness at meals, excessive noise, chatter or activity are uncomfortable diversions from totally enjoying and tasting your food.

Part of the training guests at our Health Center receive is learning to eat in this conscious way. They have shared with astonishment the experience of really tasting a carrot or an orange for the first time. Such is the power of concentration and one-pointed awareness! Ideally, mealtimes are meant by nature to be times for re-energizing, and you can then leave meals feeling quietly rejuvenated, instead of draggy and fatigued, as so many of us experience after a heavy meal.

There are many benefits to be derived from eating with conscious awareness. Perhaps the greatest joy of all is the moderation in diet that inevitably follows. Eating slowly, chewing and savoring each bite, you are better able to take stock of what and how much you need and to own responsibility for the act of nourishing yourself. You thus have a more fulfilling eating experience and need less food for satisfaction. If you're listening, your prana, or inner voice, will signal you when the body is just full enough. If you end at the moment that signal comes, an almost sweet, steady energy will be yours throughout the day, a feeling of your meal being efficiently digested and assimilated by your system.

Overeating, on the other hand (and undereating as well) is almost always related to emotional stress and anxiety. Quelling tensions and conflicts that arise in our lives through overeating, we attempt to anesthetize ourselves from feeling whatever we need to feel, or we use food as a diversion, "reward", or antidote to boredom.

At the Retreat we come face to face with our diverse eating habits, and in exploring inner motives, we are often rewarded not only by improved, healthier diets, but also by deeper understanding of what makes us "tick." Eating consciously is the key; it is an entry for initiating this process of which moderation and joyful eating are the result.

Join us, if you will, in a conscious eating experiment. You may make some exciting discoveries, and above all you'll have a chance to enjoy your meal with peaceful appreciation. Adapt the following guidelines so that they realistically meet your own situation, work, and family needs. But take the time to experience eating once again from the simplicity and wondrous vantage point of a child!

GUIDELINES FOR CONSCIOUS EATING

1) Eat only when you are truly hungry.

2) Take your meal in a quiet, peaceful surrounding with minimal distractions. If away from home, try to find a local park or even a patch of lawn where you can take your lunch. In a restaurant, choose a quiet booth, if possible, where you can relax and be fairly quiet.

3) Try to eat at least one meal a day in silence. Allow yourself to be concentrated on your food, arranging your meal so that you do not need to extend yourself verbally while eating.

4) Before you eat, take a moment to close your eyes; take a few long, deep breaths and relax your body. Forget about the meal for a moment and let all of your awareness flow over your body, relaxing any tense or tired places. Affirm that you are a healthy, whole reflection of energy and well-being, and see yourself in your mind's eye in this way. (You might want to use the affirmation we have adapted for this purpose at the end of this chapter.)

5) Taking your food in your hands, give thanks for the simple nourishment before you and acknowledge that you are receiving it.

6) Eat your meal slowly, chewing each mouthful well. Liquefy the solids in your mouth before swallowing. Even liquids should be held in the mouth a moment to mix with your saliva, increasing their digestability. While chewing, be relaxed and calm, without thinking or rushing on to the next bite. Allow yourself to fully experience the taste, aroma and consistency of whatever it is you're eating.

7) When you feel the subtle "full" signal from your body, put away your dishes and sit quietly for a few moments, letting digestion happen as you allow the experience of contentedness and real "nourishment" to permeate every cell of your body.

Realize that the food you have taken will nourish you throughout the day, as the positive energy you've invested in it will nourish your mental attitude and emotions as well as your physical body.

Affirmation
To ⚬ My Body

I recognize you are the temple in which my spirit and my creative energy dwell.

You are my responsibility to care for. I have the ability to make you ill or healthy.

I must offer you the most alive, healthiest food so that you may continue to sustain my creative energy, my spirit and my soul.

I have created you from my need to have my spirit manifest on earth, so that I may have this time to learn and grow.

I offer this food to you with love and a sincere desire for you to remain free from disease and disharmony.

I accept you as my own creation.

I need you.

I love you.

6·
Purification
and Fasting

Sukanya

When I first heard of fasting and purification many years ago, visions of castor oil, enema bags, plain salads with no dressing, and the howls and growls of my empty stomach danced in my head. I imagined that I would need to lie flat on my back drinking gallons of water until it almost came out of my ears and taking enemas until my rear end got sore. Ugh!

My very first "fast", undertaken in order to lose weight, consisted of two bottles of diet-cola drunk on a hot muggy summer day with no other food or drink. I arrived home at the end of the day with a splitting headache, stomach pain and nausea that lasted all night. Breaking the fast with a piece of toast and a glass of orange juice, I resolved never to undergo such an experience again. And that held true for me until I moved to Kripalu Retreat and had an opportunity to learn what real fasting and purification are all about.

To understand the need for purification and simplification in diet, it is helpful to focus upon the idea of toxicity. Most commonly we view toxicity as a "dis-at-ease" state of the body, brought about by over-eating, poor food combining or the consumption of devitalized, processed foods. Through yogic training and what our experience has taught us, we have expanded the definition of toxicity to include a state of imbalance or impurity brought about not only by external agents but also as the result of poor living habits on our part: lack of exercise, sleeping too much or too little, or experiencing stressful feelings such as fear, anger or negativity. Body, mind, emotions, spirit are all one; as such, any disruption in one area immediately has its effect in all the rest. Thus, when we undertake a purification diet, we are contributing to our well-being on all levels, correcting abuses or imbalances which may have existed for a long time.

In the realm of diet, there is almost universal need in our society for change and purification because of the poor dietary habits most Westerners follow. Many of our bodies have been deprived of vital nutrients and clogged with unnecessary food substances for many years. Many of us have unwanted fat deposits, cholesterol build-up or toxic residues lodged in the tissues of our bodies, of which we are often unaware. Embarking on a purification diet in itself is an excellent remedy for improving body awareness, giving us a deeper understanding of the way our eating habits have contributed to our present state of being. Only by stepping back from our normal habits for any length of time are we able to see their real effects in our life.

Although the body has several detoxifying stations, including the liver and kidneys, we often take in more harmful substances than the body can effectively filter at one time. As a result, these residues are circulated through the blood stream and deposited in tissues and arteries to be taken care of at a later time. For far too many people, that "later time" never comes. More and more residues build up without ever giving the body a chance to stop and clean house. The result can be a serious disease in later life, or simply a chronic feeling of fatigue and general lackluster spirits. This physical housecleaning is the purpose of a fast or purification diet.

Each night as we go to sleep, our body is afforded an opportunity to slow down and flush itself clear of undigested food substances. When we snack frequently or eat late at night, we force the body to continually process food without a chance to rest or empty out in-between. Similarly, when we eat heavy, more complex foods such as proteins and fats, our digestive system must work for a longer time to process them. Eating only two or three meals a day without snacks, on the other hand, gives the body a chance to digest everything properly and empty itself before the next meal comes through.

By consciously choosing to eat lighter, more readily digested foods such as plain fruits, vegetables, or juices during a cleansing diet, we give the body a chance to clear itself adequately, and to rebuild old cells and tissues. Residues that have long been lodged in tissues and organs will be drawn out once again into the blood stream to be filtered through the liver and kidneys and excreted from our bodies.

WHAT IS A PURIFICATION DIET?

Although there are many types of purification diets suited to different needs, the main effect of such diets is a cleansing and rejuvenation of the body's tissues and vital organs. Any diet including a preponderance of either fresh fruits, juices, or vegetables can be considered a cleansing diet. At the Retreat we have a yearly purification schedule which is included at the end of this chapter to give you further insight and understanding.

Depending on the type of purification and the condition of the body, the cleansing process could be a slow and subtle one or a relatively abrupt and dramatic process. During a purification diet, it is our purpose to feed the body with vital, easily digested foods, such as juices. These juices are used within the body system to nourish new cells and tissue growth as the removal of unwanted material is speeded up and flushed from the system. Many people experience such things as old waxy lumps of bile, strings of mucus, and old fecal matter being removed from the system during extended purification diets.

As the cleansing process continues, we may feel symptoms such as dizziness, headache, slight nausea, or tiredness. These are signs that the purification is happening and was much needed by the body. Don't be alarmed. Simply drink plenty of water, and give your body extra rest, plenty of fresh air and exercise, perhaps a sauna or massage, and daily enemas. Because you will be putting very little bulk into your system, peristalsis may be slowed down and even stopped temporarily. As toxins accumulate in the colon they will need to be flushed out of the system. This is why the daily enema is suggested. The only time we recommend the use of enemas (it can be habit forming) is during a purification diet or in times of illness. No purification diet should be embarked on without knowledgeable supervision and thorough understanding. Before embarking on any cleansing diet regime which lasts longer than a day, you should gradually prepare the body by following the suggested guidelines for good eating enumerated in the first four chapters of this book. Particular attention should be paid to the practice of drinking only fresh juices for one day out of each week for several months before attempting a longer cleansing program.

RAW JUICE FASTING

The following fruit and vegetable juices are particularly effective for use in fasting. Each juice has its unique benefits, and you may wish to consider these before choosing a fast.

APPLE JUICE

An especially nice juice in the fall when apples are abundant and ripe from the tree, apple juice is a good digestive tract cleanser and a mild laxative. (Be aware of its tendency to produce gas in some, however.) The apple stimulates all body secretions and is an overall tonic, containing many nutrients: Vitamins A, B, C, calcium, phosphorous, iron and potassium. Apple juice can help such disorders as skin disease, arthritis, lung problems, anemia, and bladder and kidney ailments.

BEET JUICE

Here's the perfect blood-builder! Beet juice helps rebuild red blood cells due to good proportions of phosphorous, sulfur, potassium, Vitamin A and iron, and it is also very cleansing to the liver. (Thus it's good to take it in small quantities or blended in with other juices.) It has an extremely cleansing effect upon the whole body and has been recommended in use for such ailments as constipation, skin disorders, liver problems, anemia and menstrual disorders, as well as obesity.

CARROT JUICE

One of the most versatile of the veggie juices, fresh organic carrot juice is a very popular choice on our cleansing and purification diets. Rich and full-bodied, carrot juice provides Vitamin A as well as calcium, phosphorous, and Vitamins D, E, G and K, and is helpful in improving vitality and vigor, enhancing our resistance to infection, and providing for the health and integrity of the respiratory tract and mucus membranes of the body. It has been recommended for use in cases of asthma, lung problems, ulcer or cancerous conditions, gall and kidney stones and for improvement of eyes, hair and skin. Often we make a fresh veggie "cocktail" which has carrot juice as its base and includes combinations of beet, celery, cucumber, green pepper, or parsley juice.

CELERY JUICE

Good for the nervous system, celery juice has a soothing effect on the nerves and helps strengthen the nerve sheaths. Its increased percentage of sodium and magnesium is helpful in dissolving wastes, eliminating carbon dioxide from the body and improving the circulatory system. In addition celery juice helps cool the body. Try it in a "green drink" -- along with parsley, green pepper, and cucumber, or alone with carrots; it's quite refreshing!

GRAPE JUICE

When extracted from fresh grapes, this juice is highly cleansing and has achieved acclaim as an offspring of the famous "grape cure". Very easily assimilated by the body, grape juice aids in elimination and detox-ification, at the same time strengthening and rebuilding tissues of the body. With varying amounts of calcium, magnesium, iron, sulfur, and Vitamins A, B, and C, grape juice is a good nutrient and can be satisfying and pleasant on a fasting/purification diet because it is high in natural sugars. Widely used for a variety of conditions, it has been shown to be particularly effective in cases of anemia, low blood pressure, sluggish liver, obesity, skin disease or where ulcers or cancerous conditions are present. Those with high blood sugar should use under supervised conditions only.

ORANGE JUICE

Antiseptic and highly cleansing, orange juice provides high quality Vitamin C as well as B, calcium, phosphorous, potassium, and bioflavanoids to the body, and is useful in promoting the healing process, rebuilding teeth and bones and preventing infection. Orange juice is recommended for a variety of dis-orders, including asthma, bronchitis, rheumatism, arthritis and high blood pressure. Anyone suffering from stomach ulcers or inflammation in the stomach or intestines should proceed cautiously with the use of orange juice. Used in a purification diet, orange juice provides high energy and good taste and is very alkalinizing to the system, thus decreasing the chances of infection and stimulating the liver and digestive organs.

WATERMELON JUICE

Very helpful in purification diets because of its diuretic qualities, watermelon juice is a pleasant-tasting drink which contains Vitamins B, C, calcium, phosphorous and a large proportion of potassium. Watermelon is very helpful in ailments of the kidneys and bladder and in alleviating high blood pressure.

It is important to maintain a lighter diet, such as the one described in our sample program, before beginning the juice diet and for several days following it. This gives the body a chance to gradually adjust to the change and to begin to release toxins slowly. Otherwise the system could be flooded too abruptly with toxic matter, and might become overtaxed.

Occasionally the second day of juicing may be replaced by a day of water fasting. This is recommended only for those who are experienced and comfortable on a juice diet. Water fasts tend to release toxins quickly. They do not feed the body as a juice diet does with needed vitamins and minerals, and cannot be recommended for general use. With experience and supervision they can occasionally be helpful.

If you are a meat-eater, it is best to gradually adapt your diet so that a purification plan is practical, rather than making an abrupt transition. First begin one day a week cutting back on heavy protein sources and see what results you get. Then attempt one or more days per week without meat or fish. If you feel comfortable and wish to experiment further, you may try eating fruits only one day a week, or incorporate Day 1 or 2 of our purification program once a week into your diet.

BENEFITS OF A PURIFICATION DIET

Although some symptoms of toxic release may occur during a purification program, there are long-term benefits that far outweigh these temporary inconveniences. During the program you will have days when your body feels energetic and flexible, your senses are sharp, and your mind is clear. As you begin to eat again you will probably notice that food never tasted so good, so vibrant, so satisfying. Small amounts of food will satisfy your hunger. Your body weight will probably drop in the beginning, but will eventually level out. People who were originally underweight often find that because their assimilative processes are improved, they are able to gain weight more easily following the purification program. Overweight people will be able to maintain their weight loss providing they return to moderate eating on a nutritionally balanced diet.

A Purification Diet

The following are daily and yearly purification schedules which we employ at the ashram. Feel free to borrow from, adjust or adapt these programs to meet your own dietary needs.

Daily

1. Eat 2 moderate meals each day with a third small meal consisting of either fruit or salad only, in the evening.

2. Avoid eating between meals.

3. Avoid eating after 6:00 in the evening so that all food can be processed during your waking hours and the body can be at rest in the evening.

Weekly

1. Choose one day each week to eat a mono diet consisting either of one kind of fruit or of fresh fruit or vegetable juice. (Fresh juices/fruits are preferable to canned or frozen varieties since they maintain the highest food value and are the most "alive" sources of enzymes, minerals and Vitamin C, which are highly susceptible to loss through processing.)

AN 8-DAY PURIFICATION DIET

At the change of each season, we embark on a longer purification program. A suggested menu is listed below:

First Day

Breakfast - Fresh applesauce with raisins, herbal tea.
Lunch - Garden salad, Hearty Vegetable Soup, sprouts (see Ch. 22)
Dinner—Garden salad and light soup.

Second Day

Breakfast - Grated apples and dates
Lunch - Garden salad, sprouts.
Dinner - Stewed tomatoes.

Third to Fifth Days

Fresh fruit or vegetable juice—from 6-8 cups daily with sufficient water or rejuvelac (p. 247), taken in between.

Sixth Day

Breakfast - Vegetable broth, sprouts
Lunch - Broth, spinach-sprout salad
Dinner - Stewed tomatoes

Seventh Day

Breakfast - Lightly stewed prunes and apples
Lunch - Spinach-sprout salad
Dinner - Vegetable soup

Eighth Day

Breakfast - Hot applesauce with raisins
Lunch - Salad and a steamed vegetable
Dinner - Light soup

Ninth Day and Following

Begin gradually adding grains and more steamed and cooked foods until normal diet is resumed.

7· Setting Up Your Kitchen

Your kitchen: much more than simply a place to store and prepare food, the kitchen, throughout history and in all cultures, has been a place of warmth, sustenance, creativity and comfort. Practically speaking, how you utilize the space in your kitchen may settle the question of whether your cooking process is an inspired and enjoyable flow or a jarring ordeal ("where *did* I put the garlic press?"), jogging your memory to the limits and keeping you on the run.

SPATIAL ARRANGEMENT

Equally important as the ingredients you cook with are the utensils and environment in which you create your meals. When I first began to cook at the ashram, I was working in a yet-unfinished room which, organizationally, was not an ideal set-up. I had to walk half-way across the kitchen each time I wanted another piece of equipment and into another room to locate staple items. I used to wear sneakers, feeling that a marathon runner could get no better training than to spend the day running circles with me around the kitchen. Since that time, our carpenters have completed the kitchen, and with help from family members and friends we've been able to organize our work space to cut back on fully half of our preparation time. The kitchen looks neater, feels more spacious and less cluttered, and the staff is able to work more effectively than ever before.

Although ours is a large kitchen feeding up to several hundred people, the same principles of organization and spatial arrangement are effective on a smaller scale. Our basic organizational principle is that all equipment should be easily accessible and in close proximity to the space in which it is most often used. Equipment that you use most often should be the most easily accessible. In other words, to keep measuring cups in the back of a drawer filled with knives, wooden spoons and spatulas may not be the most efficient arrangement. Most important is that each piece of equipment should have a designated space to which it is returned after every use. Cluttered drawers and cabinets which contain a variety of objects are usually time wasters and eventual (if not immediate and continual) sources of frustration.

There are several major pieces of equipment around which you will want to create your kitchen. They include: refrigerator, stove, sink, cabinet and shelving space, and, hopefully, a large table. A butcher block is ideal, although any table will do, as you can use a larger cutting board on top of it. Once these large pieces of equipment are fitted into the space available in your kitchen, you're ready to begin arranging pots and pans, spices and staple goods around them.

You'll want to store cutting boards, knives, mixers, blenders, and mixing bowls near the table or counter top on which you are planning to use them. A convenient, easy to find method of storing large knives, slotted spoons, spatulas, etc. is to hang them from designated nails or hooks on a large wooden board, occupying space on one wall. We've even drawn a picture of each item right on the board so that there's no question about what goes where, and no time lost hunting through large disorganized drawers. Pots and pans can be hung in a convenient corner of the room overhead wherever they are high enough not to get bumped into and low enough to be within easy reach. We hang all of our larger pots up this way. We suspend small saucepans from hooks along one wall. Pot lids can be organized in narrow sections on shelving space according to size. We like to keep bread pans, pie pans, and casserole trays on shelf space in our baking area. This way they are within easy reach yet not mixed up with a myriad of other assorted cooking equipment. Spices are kept filled and labelled on shelves in two areas of the kitchen, near the stoves, and near the mixers and blenders. We find this to be a convenient arrangement since we use the spices primarily near the mixer and blender for putting together basic recipes, and near the stove for spontaneous creations.

BUYING EQUIPMENT

Before buying equipment for your kitchen, there are several key questions to think about.

1) How many people am I planning to feed on a regular basis?

2) How much space do I have?

3) How much money can I spend?

4) What kinds of equipment will last the longest?

5) How will different metals, woods, etc. affect the food I am planning to prepare?

At this point, you can begin to make up two lists. One list will contain pieces of equipment that you feel are essential, and the other will contain the equipment you would like to have but could do without. For a moderately sized kitchen in which you are regularly planning to feed about 4 to 7 people, we have provided a listing of suggested equipment on page 47.

BUYING AND STORING FOODS

When you begin to change your diet from one in which meat is the staple food to a more vegetarian approach, you may find that the corner grocery store is no longer sufficient for filling all of your needs. You'll want to have sources of more natural, wholesome products. The local farmer's market and health food store are two good places to shop for fresh produce and organically grown and prepared staples. Mail order from reputable organic suppliers is also helpful. If you have your own garden, then you have an ideal set-up for ensuring the availability of wholesome, organically grown produce. Becoming a part of a food-buying co-op or beginning your own can also go a long way toward saving money on foods that you can count on to be more natural and healthful.

Once you've purchased healthful foods, the next step is to ensure their staying that way through proper storage. All spices, grains, legumes, nuts, and seeds keep best in a cool, dry place in air-tight containers. Spices are best kept in colored glass jars as they are easily affected by light. All natural oils and high oil content products such as wheat germ, soy flour, etc. are best kept refrigerated to protect against rancidity. Sweeteners such as honey and molasses can be kept in tightly closed containers at room temperature; when kept in the refrigerator they thicken and become hard to pour. Fresh produce should be kept airtight in the refrigerator until needed. They can be washed ahead of time if they are thoroughly dried before refrigerating. Potatoes, beets, apples, pears, winter squash and pumpkins can be kept in a cool dry place rather than the refrigerator. Bananas should be kept at room temperature, as they turn brown quickly when refrigerated. A general rule of thumb to follow in the storage of all foods is that they are most easily affected by heat, light, and water. These three leach vitamins and should be eliminated in storage as much as possible.

Kitchen Companions

Basic Smaller Things

1 grater

1 blender

1 mixer

5 mixing bowls in graduated sizes

5 bread pans

4 muffin tins

4 cookie sheets

3 casserole trays

2 cake pans

2 sets of measuring spoons

1   4-cup measuring cup

1   2-cup measuring cup

2 sets of graduated measuring cups

2 strainers, 1 small and 1 medium

2 cutting boards

1 wire whisk

Pots and Pans

2   1-quart saucepans

1   2-quart saucepan

2   2-gallon saucepans

1 medium-size wok

2   12-inch skillets

Utensils

2 slotted spoons

4 serving spoons

2 wooden spoons for mixing

2 spatulas

1 pancake turner

1 apple corer

3 large knives for chopping

2 paring knives

1 can opener

1 church key can opener

3 ladles - 2 large (for soups) and 1 small (for dressings and sauces)

2 sets of tongs

Miscellaneous Friendly Items

cheese cloth and rubber bands (for sprouting)

3-4 sprout jars (old clear glass jars do fine)

vegetable steamer

citrus hand juicer

Handy but not essential

grain grinder

ice cream maker

juicer

pastry cutter (can use knives instead)

sifter (can use a strainer)

small tofu press and pressing cloths

food mill

hand cheese slicer

We recommend that all equipment be either stainless steel, glass or wood. Wood has a nice, earthy feel for mixing spoons and bowls. Metals such as iron, tin and aluminum leach into the food that is cooked in them, and sometimes rust. Glass and stainless steel do not. We prefer them for this reason. Stainless steel lasts a long time and is worth the extra money that it initially costs.

ADDING HEART

When the utensils are neatly hanging on the walls, the pots and pans stacked and stored for easy grabbing, the wheat, rice and lentils tucked carefully away in their own labelled containers, and the herbs and spices stacked across your kitchen shelf in order and clarity, you have still one more element to consider: the *heart* of your kitchen. With order, cleanliness, and a sense of organization, the foundation is laid. Let your kitchen now become a place of beauty, a place of light, a place that, for you, nurtures your own unfolding cooking wizardry. Perhaps you have sparse, clean tastes, and find a simple pottery vase of dried weeds all the added beauty you prefer. You may want to hang wooden or glass wind chimes in the window, place prisms in the sun to catch and distribute rainbows as you work, or bring in your favorite art prints, posters, or a picture which evokes a mood of peaceful contemplation, joy, or simple good feeling for you. Music and cooking harmonize nicely, so haul in a speaker if possible, and by all means, sing as you work. (Your dishes will certainly improve.) Green hanging and flowering plants will lend general good cheer and liveliness to your cuisine environment. The possibilities are endless, and often "less is more", more or less. In a nutshell (forgive our punning), your kitchen is a place of creativity, purposeful activity and giving: let it reflect your heart as well as your (organized and efficient) thinking, and true cooking will begin to take place within its four walls.

8·
Creative
Menu Planning
and Cooking, Demystified

"What shall we do about poor little Tigger?
If he never eats nothing he'll never get bigger.
He doesn't like honey and haycorns and thistles
Because of the taste and because of the bristles.
And all of the good things which an animal likes
Have the wrong sort of swallow or too many spikes…"[1]
—Winnie the Pooh

Unlike the daily fare of Tigger and Winnie the Pooh, meal planning for most of us is more complex than combining haycorns and thistles. At Kripalu Retreat, people's tastes are an important determinant in our menus, as well as knowledge of what's on hand and what's in the market. Gazing into my vegetarian crystal ball, I get a misty picture of what folks may be wanting one and a half weeks hence, and what the produce stores may be providing. Sometimes it comes out like this:

"Hmm, let's see. For Monday we'll have nutty carrot and rice loaf, and Tuesday stuffed acorn squash with peas. Let me call Lee at the Reading Produce Market and find out the going food prices." (After call): "Well, with acorn squash at $15.00/bushel and zucchini at $9.50/bushel, we'll be having stuffed zucchini instead for Tuesday lunch."

I love the challenge of planning our meals! Menu planning requires adroitness of mind, eye-hand coordination (to shuffle the various dishes, ingredients and whims of the diners), some knowledge of agrarian economics, rain and crop factors, and of course, a sturdy acquaintance with soup, stove and skillet.

Our meal planning has gone through continuous evolution as we invent new recipes, revive and dress up old ones, witness a change in our tastes and food preferences and grapple with what's available on the market. We're just now considering putting the raisins in our raisin bread (or cookies), since for so long they've been out of our community price range. Our meal planning is an organic event, growing up out of the changing times and our own evolving nutritional consciousness as individuals and as a community.

Through the years we've changed, adapted, or assumed new dishes, food combinations or dietary approaches. As our nutritional understanding becomes more sophisticated, our culinary habits change. Thus grain coffees and herbal teas replace caffeinated blends; whole, fresh vegetables the overcooked, oil-saturated versions, and rich, subtle grains such as bulgar, millet or buckwheat are used in place of polished, lifeless, instant-style supermarket varieties. Gradually, our taste buds seem to be moving toward simplicity, towards food closest to their natural state. Our weekly raw veggie day offers peppers, beets, carrots, celery, radishes and all manner of dips and spreads a chance to parade in riotous rawness right onto our plate and palate, and is becoming our favorite fare. Still, we love the flourishes of a well-made casserole or crepes served a la francaise. Our Saturday evening dessert is generally well-attended, proving that we enjoy a sweet carob pudding or banana cheese pie with as much gusto as the grainy grains and veritable vegetables we're reputed to eat so much of. Eating is a pleasurable experience for us. In fact, we focus our senses, mind and heart one-pointedly and make our eating into a meditation -- a truly joyful act of receiving and nourishing ourselves. (See Chapter 5 on conscious eating.)

Below is a checklist to help you incorporate new ideas into your meal planning or merely to evaluate your current approach to shopping, cooking or serving meals. This checklist is especially helpful if you're planning meals over a period of time, for many people, or if you need to take several variables into consideration. Use these as questions to ask yourself as you plan.

CHECKLIST FOR MEAL PLANNING

1) Who am I cooking for? What are their special dietary needs, whims, etc. How many am I cooking for? How hard is their work? How much will they want to eat, and in what variations?

2) What foods are available, and what is the best price? What foods do I most enjoy preparing? What new things might I experiment with? What will provide my family (friends, etc.) with the most nutritious options (i.e., serving complementary proteins as much as possible; for example, a hearty rice and bean dish or cornbread and split pea soup)?

3) When am I planning for? Time of year is a great determinant -- available foods change, seasonal crops vary, etc. (It's better not to buy produce shipped across the country that has sat in refrigerator trucks for weeks, if a local variety comes cheaper or more quickly. Or if there are no local varieties, then perhaps for health's sake, it's better to sit out the season and buy blueberries, snap beans, or melons when they're truly in season locally.)

4) How much do I have available to spend? Working with a budget is both a discipline and a delight -- especially if you allow yourself a few dollars/week just to have unusual or favorite treat alternatives. Then an avocado dip, cooked artichokes, or a fruit salad with strawberries, pineapple and concord grapes is a welcome sight!

5) How far can my creative imagination go? Play, have fun and experiment to come up with some sparkling new eating alternatives. Try using leftover cereals in freshly baked breads, and crusty old breads in croutons or spicey bread pudding. See what new ideas occur to you...

No one ever said meal planning had to be dull or repetitive. The following is a list of some tasty menus for you to sample; the recipes are listed throughout this cookbook.

COOKING TERMS, DEMYSTIFIED

Cooking itself, according to our recipes, is fairly simple and straightforward. We assume however, that you have had some kitchen experience and can tell a wok from a sieve. Just to be safe, though, we include here some basic cooking terms.

Boiling: We prefer steaming to boiling in almost all cases, since it preserves vitamins so much more effectively. Boiling is done by placing raw vegetables or grains directly into boiling water and maintaining a high temperature until the vegetable or grain is cooked.

Steaming: Here, the food is cooked with the steam, not the boiling water, and is placed in some type of basket that raises it above the water. Once the water has reached a boil, the fire is turned off and the food cooks, with covered lid, in the steam produced.

Walnut-Cheese Spread on
Whole wheat bread with honey
Carrot and Celery Sticks

Tomato Sun Spread
Cucumber Marinade
Raw Veggies
Malti's Melty Muffins

Merry Miso Veggie Broth
Tofu Curry Dip on Bali's
Toasted Rye Bread
Cider Beans

Saturday Night Tomato Soup
Toasted Cheese 'N
Cuke Sandwich

Cream of Celery Soup
Humus Pita Sandwich and
Salad fixins

Chickpea Patties with
Tahini Sauce
Peas-Carrot Curry

Hira's Multi-Bean Soup
Crunchy Cheese Crackers

Dinner

Zucchini Cheese Soup
Sesame Crackers
Garden Salad with
Carrot Dressing
Strawberry Pie

Sauteed Chunk Tofu
Feast of Wok Veggies
Brown Rice/Salad with Cuke-
Lemon-Dill Dressing
Date Bars

Horish
Spinach Celery Toss
Greeny Tahini Dressing
Banana Nut Ice Cream
Date Prasad

Soyburgers with catsup
Sunny Beans
Salad with Parsley Tahini
Walnut Raisin Cookies

Scalloped Potatoes
Steamed and Herbed Broccoli
Raisin Sun Slaw
Carrot Cake with
Cream Cheese Icing

Cabbage Rolls
Golden Breaded Carrots
3-Bean Salad
Soy Mocha Ice Cream

Sunseed Gazpacho
Potato Eggplant Maharaj
Garden Salad with
Italian Broccoli Dressing
Carob Tofu Cream Pie

Hearty Red Lentil Soup
Carrot Raisin Salad
Spinach Elegante

Nutty Carrot/Rice Loaf
Spinach-Pea Soup
Alfalfas, mung sprouts
Pickled Beets
Chitra's Orange Yogurt Cake

Eggplant Bella Mozzarella
Lemony Beets
Romaine with Pleasing Peas-
Tomato Dressing
Peanut Butter Swirl Bars

Chili Con Veggies
Sourdough Bread
Herbed Zucchini
Tossed Romaine with
Beetnut Dressing
Honey Cake

Eggplant Parmigiana
Garden Salad with
Russian Dressing

Part 2:
Food for the Soul

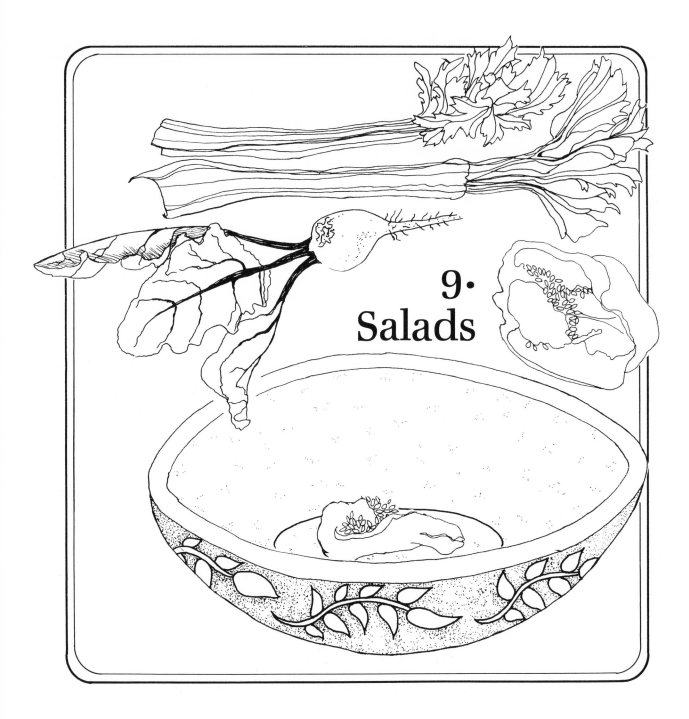

9.
Salads

Just visualize, if you will, the salad you've been wanting to prepare. See yourself gathering the ingredients, washing each of the radishes, greens, cukes or carrots. See each vegetable as it is dressed (or undressed) for such a splendid occasion: a fresh, glowing salad of many colors to adorn your table. (Actually, for many of us at Kripalu Retreat, salad may well be the mainstay of the meal, and there is no set notion about when to eat it or for which meal.) Just as an experiment, try eating salad for breakfast one morning, with lots of sprouts and freshly cut greens. You may be delightfully surprised! It's satisfying, nutritious, yet nice, and easy to digest. And what a beautiful way to commune with nature and continue to maintain contact with the freshness and vitality of life!

Salads hold a prominent position in our menu. Their fresh, crisp goodness adds valuable nutrients to our meals. We prefer a combination of the dark, crunchy greens such as spinach, endive, romaine, parsley, and watercress, with less attention to iceberg lettuce, since it offers few nutrients.

MAKING GREAT SALADS

The key to making successful salads, enjoyed to the last leaf, is to use fresh, crisp ingredients that are thoroughly washed and dried before entering the salad bowl. The following are some hints for keeping your salads attractive and fresh:

1) Wash salad greens in cold water, and dry immediately and thoroughly on terry towels. Greens can be stored this way under refrigeration in plastic bins topped with a layer of damp paper towels and covered on top with plastic wrap—that way they'll keep longer. We've effectively stored, washed and dried romaine or spinach for as long as 2-5 days using this method.

2) Speaking of spinach, it often needs two to four rinsings to remove all of the sand and dirt that have come along. The rinsings are well worth the extra time for the fresh flavor and vitamins spinach brings to the salad bowl.

3) Parsley may wilt after a day or two in the refrigerator but can be revived simply by being placed in a bowl of ice-cold water for an hour.

4) For salad preparation, separate the leaves of lettuce or romaine by hand, gently tearing and tossing them into the salad. Cutting these with a knife leaves brown edges if the greens are refrigerated for any amount of time. Remember that these plants are alive and responding to your energy! Build up your basic bed of greens, and add it to sliced or shredded carrots, celery, cabbage or assorted fresh veggies as you go. A sprinkling of fresh lemon juice keeps your salad fresh and tangy until serving time.

5) If you are making a salad several hours in advance of the meal, leave out all tomatoes, cucumbers, and shredded vegetables until the last minute, as these make your salad soggy and unappetizing. You can prepare and store these in separate bowls until needed.

6) Add dressings right before serving or keep them on the side for everyone to choose their own. Added ahead, they will quickly wilt the salad before you're ready to serve.

7) We often like to add such delicacies as young dandelion leaves (picked before plant flowers to avoid bitterness), fresh wild onion greens, fresh comfrey, or even tiger lily blossoms for an exciting touch!

8) Other things you might experiment with in different combinations, once you've prepared your basic bed of greens, include:

a) Tomatoes cukes and Cucumber Marinade Sauce (p. 67).

b) Shredded beets carrots and turnips (you can arrange in lovely rainbow fashion with rows of the shredded veggies alternated with lettuce).

c) Chopped watermelon pickle or green and ripe olives, sliced.

d) Three-bean salad (p. 63), or cooked chick peas with marinated artichokes.

e) Cheese chunks (Colby, Cheddar, Feta or naturally-aged Swiss).

f) Croutons (p. 236), cracker bits, or toasted sun seeds.

g) Pickled beets or corn (p. 63).

h) Sprouts: sunflower seeds, mung beans, or alfalfa seeds (See Chapter 21).

i) Red or white cabbage or already-prepared cole slaw (p. 61).

j) Raisins, apple chunks, walnuts (add celery and homemade mayo, p. 131, and you have a mouth watering Waldorf salad).

k) Watercress, asparagus, leeks.

l) Fresh cauliflower, chard, mustard greens.

m) Avocado and a squeeze of lemon or lime.

n) Chinese cabbage, water chestnuts, snow peas (for a Chinese touch).

As other options you might try our marinated Rice N' Bean Salad (p. 64; nice for a picnic); or Taboulie (p. 65), a salad offering from the Middle East which combines bulgar wheat, fresh vegetables and delicate seasonings to give you an easy-to-tote meal-in-itself for your luncheon choice. Try several of these salad combinations and give the fresh veggies, sprouts n' fixins a chance to brighten your day. See Soymaking (Chapter 17) for good-tasting recipes for tofu salads and spreads.

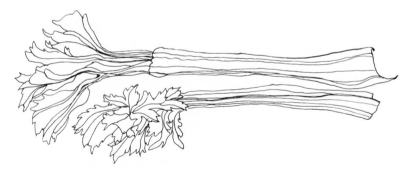

Spinach-Celery Toss

4 cups spinach
½ head romaine or head lettuce (large whole head of romaine)
2 small carrots
1 green pepper
1 large or 2 small sticks celery
1 bag radishes

Wash all the vegetables. Leaf or cut spinach and romaine and place in a salad bowl. Slice the carrots, dice the pepper and celery, and slice radishes. Mix all contents together well. Serve with your favorite dressing.

Serves 6-8.

Tossed Romaine

1 head romaine lettuce
¼ head purple cabbage
1 (medium) carrot
½-1 cup parsley (1 bunch)
½ bag radishes
2 peppers

Wash all the vegetables. Gently tear romaine lettuce, and place it in a large salad bowl, chop the cabbage and remaining vegetables (carrots can be made into flower or star shapes), and mix together well. P.S. Your salad will keep longer if the greens are well-dried.

Serves 6-10.

Raisin Sun Slaw

½ head small white cabbage
½ head small red cabbage
2 cups shredded carrots

Dressing:
2 cups yogurt
⅓ cup lemon juice
1 tsp. celery seed
1 tsp. mustard
1 tsp. salt
½ cup sunflower seeds
½ cup raisins

Shred your cabbage and carrots. Blend together all the ingredients for the dressing. Add the sunflower seeds and raisins to cabbage and carrots. Fold the dressing into vegetable mixture, then chill and serve.

Yield: 12 cups.

Carrot-Raisin Salad

½ cup sunflower seeds
1 cup celery (diced)
3 cups shredded carrots
½ cup raisins
¾ tsp. salt
1 cup yogurt
1 Tbs. lemon juice
1 Tbs. honey
dash pepper
2 Tsp. lemon peel

Toast the sunflower seeds. Dice the celery and shred carrots, and add the raisins and sunflower seeds to the vegetable mixture. Blend together the remaining ingredients and stir into the carrot salad. This is a light, pleasant dish which balances a heavier bean or grain entree.

Yield: 4 cups.

Cucumber Salad

3 cups thinly sliced cucumbers
1 cup yogurt
2 Tbs. honey
1 tsp. salt
1/8 tsp. pepper
6 Tbs. vinegar

Slice the cucumbers. Blend together the other ingredients and toss gently with cucumbers. (If yogurt is thin in consistency, add proportionately less. Garnish with parsley; chill and serve.

Yield: 3½ cups.

Cucumber Marinade

2 cups cucumbers
Marinade:
¼ cup vinegar
¼ cup water
¼ cup lemon juice
1/8 cup honey
¼ Tbs. dill
½ tsp. salt
Dash powdered mustard

Peel and cut the cucumbers. Prepare the marinade, and let the cukes sit in the marinade at least 3-4 hours. Drain the cukes thoroughly and then blend them up in your blender. This is an excellent dressing, and also serves as a base for a cold vegetable soup, to which you can add fresh tomatoes, cauliflower, green peppers, or any other of your favorites.

A variation would be to add 1½ cups of sliced tomatoes in with the cucumber, omitting the water from the marinade. Add 1 tsp. dill weed and 1 tsp. salt, and follow the directions for the regular cucumber marinade.

Yield: 2 cups.

Pickled Beets

4 cups cooked diced beets
5 cups water
1 tsp. salt

Marinade
½ cup lemon juice
1 cup vinegar
¼ cup honey
½ Tbs. dill
¼ tsp. mustard powder

Cook the beets, and remove them from the heat. Soak and chill the beets in water and salt for several hours and then drain off the water. Prepare all the ingredients needed for the marinade, mix them together and pour marinade on top of the beets. Allow this mixture to marinate overnight and serve the next day. This has a tangy sweet taste, perking up your lunch or dinner vegetables.

Yield: 5 cups.

Three Bean Salad

1 cup chick peas (dry)
1¾ cups green beans (2 in. pieces)
1 cup kidney beans (dry)
½ cup chopped celery

Marinade
½ cup oil
1½ cups vinegar
1½ tsp. honey
¼ tsp. black pepper
1 tsp. oregano
½ tsp. basil
½ tsp. salt
¼ tsp. marjoram
1/8 tsp. dill
pinch cayenne
2 Tbs. tamari
¼ cup water

Soak the dry beans overnight. Mix the spices, oil, vinegar, honey and water in a shaker bottle and set aside. Cook all the beans. Then mix the beans in a bowl, and pour the marinade over them, blending it in thoroughly with the beans. Refrigerate mixture overnight so that the flavors have a chance to penetrate the bean mixture. Serve the next day. Especially wonderful on a picnic or outing.

Yield: 6 cups.

Cider Beans Salad

4 cups green beans
1 cup grated sharp cheese
6 Tbs. oil
½ cup cider vinegar
⅓ cup chopped parsley
1 tsp. salt
¼ tsp. pepper
½ tsp. mustard powder

Cut the beans into ½ in. slices, and cook them until just tender. Drain. Toss the beans with other ingredients and chill (preferably overnight so flavors can set in), and then serve.

Yield: 4½ cups.

Marinated Rice N' Bean Salad

1½ cups cooked brown rice
1 cup cooked green beans
¾ cups sunflower seeds
2 Tbs. butter
½ cup vinegar
¼ cup oil
1 tsp. dill
1 tsp. salt
½ tsp. pepper

Cook the rice (see chart on p. 114 for cooking time) and set aside. Cut the green beans in 1 in. pieces; steam them until just tender, and set aside. Brown sunny seeds in butter in a skillet on medium heat. Mix all the ingredients together. Chill and serve.

Yield: 3 cups.

Tater' Salad

7 medium potatoes
½ cup diced green pepper
½ cup diced celery
¼ cup chopped parsley
¼ cup chopped radishes
1 Tbs. vinegar
1/8 tsp. mustard powder
¼ tsp. paprika
1½ tsp. salt
½ tsp. pepper
2 cups eggless mayo

Boil potatoes until soft. Allow them to cool for a while, and then dice. Add the other ingredients together, and toss in with the potatoes. Serve either hot or cold.

Yield: 7 cups.

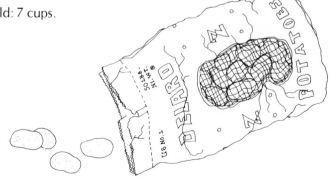

Taboulie

1 cup water
¼ tsp. salt
1 cup dry bulgar wheat
1 cup tomatoes, diced fine
1½ cups chopped broccoli
½ cup diced cucumbers
2-3 stalks, or 1 Tbs. fresh or dried parsley
½ tsp. oregano
½ tsp. salt
1 Tbs. basil
1 Tbs. oil
black pepper to taste
⅓ cup lemon juice

Boil the water with ¼ tsp. salt added. Mix the bulgar into boiling water, cover it and turn off the heat. After 20 minutes, place bulgar in the refrigerator to cool. Chop the vegetables and add them to the cooled bulgar along with spices, oil and lemon juice, and mix thoroughly. If you like, try adding some of your own favorites: green peppers, cauliflower or carrots, and try seasoning with some fresh mint, if in season.

Yield: 2¼ cups

Herbed Cottage Cheese

4 cups cottage cheese
1 cup sunflower sprouts
1 cup chopped radish
¾ tsp. poppy seeds
¾ tsp. caraway seeds
¾ tsp. sesame seeds
1 tsp. marjoram
1 tsp. thyme
1 tsp. basil
½ bunch parsley
¾ tsp. dill
1 cup chopped celery
¾ tsp. salt
1/8 tsp. pepper

Combine all the ingredients together in a large salad or mixing bowl. Garnish with extra parsley on top and serve. This recipe may also be made with tofu, made from soy flour (p. 174), in place of cottage cheese. Add sunflower or safflower oil to moisten slightly if needed.

Yield: 6 cups.

Sesame Macaroni Salad

¾ gallon water
1/8 tsp. salt
1 tsp. oil
3 cups elbow macaroni
1½ cups diced green pepper (or celery)
¼ cup sesame seed
1½ tsp. salt
1½ cups mayo (see mayo recipe)
½ tsp. mustard
¼ tsp. pepper
1 Tbs. dill
¼ cup fresh chopped parsley
½ cup chopped radishes

Boil the water with salt and oil added. Add the dry macaroni and cook for 12-15 minutes. Be sure to stir them or else they'll stick to the bottom of the pan. Strain off the macaroni and rinse it with cold water. Prepare the remaining vegetables, spices and ingredients and add to the macaroni in large mixing bowl. Chill and serve.

Yield: 2 quarts

Beet Raita

2 Tbs. oil
½ tsp. mustard seeds
3 cups grated beets
¾ tsp. salt
2 cups yogurt
1 Tbs. honey
½ tsp. cumin

A "raita" is an Indian side-dish, often made with a yogurt base, which helps balance the hotter, more heavily seasoned dishes of the main meal. You can serve it in like manner or just eat it as a yogurt salad -- it makes for very tasty dining! Heat the oil, add the mustard seeds and wait until they pop; then add beets and salt, sauteeing until the beets are tender. Remove from heat. When the beets have cooled sufficiently, add the yogurt, cumin and honey. Chill and serve.

Yield: 2½ cups.

10·
Vegetable Entrees & Side Dishes

Suk

From the bright rich orange of acorn squash to the deep purple of beets and the rainbow of greens, from peas to spinach, vegetables contribute the most colorful part of a meal. What could be more appealing than the warm golden yellow of a freshly steamed ear of corn lying beside a creamy potato salad sparkling with bits of red and green peppers? Or the shiny green of garden snow peas adrift in a light sauce of stir-fried orange carrots? Attractive, versatile and delicious, vegetables have a diversity of unique flavors and a special sweetness to contribute to any meal.

In our preparation of veggies, we view each aspect as meditation. It is not the cooking alone which requires creativity, but the entire preparatory process -- from the point when the carrots are scrubbed shiny clean to the moment they emerge buttery and steaming from the oven -- all this is the creative act in which we take part.

If you have not had a chance to make your acquaintance with diversely shaped spinach leaves -- or the art of slicing butternuts or beet-gazing (staring at the woody texture of beets after they've been soaked and sliced) -- then a new and unexpected vegetable meditation awaits you. Slow and careful preparation of all ingredients with an attitude of serenity and gratitude transforms your "veggies" (and you as well) and changes cooking from a humdrum routine into a joyful creative act. Try this simple, meditative approach and see how you feel (unless of course, you're a seasoned cook, in which case we imagine you're fast approaching haute-cuisine "nirvana . . . ").

But, getting back to the cooking . . . Whether you use vegetables as an entree, relish, soup or sidedish, you will want to maintain their high quality nutrients, vitamins, and minerals through attentiveness to proper preparation and cooking. The following are some helpful hints to guide you:

1) Wash and scrub vegetables in cold water. Don't let them sit in the water too long, as water may leach some of the vitamins (especially the water-soluble ones: B-complex and C).

2) Peel only if waxed, as most of the nutrients are just beneath the skin.

3) Cut vegetables with care. Depending on the type of dish you're preparing, you can choose to cut your veggies in a variety of ways, including:

   a) Slicing - either with a straight cut for soups and salads or on the diagonal for sauteeing and oriental dishes.

   b) Chopping - a straight cut into pieces that are smaller than sliced pieces, but not as small as diced pieces. Pieces may be irregular in shape.

   c) Dicing - usually refers to very small pieces with a square shape. Used in a variety of salads and cooked vegetable dishes.

   d) Grating - can be finely or coarsely done, depending on the type of food. Usually done with a hand grater.

4) Serve your vegetables raw as often as possible (See Chapter 9 for creative suggestions on salads.)

5) When cooking vegetables, you have several options: steaming, baking, sauteeing, or frying (see Chapter 8; pages 52-53). Steaming is our preferred method. Steaming can be done in the oven, or on top of the stove. In the latter case, the saucepan is filled with water, and a rack or steamer basket is placed on top

and filled with fresh vegetables, which then cook without losing nutrients. We generally use the oven method for vegetables such as pumpkin and winter squash, which are cut in half and placed cut-side down in a shallow pan filled with about an inch of water. The squash then cook in the steam created by the water; for the final 10-15 minutes of cooking time, the water can be drained from the pan and the squash placed cut-side up and stuffed, if desired.

Regardless of the method of cooking, it is very important not to overdo it; vegetables should be on the crunchy side rather than completely soft. Overcooking destroys valuable vitamins and enzymes.

6) Save all vegetable peels, tops, withered parts, etc. and cook them down to make a delicious soup stock or broth. Then compost the remains in your garden.

7) Use leftovers right away. Plan your menu so that a soup or mixed vegetable casserole follows a day of steamed or sauteed vegetables. Vegetables lose large quantities of nutrient content quickly when left to sit in the refrigerator.

Enjoy the colors, flavors, textures and aromas -- there is such a splendid variety in the vegetable kingdom. You can mix, arrange and plan with such diversity as to never quite duplicate a vegetable dish twice. As you try our recipes, let your imagination take you into spices and subtle blends of your own.

Vegetable Entrees

Vegetable-Noodle Casserole

4 cups tomato sauce
3½ cups cooked noodles
¾ cup broccoli
1¾ cups string beans
2 cups carrots
1¼ cups celery
2 Tbs. fresh parsley
Pinch black pepper
1 Tbs. oregano
1½ tsp. basil
½ tsp. salt

Sauce:
1¼ cups tomato paste
2¾ cups crushed tomatoes
1/8 tsp. thyme
1/8 tsp. oregano
¼ tsp. salt

Make tomato sauce by combining sauce ingredients and blending them. Set aside. Wash and chop all the vegetables, and steam or saute them until almost tender. In a large bowl, combine veggies, tomato sauce and spices. Pour into a 9 x 13 in. casserole pan and cover with foil. Bake at 375° for 30 to 45 minutes.

A simple but tasty, colorful dish that enhances any meal or serves practically as a meal in itself.

Yield: One 9 x 13 in. casserole.

Millet With Potatoes & Carrots

4 cups cooked millet
½ cup chopped green pepper
1 medium diced carrot
2 medium diced potatoes
5 Tbs. oil
1 tsp. mustard seed
1 tsp. turmeric
2 tsp. salt
1 cup water

Cook the millet and cool. Wash and chop the green pepper, and dice the carrot and potatoes. In a heavy skillet, heat oil and add mustard seeds. When the seeds begin to pop, add turmeric and the veggies, plus 1 cup water. Mix well. Cook until the veggies are almost soft. Add salt and millet and continue to cook until the veggies are completely cooked and millet is hot.

Yield: 6 cups.

Veggie Shish Kabob

Vegetables:
Enough to make 4 cups total:
Eggplant
Mushrooms
Zucchini or summer squash
Tomatoes
Celery

½ cup melted butter
Soy sauce to taste

Preheat your oven to broil temperature or use a toaster oven set on broil. (Or best of all, prepare the shish kabob over a grill for that delicious charcoal flavor . . .) Using regular shish kabob skewers, or hot dog grilling forks (or some variation -- perhaps even coat hanger wire), pierce the cut veggies (should be cut into big pieces) and place on aluminum-foil covered broiler or on the grill. Cook at broiling temperature approximately 8 to 10 minutes per side, depending on how crispy you like the veggies. Continually baste with the melted butter. Top with soy sauce when the veggies are complete, and serve over a bed of rice or stuffed inside of pita pockets! You may enjoy preparing a barbecue sauce (p. 139), or one of the tasty brown sauces (pp. 138, 139). Try a number of different variations and whoever's eating can dip their veggie chunks in the variety of sauces you've prepared.

Yield: 4 cups.

Chop Suey

3 cups fresh celery, sliced diagonally
3 cups fresh green peppers, sliced in strips
½ cup fresh parsley
2 cups mung bean sprouts
1 cup fresh green peas
4 Tbs. oil

Sauce:
1¼ Tbs. arrowroot
1¼ cups water
2 Tbs. butter
½ tsp. ground ginger
½ tsp. mustard powder
5 Tbs. tamari

You never knew how easy it was to be Chinese. Try this recipe for starters. Wash and slice your vegetables. Chop the parsley. Saute veggies and sprouts in the oil until just tender, then add parsley. Cook for another two minutes only. To make the sauce, stir the arrowroot into water, and saute spices in butter. Stir in the tamari and arrowroot mixture, and cook until thickened over a medium flame. Pour the sauce over the vegetables. Serve over a bed of rice or with chow mein noodles. Then enjoy your Chinese cooking -- perhaps with some egg rolls or a pot of steaming green tea.

Yield: 6 to 8 cups.

Eggplant Bella Mozzarella

1 medium eggplant
3 cups grated mozzarella cheese (loosely packed)
1 tsp. salt
1 Tbs. oregano
1½ tsp. basil
¼ tsp. cayenne

An easy to prepare, mouth-watering dish, this makes a tasty lunch or dinner as well. Wash and slice the eggplant in ¼ in. - ½ in. rings. Place on a lightly oiled baking tray. Sprinkle cheese on the eggplant rings, then combine your spices and sprinkle over the cheese. Bake at 350° until the cheese bubbles to a golden brown. For a variation, put light tomato sauce on eggplant before adding the cheese.

Make sure you've cut your eggplant thin enough; that's one of the secrets for making this dish perfect everytime. And watch out for the "cheese snatchers" -- every so often someone may come along when you're not looking and snatch the cheese off of the eggplant. Ah well . . .

Serves 3.

Carrot Casserole

6 cups carrots

Sauce:
1 Tbs. lemon juice
½ tsp. fresh lemon rind
⅓ cup honey
½ tsp. cinnamon
1/8 tsp. ground cloves
¼ cup raisins
2 Tbs. butter

Wash and dice the carrots. Steam lightly, so that they're still a bit crisp. Grate the lemon rind. Combine the lemon juice and rind, spices, honey and raisins. Drain the carrots and place them in a small baking dish. Pour the sauce over the carrots, and dot the top with butter. Bake at 350° for 30 minutes. So good you may not be sure if this is a main meal dish or a dessert!

Yield: 4 cups.

Spinach Elegante

2 lbs. spinach
1½ cups cottage cheese
3 cups grated Cheddar cheese
2 cups whole wheat bread crumbs
¼ tsp. nutmeg
¼ tsp. salt
¼ tsp. black pepper

Wash the spinach well and let it drain. Chop it into bite-size pieces. Then grate your cheese. In a large bowl, mix together the spinach, cottage cheese, grated cheese, bread crumbs and spices. Pour the entire mixture into a 9 x 13 in. baking pan. Cover it with foil and bake in the oven for 30 to 40 minutes at 350°.

An "elegant" meal by itself. Believe it or not, it tastes like it has a smidgeon of garlic! Everyone will love it.

Serves 6 to 8.

Cheese Broccoli Bake

1 bunch broccoli (12 spears)
2 cups Cheese Sauce (see p. 142)
½ cup whole wheat bread crumbs
1 Tbs. butter

Wash and cut the broccoli into spears (lengthwise). Steam them until almost tender. Place the broccoli in a casserole dish, alternating with layers of cheese sauce, and top with bread crumbs. Dot the top with butter. Bake at 350° for 30 minutes or until the cheese turns golden brown. For variation, use steamed cauliflower with broccoli ("Treetop Casserole") or mix steamed green beans with either broccoli or cauliflower.

Serves 3 to 4.

Old World Cabbage Rolls

1 head cabbage
3 cups cooked brown rice, millet, or bulgar

Sauce:
2½ cups stewed tomatoes
1 Tbs. tomato paste
¼ tsp. salt
Dash pepper
½ tsp. oregano

2⅓ cups finely grated celery
1½ cups finely grated carrots
1 Tbs. oil
3 Tbs. tamari
¼ tsp. pepper
½ Tbs. paprika
1 Tbs. basil

Boil the water in a large pot. Drop the whole head of cabbage in the water for 3 to 5 minutes; drain. Carefully peel off the leaves and set them aside. Wash and chop the celery in very small pieces and grate the carrot. Saute the celery and carrots in oil, adding tamari and spices. Then mix the sauteed veggies with the cooked grain. Place ½ cup of this mixture on each cabbage leaf and roll up the leaves. A toothpick can be used to hold the cabbage leaf together, if desired, but be sure to let folks know they're there before they begin eating! Place cabbage rolls in a baking dish and cover with the sauce. Bake at 375° for 45 minutes.

These cabbage rolls bring you the gentle taste of Eastern Europe. They taste even better if allowed to "age" a wee bit; prepare them on a leisurely day, then refrigerate for one or two days; then bake and serve. An extra special meal!

Yield: 12 rolls.

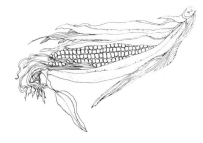

Peas-Pocket Squash

2 medium butternut squash
1⅓ cups peas
4 tsp. butter
2 Tbs. honey

Wash and cut the squash in half, lengthwise. Scoop seeds out of the center. Place squash cut-side down in a shallow baking dish filled with 1 in. of water. Cover with foil or baking lid. Bake at 375° for ½ hour. Turn the squash over so the cut side is facing up. Put butter, 1½ tsp. honey and ⅓ cup peas in the hole of each squash. Bake uncovered for ½ hour, and serve.

Serves 4.

Hira's Ukrainian Goulash

2 cups carrots
3 cups potatoes
1/8 cup butter
½ tsp. salt
1 Tbs. parsley
½ tsp. tarragon
¼ tsp. basil
¼ tsp. pepper
¼ cup whole wheat pastry flour
1 cup tomato paste
2 cups water

Wash and chop the carrots and potatoes into bite-size pieces. Then steam them until soft. Melt the butter in a frying pan. Add the spices and then stir in the flour to make a smooth paste. Add the tomato paste and water, stirring until smooth. When this sauce is hot, gently stir in carrots and potatoes. Let it cook until it gets nice and hot. A fine hot stew with a tomato taste, this will go a long way on a cold winter day.

Yield: 5 cups.

Eggplant Parmagiana

1 large eggplant
½ cup milk
1 cup wheat germ
½ tsp. salt
1 tsp. oregano
1 tsp. basil
½ tsp. black pepper
3 cups grated cheese
2 cups cottage cheese
2½ cups lasagna sauce (p. 142)

Here's an old favorite Italian-style meal you'll enjoy. Wash and slice the eggplant into ¼ in. rounds. In a mixing bowl, combine the wheat germ and spices. Dip the eggplant slices first in milk, then in wheat germ mixture. In a skillet fry the coated eggplant in ¼ in. of oil until light brown. Set the cooked eggplant aside on a paper towel. In a separate bowl, mix the cottage cheese and 2 cups of grated cheese. Spread ½ cup of lasagna sauce in shallow baking dish. Cover the sauce with a layer of browned eggplant. Then spread one layer of cheese mixture, ½ inch thick, over the eggplant. Repeat this process until you have used up all the ingredients. Top with remaining 1 cup grated cheese, and bake at 350° for 45 minutes.

Serves 6.

Vegetable Pie Crust

¾ cup melted butter
1⅓ Tbs. milk
½ cup boiling water
¾ tsp. salt
3 cups + 2 Tbs. whole wheat pastry flour

Melt the butter, and boil the water. Mix together the butter, milk, water and salt. Sift the pastry flour into the liquid. Stir until dough sticks together. Form 2 balls, then roll out the crusts to a thickness of ¼ in., in a 9½ in. square oiled pie pan.

Yield: Bottom and top for 9 in. pie.

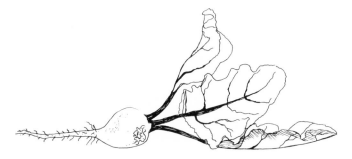

Vegetable Pie

Filling:
4 cups raw chopped carrots
4 cups raw chopped broccoli
4 cups raw chopped green pepper
2 cups fresh or frozen peas

Gravy:
½ cup butter
3 cups cold water
½ cup arrowroot
¼ cup tamari
1/8 tsp. powdered sage
½ tsp. tarragon
2 tsp. savory
1 Tbs. dill
½ tsp. salt
¼ tsp. pepper

Wash and chop the vegetables. Steam (excluding peas) lightly. Set aside. In a saucepan, melt the butter; measure out the cold water and add arrowroot; whisk well. Add this mixture and the rest of the gravy ingredients to the butter and heat slowly, stirring with a whisk constantly until very thick.

Take prepared vegetable pie crust (above) in pan and pour the filling (vegetables and gravy) into the crust. Cover with the second crust and pinch the edges of the two crusts together. Make several indentations in the crust with a fork. Bake for 45 minutes at 350°, or until the crust is golden brown.

Yield: One 9 inch pie.

Potato Latkes

5 cups finely grated raw potatoes
1 cup finely grated carrots
3 Tbs. minced green pepper
½-1 cup yogurt (depending on how juicy your veggies are)
1/8 tsp. hing
2 tsp. salt
¼ tsp. pepper
½ cup cornmeal
¼ cup nutritional yeast
2-2½ cups whole wheat flour
Oil for frying

These pancakes will give you the feeling of sitting in a Jewish household on the first night of Chanukah, when candles are lit, children play with "dreidls", and hot latkes are served right off the stove.

Wash and finely grate potatoes, carrots, and green pepper. The potatoes should be grated as finely as possible. In a large mixing bowl, combine the grated veggies, yogurt and spices, stirring well. Add cornmeal, yeast, and 1 cup of flour. Mix thoroughly. Add the remainder of flour as needed -- the mixture should be mushy but capable of being dropped into rounded pancakes. Let the frying pan get very hot and add a small amount of oil. Spoon out the potato mixture, flattening into pancakes in the pan. Cook on both sides until crispy, about 10 minutes. Serve piping hot with plenty of yogurt or sour cream.

Yield: 20 medium pancakes.

Scrumptious Scalloped Potatoes

3 cups thinly sliced potatoes
2 cups grated Cheddar cheese
1 cup whole wheat bread crumbs
1 cup milk
1½ tsp. salt
Pinch pepper

Always a favorite and easy to do! Preheat oven to 350°. Slice the potatoes and grate your cheese. Spread a layer of potatoes in a lightly oiled 9 x 9 in. baking dish. Cover them with a layer of cheese and next a layer of bread crumbs. Pour ¼ cup of milk over this and begin again with a layer of potatoes. Repeat until all ingredients are used. Cover with foil and bake at 350° for 1 hour or until the potatoes are tender.

Hint: you can pre-cook the potatoes separately for faster baking time, if desired. But don't cook them until they're too soft, because then they will be very difficult to slice thinly.

Yield: 9 x 9 in. dish.

(continued from page 137)

SPINACH AND TOFU LASAGNA

Serves 8

Preparation time: 30 minutes
Cooking time: 50 minutes

ALMOND BUTTER ADDS A UNIQUE RICHNESS, BUT YOU CAN SUBSTITUTE PEANUT BUTTER.

12-ounce block firm tofu, drained
4 tablespoons lemon juice
2½ tablespoons almond butter
1 tablespoon low-sodium soy sauce
1 tablespoon extra-virgin olive oil
1 large yellow onion, diced
2 large cloves garlic, pressed
Freshly ground pepper
1 teaspoon oregano
1 teaspoon basil
½ pound fresh mushrooms, sliced
¼-inch thick
½ cup dry sherry or nonalcoholic
wine
2 packages frozen chopped spinach,
thawed and squeezed dry
½ cup fresh parsley, finely chopped
¼ cup fine bread crumbs, lightly
toasted
½ cup toasted walnuts, chopped
4 cups tomato sauce
9 lasagna noodles, cooked al dente
Grated Parmesan cheese

In a food processor or blender, puree the tofu. Add the lemon juice, almond butter, and soy sauce, and blend until silky smooth. Warm a large, nonstick skillet or a Dutch oven over medium heat and add the olive oil. When the oil is hot, add the onion and sauté until it begins to turn golden brown. Stir in the garlic, pepper, oregano, basil, and mushrooms, and sauté for about 5 minutes. Add the sherry, spinach, and parsley. Sauté for a few minutes longer.

Add the sautéed vegetable mixture to the tofu in the food processor and

blend it with a few chopping strokes so that it's not overly smooth.

Preheat the oven to 350 degrees. Lightly oil a 9-by-13-inch glass baking dish. Distribute half of the bread crumbs across the bottom and sides of the dish. Spread a third of the walnuts on the bottom and top with a quarter of the tomato sauce. Lay 3 noodles side by side over the sauce and spread half of the tofu mixture on top. Repeat with a second layer of walnuts, sauce, noodles, and tofu mixture. Then add a third layer of walnuts, sauce, and noodles. Top with the remaining sauce. Use the rest of the bread crumbs to dust over the top.

Sprinkle with Parmesan and bake, covered, for 30 minutes; then uncover and bake for 10 minutes longer to crisp the top. Allow the dish to cool for 20 to 30 minutes before serving.

● *Per serving: 377 calories, 18 g protein, 14 g fat, 47 g carbohydrate, 932 mg sodium, 0 mg cholesterol.*

Potato Eggplant Maharaj

1 medium eggplant
1 medium potato
¼ cup chopped green pepper
3 Tbs. oil
½ tsp. mustard seed
½ tsp. fenugreek seed
1 tsp. turmeric
1½ tsp. salt
1 tsp. ground coriander
½ tsp. black pepper
½ Tbs. honey
½ cup water

The use of delicate or unusal spice combinations turns ordinary eggplant and potatoes into an extraordinary dish fit for a Maharaj.

Cut the eggplant into 1 in. cubes and slice the potato thinly. Chop the green pepper. Heat your oil, adding the mustard seed. When the seeds pop, add the fenugreek, turmeric and potatoes. Cover and cook for 5 minutes over medium heat, stirring frequently. Add the remaining ingredients and mix well. Cook over medium heat for 10 minutes, stirring frequently or until the vegetables are tender. Serve with a bed of rice, any other species of curry and a soothing yogurt dressing or "raita" (see Chapter 14) for a tantalizing meal.

Yield: 4 cups.

Potato Carrot Patties

5 medium-size potatoes
3 cups grated carrots
1 tsp. salt
½ tsp. curry powder
4 Tbs. oil
½ tsp. mustard seeds
1 Tbs. honey
½ tsp. black pepper
1 Tbs. sesame seeds
1 Tbs. shredded coconut

Boil the potatoes in their skins. While the potatoes are cooking, grate the carrots. When the potatoes are soft, cool them slightly; then mash them, leaving skins on for nutrition. Add ½ tsp. each salt and curry powder to the mashed potatoes. In a medium-sized saucepan, heat the oil and add the mustard seeds. When the seeds pop, add grated carrots and ½ tsp. salt. Cook over a low heat 10 to 15 minutes, stirring frequently. Add the remaining ingredients and mix well. Cool and combine the potato and carrot together. Form them into balls, then flatten into patties. Heat a heavy skillet, adding enough oil to keep the patties from sticking. Cook patties over low heat until brown on both sides.

As a variation, add chopped parsley to mashed potatoes. Serve with yogurt chutney and fresh salad.

Yield: 10-12 patties.

Feast of Wok Veggies

1½ cups carrots
1½ cups celery
1 cup cauliflower
1 cup broccoli
1 cup green pepper
1 cup zucchini
1 tsp. oil

Wash and cut the vegetables. For traditional style, cut the carrots, celery, broccoli stalks and zucchini on an angle. Cut the peppers into long thin strips, and the cauliflower into bite-size pieces. Saute in a wok or heavy skillet in the above order, allowing each vegetable to cook slightly before adding the next vegetable. With experience, you'll know the exact point at which to add each vegetable so that each one can be cooked to perfection, not over or undercooked. You can add any of your own favorites to this basic recipe as well. Serve with Ginger Soy Sauce (see p. 140).

Yield: 4 cups.

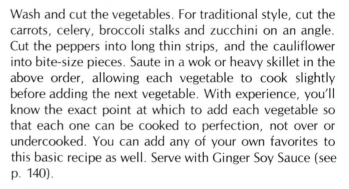

Stuffed Peppers

3 large peppers
1 cup chopped tomatoes
1 cup shredded carrots
¼ cup butter
1 tsp. oregano
1 tsp. basil
½ tsp. salt
½ tsp. marjoram
2 cups cooked brown rice, millet or bulgar
¾ cup water
2 Tbs. tomato paste
1 cup tomato juice

Wash the peppers, slice off their tops, and clean out the centers. Chop tomatoes into bite-size pieces, and shred the carrots. In a frying pan melt the butter; add the carrot, spices and grain. Saute. Add the chopped tomatoes, ¼ cup of water, and 1 Tbs. of tomato paste. Saute until the tomatoes are soft. Stuff the peppers with this mixture. In a separate bowl, mix together 1 cup tomato juice and ½ cup water and 1 Tbs. tomato paste, and pour into a baking dish. Place the peppers in this sauce and bake at 375° for 30 to 45 minutes. For added variety, top peppers with bread crumbs, wheat germ, or grated cheese.

This is another dish that tastes extra savory if you refrigerate, allowing the flavors to seep in, and serve up several hours (to several days) later!

Serves 3.

Malti's Veggie Stew

3 cups diced potatoes
3 cups diced carrots
3 cups broccoli
1 cup corn or peas
5 cups water or veggie stock
½ tsp. pepper
3/8 cup arrowroot
1/8 cup nutritional yeast
1/8 - 1/4 cup tamari

Here's an old-time simple veggie stew that will taste more exquisite the longer you allow it to cook. Wash and dice the veggies into small cubes -- the smaller the better. Place the veggies in a saucepan, covering them with water. Bring to a boil, then simmer as low as possible for one to two hours. The veggies should remain firm. Add pepper while the veggies are cooking. When the veggies are cooked but still firm, remove 1 cup broth and add in arrowroot and yeast, stirring to a smooth consistency. Stir this mixture into the simmering veggies, and simmer 15 minutes more, stirring occasionally and allowing time for the arrowroot to thicken and cook. Add tamari to taste. Be patient with the arrowroot and your efforts will be rewarded. The key to success in this recipe is the slow cooking of the veggies. Enjoy!

Yield: 8 cups.

Ratatouille

1 cup zucchini
1 cup eggplant
1 Tbs. oil
¼ tsp. basil
¼ tsp. oregano
Pinch parsley
½ bay leaf
1/8 tsp. tarragon
Pinch black pepper
¾ cup stewed tomatoes
¼ cup tomato paste
1 tsp. honey
¼ Tbs. tamari

This is a more "tomato-ey" blend of ratatouille -- thick and hearty -- and good alone or as a filling for crepes or tacos. Wash and chop the zucchini and eggplant into bite-size pieces. Saute the spices in oil for 2 minutes. Add stewed tomatoes, tomato paste, honey and tamari, and simmer for 3 minutes. Add the veggies, and simmer until they are tender, stirring occasionally.

Yield: 1½ cups.

Potato Patties

12 cups potatoes
¼ cup milk
1½ Tbs. butter
1½ cups bread crumbs
2 tsp. salt
¾ tsp. pepper
Enough corn meal to cover patties
2 Tbs. oil

Wash and cut the potatoes into large chunks. Steam, then mash the potatoes, adding the rest of the ingredients. Mix well, and form them into patties, sprinkling with cornmeal. Heat oil in a pan. Over low heat fry the patties until they're golden brown on each side. Cover the pan while they're cooking.

Yield: 16 patties.

Goldenrod Potatoes

3 cups diced potatoes
1 cup diced carrots
1/8 cup oil
½ Tbs. mustard seed
1 tsp. turmeric
3 Tbs. + ¼ tsp. tamari
½ tsp. salt
¼ tsp. pepper
1/8 cup water

Wash and dice the potatoes and carrots into bite-size pieces. In a medium sized saucepan, heat the oil and add mustard seeds. When the seeds begin to pop, add turmeric and stir well. Stir in the carrots and potatoes, and saute. Add tamari, water, salt and pepper, cover and cook until the potatoes and carrots are tender. This is a pleasant, nicely spiced potato dish.

Yield: 3 cups.

Creamed Cauliflower & Broccoli

2 cups chopped broccoli
2 cups chopped cauliflower
1½ cups white sauce (see p. 138)
½ cup milk
2 cups grated cheese
Salt and pepper to taste
¼ cup wheat germ

Wash and chop the broccoli and cauliflower. Lightly steam them until almost tender, and then place them in a baking dish. Make a white sauce with ½ cup of extra milk, and sprinkle the grated cheese into the sauce. Pour this mixture over the broccoli and cauliflower. You might want to add extra salt and pepper, to suit your own taste. Sprinkle the top with wheat germ, and bake at 350° for 30 minutes.

Yield: 5 cups.

Sunny Bean Casserole

6 cups green beans
1/8 cup oil
½ cup sunflower seeds
2 Tbs. tamari
1½ tsp. tarragon
1½ tsp. oregano
1 tsp. parsley
1½ tsp. salt

Wash and cut the beans. Saute the beans for 5 minutes in oil and tamari. Add seeds and continue cooking until the beans are firm but tender. Add the spices, mix well, and let sit covered, with the heat off, for 10 minutes.

This is a very esthetically pleasing dish, and blends well by color, not to mention taste, with your meal. If you feel in the mood to splurge, replace sunny seeds with slivered almonds and cook in the same manner.

Yield: 5 cups.

Country Mashed Potatoes

4 cups potatoes
½ cup milk
1/8 cup butter
1½ tsp. salt
Dash pepper
2 Tbs. parsley

Steam the potatoes until soft, approximately 20-30 minutes. Drain and mash them with a hand masher or electric mixer. Add spices, milk, butter and parsley; blend in a blender for smoother potatoes or mix by hand. Serve as is with butter or use as a base for shepherd's pie, vegetable pie, or other dishes.

Yield: 4 cups.

Yam Casserole

5 cups yams
1 Tbs. butter
¼ tsp. cinnamon
1/8 tsp. vanilla
¼ Tbs. honey
¼ Tbs. molasses

Here's an easy-to-prepare casserole, reminiscent of Thanksgiving and the winter holidays. First cook the yams in boiling water, then drain. Place the yams along with other ingredients in your electric mixer and blend together thoroughly. (You can, by the way, substitute coriander for the cinnamon in this recipe. Also, for added spice, dot with raisins.) Place in casserole dish and heat 10 minutes in medium oven before serving.

Yield: 5 cups.

Vegetable Side Dishes

Chinese Egg Rolls

GENERAL INGREDIENTS

Eggroll shells
Fillings
Mustard Sauce (see p. 142)
Sweet & Sour Sauce (see p. 143)
5 cups soy oil for frying

RICE VEGGIE FILLING

½ cup cooked brown rice
½ cup finely grated carrot, celery, cabbage combined
1/8 cup grated scallion
1/8 cup mung sprouts
1 Tbs. hot mustard (see p. 142)
1 tsp. tamari
¼ tsp. parsley (dried)
1/8 tsp. dill weed
1/8 tsp. cumin

EGGROLL SHELLS

2 cups pastry flour
3/4-1 cup water
2 tsp. salt

TANGY VEGGIE FILLING

¾ cup finely grated carrot, celery, cabbage and scallion, combined
½ Tbs. hot mustard
¼ tsp. curry powder
Dash chili powder
¾ tsp. tamari
¼ tsp. lemon juice

Preparation of eggrolls can be done in two steps (the first step ahead of time, if you like). For the first step, prepare the Mustard Sauce (see p. 142) and the Sweet and Sour Sauce (see p. 143) and mix the flour for the eggroll shells. The second step entails preparing the fillings, rolling out the shells, and frying or baking them with the fillings added.

STEP ONE (Can be done ahead)

1. Prepare the dough for eggroll shells by combining the pastry flour with the water and salt, and shaping it into a big ball. The texture should be thick and manageable as bread dough. It can be stored under damp toweling in your refrigerator overnight.

2. Prepare the hot mustard and sweet and sour sauce according to recipe instructions and set aside.

STEP TWO (Preparing and cooking eggrolls)

1. Assemble all ingredients needed for your fillings. For the Rice Veggie Filling, cook the rice and set it aside.

2. Make sure all your vegetables are very finely grated.

3. Add rice and vegetable mixture together along with remaining ingredients for Rice Veggie Filling, and stir it with a wooden spoon. When all ingredients are evenly stirred in, set mixture aside.

4. Prepare the Tangy Veggie Filling, combining the vegetables with the mustard, spices, tamari and lemon juice, and mixing together well.

5. Frying the eggrolls: It's best not to use cold-pressed oils when frying, as frying with cold-pressed oils takes longer and is very uneven. Place 5 cups soy oil in a deep frying pan or suitable frying pot which is deep enough so that hot fat won't sizzle over the sides. As you begin rolling out the dough, place the pan with oil in it over a very low flame so it can begin heating.

6. Preparing the dough: On a wooden board or suitable surface, take a lump of dough in your hand, press it flat, and then roll it very flat with a dowel or rolling pin, preferably less than 1/8 in. thickness. Have on hand some whole wheat flour for sprinkling if the dough gets too wet. Once the dough is the desired thickness, take a knife and square off the edges, cutting each piece into a 4 in. by 4 in. square. Place a spatula gently under each corner, making sure you're able to lift it off the surface before you're ready to roll it up. In the center and closer to one edge, place 1½ Tbs. of whichever filling you're using, rolling the eggroll up from one side. Gently tuck in the outer edges, removing excess dough and lightly pressing on the center so that the dough molds closely to the filling mixture (without having it break through). Place the finished eggroll on a lightly floured tray.

7. When all the eggrolls are prepared, deep fry about 4 at a time in sizzling oil for 5-8 minutes. Turn once while frying. When done, place on several thicknesses of paper towelling to drain.

Serve eggrolls with Hot Mustard Sauce and Sweet and Sour Sauce. You'll soon hear family and friends exclaiming, "Ah. So . . . Good!"

Yield: 10-12 eggrolls.

Carrots N' Curry

4 cups finely sliced carrots
2 Tbs. oil
¾ tsp. turmeric
¼ tsp. cumin seed
½ tsp. curry powder
¾ tsp. salt
⅓ cup water
1 tsp. honey

Wash and thinly slice the carrots. Saute the spices in oil. Add the water, carrots and honey, and continue to saute until the carrots are tender.

Yield: 3 cups.

Lemony Beets

3 cups beets
⅓ cup beet juice
2 Tbs. honey
¾ tsp. salt
1 Tbs. arrowroot
¼ cup water
3 Tbs. lemon juice

Slice and cook the beets in 1 cup water until tender. Drain the beets, saving the juice. Heat ⅓ cup of the beet juice, honey and salt. Combine arrowroot and cold water, and stir into the boiling juice, continuing to cook the mixture until it is thick and clear, stirring constantly. When thick, add the lemon juice. Pour the thickened juice over the beets. Serve hot.

Yield: 3 cups.

Curried Cauliflower

1 small head cauliflower
3 Tbs. oil
½ tsp. mustard seed
1 tsp. turmeric
1 tsp. salt
½ tsp. curry powder
1 Tbs. honey
⅓ cup water

This is a colorful, tasty, and easy to prepare dish. It makes a nice meal served with lentil soup, rice and tomato chutney.

Cut the cauliflower into small pieces. Heat oil, and add the mustard seeds. When the seeds begin to pop, add turmeric, curry, salt and honey. Add the cauliflower and water. Cover and cook until tender, about 15 minutes.

Yield: 4 cups.

Curried Veggies

4¼ cups potatoes
2¼ cups green beans
1½ cups tomatoes
1¾ cups green peppers
2¼ cups eggplant
¼ cup oil
1½ tsp. mustard seed
1½ tsp. turmeric
1 Tbs. cumin
4½ tsp. coriander
1½ tsp. curry
½ tsp. cayenne
1 tsp. salt
1½ tsp. honey
1½ tsp. lemon juice
1½ tsp. tamari

Wash and dice the vegetables. Heat the oil and add mustard seeds. When the seeds begin to pop, add the spices and saute them. Add veggies, cooking them in the order listed above. Allow each veggie to cook just a bit before adding the next one. Add the honey, lemon, and tamari. Adjust the seasonings to your taste -- you might want to add more curry or cayenne if you like your Indian food more spicy. These veggies accompany nearly all of our Indian feasts and have a mild and pleasant curry flavor.

Yield: 8 cups.

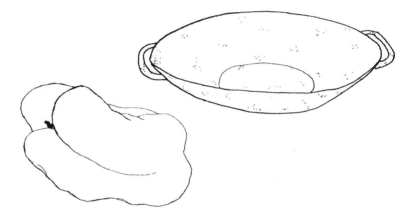

Creamed Spinach

14 cups raw spinach
¼ cup butter
3½ Tbs. whole wheat flour
1½ cups milk or soymilk
½ tsp. salt
1/8 tsp. pepper
½ tsp. nutmeg
½ tsp. grated lemon rind

This is a rich, satisfying spinach dish which is very easy for you to whip up. First, wash the spinach thoroughly. Steam it for 3 minutes only, and then drain. Melt the butter in a large saucepan. Stir in the flour to make a smooth paste, and slowly add milk, stirring constantly. Add the spices. When the sauce is thick and hot, add the spinach. Stir and cook for 3 minutes. Serve piping hot, as an accompaniment to a "well-heeled" supper or in the happy presence of salad and crackers.

Yield: 7 cups.

11·
Soups

One of my earliest recollections of soup: sitting at a picnic table on a frosty November evening, geese honking their way south overhead, a steaming bowl of hearty bean soup and a crusty hunk of hot bread before me. Since that time, some of my favorite memories have centered around soup. Like the snowy winter of my 12th year, when our new house in the country was finished enough for us to begin to move in. I can still smell the aroma of the thick and nourishing vegetable soup brought just in time for dinner by our nearest neighbor down the road. It was one of her end-of-the-season garden specials, she said, as we appreciatively eyed thick pieces of bright garden vegetables grown in her back yard. After that time, we started our own garden and found that no soup is better than the one made from whatever's left before the first frost sets in. I've had soups from pots swinging over a fire in the middle of a frozen lake, with my fingers and toes red from skating, and soups made to deliver to friends in times of sadness and need. Hot and hearty winter warmers, or cool and light summer favorites, soups are a versatile, pleasing addition to any meal.

A creative and popular way to use up leftovers, our most popular soups are made without a recipe from whatever seems to be handy and whatever spices happen to jump in the pot. So feel free to change the ingredients around and mix and match recipes to create your own new ones. I've never made quite the same soup twice. They always seem to taste a little better that way!

A word about some of the soups included here: soothing broth is a good basic to use as a building block for any number of clear soups. Just add your favorite blend of veggies or eat plain. A variation on this recipe: potassium broth is a clear soup which has a high potassium content (particularly helpful during a purifying diet or fast when the potassium as well as other minerals in the body may need a booster). This is a revitalizing and unexpectedly tasty soup, though you may want to salt it a bit. (After a fast it will taste like a "feast" to your cleansed palate . . .)

Miso soups are composed of a dark reddish-brown fermented soybean mash known as miso, a highly potent source of enzymes, protein, minerals and vitamins easily assimilated by the body. To strengthen the body during long fasts or as a healthful supplement for one who has been ill, miso broth is the perfect answer, tasteful and revitalizing. Or simply serve with vegetables and rice as hearty vegetarian fare any day…especially a cold one!

Finally, an explanation is needed for our "Stone Soup" recipe. This refers to a potpourri or add-what-you-will soup and originates in the legend of some soldiers (during an unidentified war) who entered a village, begging for food from door to door. They were overwhelmingly hungry. Suspicious of their motives, the townspeople one by one closed their door on the soldiers, saying "Sorry, no food in the house." So the soldiers, undaunted but still hungry, decided to do whatever they could for themselves and erected a pot over a big fire in the middle of town. One by one they carried big stones and put them in a pot, adding water and letting it come to a boil. Curious townsfolk peeped out of windows and doors and finally came cautiously to watch them.

"What are you doing?" they asked the soldiers.

"Why, we're cooking a stone soup," they replied.

"A stone soup?"

"Yes, it's an old recipe we have -- very good -- only we're just missing a few carrots to make it perfect."

"Oh, carrots? I've got some carrots." So carrots miraculously appeared and were tossed into the stone soup.

Others gathered, and each one asked the same question: "What kind of soup?"

"It's a stone soup, an old recipe. Only we're missing onions to make it perfect..." So the onions came. And then celery, cabbage, peas. Finally, there were enough ingredients for the soldiers to have a delicious meal -- and so pleased were they by the generosity of the townsfolk that they shared their bounty with everyone, stones removed of course. You too can make this satisfying soup, hopefully without the stones, but with all your favorite ingredients. Hearty appetite!

And enjoy the other soups as well -- as appetizers to a rich and full dinner spread or as mainstays for luncheons -- with salad and crackers on the side.

Stone Soup

5 cups water
1 cup + 1 Tbs. good tasting nutritional yeast
5 Tbs. tamari
1 tsp. celery seed
½ tsp. salt
¼ tsp. pepper
2 cups cooked sliced carrots
2 cups cooked rice

Whisk the yeast into the water and add tamari. Add the celery seed and other spices, then add the cooked carrots and rice. Heat for 15-20 minutes, stirring frequently, and then serve.

As in the "stone soup" story, this soup can have a host of variations and is a good way to use leftovers; also good for those who hanker after Mom's chicken soup, for this has a similar taste and aroma. Add cubed vegetables, tofu, or other grains according to your taste.

Yield: 10 cups.

Potassium Broth

6 cups water
2 cups grated carrots
2 cups grated potatoes
Optional: a bit of tamari or salt added to taste

Boil water; add the grated carrots and potatoes (finely grated). Simmer on low heat for 20-25 minutes and strain off the vegetables. This is an excellent broth for revitalizing the body; especially when the body is cleansing, after fasting, or as a light nourishing meal.

Yield: 3 cups.

Spinach & Split Pea Soup

¾ cup split peas
4½ cups water
3 Tbs. oil
½ tsp. mustard seed
½ tsp. turmeric
¼ tsp. curry powder
1 Tbs. lemon juice
¾ tsp. salt
¼ cup chopped green pepper
1½ tsp. ground coriander
2 cups chopped spinach

Wash the split peas and soak in 2 cup water for ½ hour. Using soak water plus remaining 2½ cups water, cook the peas and set aside. In a medium-size pan, heat the oil and add the mustard seeds. When the seeds pop, add turmeric. Add spices and oil to cooked split peas. Add all remaining ingredients except the spinach and cook for 10 minutes. Then add the spinach, and cook for an additional 10-15 minutes over medium heat. A delicious, tasty appetizer for any meal.

Yield: 7 cups.

Merry Miso-Veggie Broth

1 cup diced carrots
1 cup diced celery
4 cups water
¼ cup miso

Dice the celery and carrots and set aside. Bring a small amount of water to boil in a saucepan, add the celery and carrots and steam until almost tender. Add 4 cups of water; bring to a boil until the vegetables are cooked. Then turn off the heat and remove approximately ½ cup of broth. Add the miso to this portion only (do not boil miso, as this destroys the enzymes). Mix well and add back to the remainder of the soup. Heat and serve.

Yield: 4 cups.

Earthy Miso Soup

2 cups raw chopped cabbage
½ cup raw chopped carrots
1½ Tbs. butter
3 Tbs. flour
1 Tbs. tamari
2½ cups water
1/8 cup miso
1/8 cup fresh parsley

Chop and steam the cabbage and carrots. In a separate pot, melt the butter, add in flour to make a paste. Add tamari and miso and whisk in water, stirring constantly. As mixture thickens, add cooked vegetables. When the cooking process is nearly finished, add the fresh chopped parsley as a garnish.

Yield: 3-4 cups.

Cream of Celery Soup

4 cups chopped celery
¼ cup butter
3-4 Tbs. oil
½ tsp. savory
¼ tsp. nutmeg
½ tsp. oregano
¾ tsp. salt
6 Tbs. whole wheat flour
1 quart milk
1 quart tofu whey or water
¼ cup tamari

Saute the celery and set aside. Place the butter in a medium-size saucepan and while heating it over a low flame, add the spices, stirring gently. To this mixture, add the whole wheat flour and form a paste. As you continue stirring, gradually add in the milk, being attentive to the mixture. Allow it to come to a boil, but remember to continue mixing all the time so the soup doesn't burn. Add the water and tamari and continue cooking for 20 minutes or until the mixture thickens, stirring all the time. Stir in celery and serve.

Yield: 8 cups.

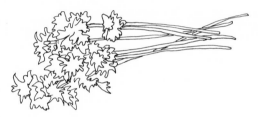

Cream of Cabbage Soup

6 cups cabbage
¼ cup whole wheat flour
¼ cup melted butter
2 cups milk
¼ cup peas
1/8 cup tahini
1/8 cup tamari
¼ tsp. celery seed
¼ tsp. basil
Pinch cayenne
¼ tsp. salt
Dash pepper

Steam the cabbage to have a final yield of 6 cups. Prepare a white sauce by adding flour to melted butter, and then whisk in milk, allowing the mixture to become even in consistency. Add the cabbage, peas, tahini and tamari. Spice the soup with celery seed, basil, cayenne, salt and pepper. Simmer the soup for 5 or 10 minutes, stirring frequently, and then serve.

For other tasty variations: try cream of cauliflower, blending a part of the cauliflower before cooking and adding the rest in pieces. Or, try cream of spinach, adding ½ tsp. thyme, 1 tsp. poppy seeds, and ½ tsp. cinnamon for each 6-8 cups of soup. This gives the soup a delicate, aromatic flavor.

Yield: 8 cups.

Cream of Broccoli Soup

4 cups chopped broccoli
¼ cup butter
½ tsp. savory
¼ tsp. nutmeg
½ tsp. oregano
¾ tsp. salt
6 Tbs. whole wheat flour
1 quart milk or soymilk

Follow directions as for the Cream of Celery Soup. Do not include any tamari, tofu whey or water, but instead cook with one quart regular or soy milk. When the mixture is hot, add the broccoli and continue cooking for 5 to 10 minutes. Remove the soup from the heat, blend the mixture well in your blender, and heat once again before serving. This has a wonderful thick texture and a sweet broccoli flavor.

Yield: 9 cups.

Cream of Carrot Soup

4 cups raw chopped carrots
2 cups water
½ cup dry milk powder
1 tsp. honey
1 tsp. salt
1/8 tsp. pepper

Chop the carrots. Steam or boil them; then blend in with the remaining ingredients until creamy. Heat the soup prior to serving.

This is the simplest cream soup recipe. Make it up for unexpected company and they will be impressed with its delicious flavor.

Yield: 4 cups.

Sunseed Gazpacho

1 cup carrot juice
1 cup celery juice
1 cup shredded cabbage
1 cup chopped green or red pepper
¾ cup tomato (fresh)
1 Tbs. tamari
¼ tsp. cayenne
½ tsp. cumin
1 tsp. honey
1 cup sunflower seeds
1/8 cup parsley

First wash and prepare all the fresh vegetables, juicing the celery and carrots and setting to one side. Then in blender add all the ingredients, with the exception of the sunflower seeds. Blend this mixture until it is liquid in consistency; then add sunflower seeds and gradually blend into the mixture. Serve cold with parsley garnish.

This is a wonderful summertime appetizer. You can play with the ingredients to your heart's content, cutting back on the sunflower seeds and adding fresh chopped zucchini or cucumber instead. Also try a bit of asafetida (hing) for that Spanish-style tomato gazpacho. Let your imagination and your blender carry you to the limits of gazpacho creation!

Yield: 4 cups.

Saturday Night Tomato Soup

3 Tbs. butter
6 Tbs. whole wheat flour
4 cups cold water
2 cups chopped tomatoes
¼ cup tamari
1½ cups tomato paste
1 tsp. cinnamon
1 tsp. cumin powder
2 tsp. oregano
1 tsp. basil
1 tsp. marjoram
1 tsp. salt
½ tsp. thyme
pinch cayenne
2 tsp. honey
pinch hing (optional)

Melt the butter, and stir in the flour to make a paste. Mix well while adding cold water. Continue stirring and add the chopped tomatoes and tamari. Whisk in tomato paste and stir until you have an even consistency. Heat, stirring frequently, and add spices and remaining ingredients; then simmer another 10 minutes or until creamy and smooth.

For variation, you can add 1 or 2 cups of cooked brown rice. P.S. You can serve this soup anytime, you like; you don't have to wait for Saturday night.

Yield: 6 cups.

Rice & Brown Lentil Soup

5 Tbs. oil
½ tsp. mustard seeds
½ tsp. turmeric
¾ tsp. curry powder
2 cups chopped carrots
1 cup cooked brown rice
1 cup cooked brown lentils
4 cups water
¾ cup chopped green pepper
1½ tsp. ground coriander
2½ tsp. salt
½ tsp. cinnamon
1 tsp. honey

In a saucepan, heat the oil and add the mustard seeds. When the seeds pop, add turmeric, curry and carrots. Cook for 3-4 minutes. Then add the rice, brown lentils, water, and the remaining ingredients. Simmer for 15 minutes over a medium heat and then serve.

Yield: 6 cups.

Red Lentil Dahl

3 Tbs. butter
2 tsp. cumin powder
1/8 tsp. cayenne
½ tsp. ginger
1½ tsp. coriander
1 tsp. mustard seeds
2 tsp. curry powder
1½ tsp. salt
8 cups water
2 cups red lentils (dry)
¼ cup + 2 Tbs. lemon juice
2 tsp. honey

A "dahl" is a thick soup, not a plaything. And a very rich, well-spiced affair at that, coming to us from the Indian tradition.

In a large saucepan, heat the butter and add all the spices, including the salt. Allow it to simmer briefly. Add the water and bring the mixture to a boil. Meanwhile wash the lentils and add to boiling water along with the lemon juice and honey. Cook over a low flame for one hour, stirring frequently.

Yield: 6 cups.

Zucchini Cheese Soup

10 cups chopped zucchini (8-10 medium)
1 cup milk
1 cup grated cheese
1 tsp. salt
¼ tsp. pepper

Steam the zucchini until tender and let it drain. Add the remaining ingredients and blend in your blender until the consistency is smooth and creamy. Heat and serve; you may like to experiment by adding a pinch of your favorite spices such as basil, dill or oregano.

Yield: 6-7 cups.

Tarrot Soup

3 cups raw chopped carrots
4 cups raw chopped turnips
6 cups water (total)
1½ tsp. salt
¼ tsp. pepper
2 tsp. honey
1 Tbs. tamari

Chop and steam the carrots and turnips until they're soft. Blend the carrots with 1½ cups of water; then blend turnips with 2½ cups of water. Place both in a saucepan and add two more cups of water, mixing together. Then add the honey, salt and tamari, and heat and serve. "Tarrot", by the way, is a cross between a carrot and a turnip, and a very delectable hybrid, as you'll soon discover.

Yield: 8 cups.

Vegan-Rice Soup

1 cup dry brown rice
1¾ cup water
1½ cups chopped carrots
½ cup chopped peppers
1½ cups chopped cauliflower
2 Tbs. butter
5 Tbs. flour
4 cups cold water
3 Tbs. Good Tasting Nutritional Yeast
1 tsp. salt
1 tsp. curry powder
1 tsp. caraway seed

Cook the rice with 1¾ cups of water and set aside. Prepare all the vegetables (you can substitute any of your favorites for those listed) and steam in a separate saucepan. In another pot, melt the butter and whisk in flour, then add cold water. When the mixture is smooth, add yeast and spices. Lastly, add the cooked rice and vegetables, and continue stirring as you cook, because the rice has a tendency to sink to the bottom and may easily burn. Heat and serve.

Yield: 7 cups.

3 Bean Soup

½ cup aduki beans (dry)
¼ cup chickpeas (dry)
¼ cup kidney beans (dry)
¾ cup raw diced carrots
½ cup raw green peppers
1 cup raw diced celery
3 cups water
½ cup tomato paste
¼ cup tamari
½ tsp. basil
½ tsp. tarragon
1 tsp. dill
¼ tsp. salt

Soak the beans overnight. Cook the beans in their soak water in individual pots (they take different cooking times; see Legume Cooking Chart, p. 107). Make sure to watch them and add water from time to time so they don't boil over. Dice the raw vegetables and steam them separately; then make a soup base using the water and remaining ingredients. (You can drain off part of the soak water from the beans for this base.) Add the beans (fully drained), and the steamed veggies, and cook for 15 to 20 minutes on a very low flame, stirring constantly.

The aduki beans make this a special dish, high in protein and nutrients. You might even like to experiment with this recipe, cooking the stock down until you have a thick, hearty bean stew instead of a soup. If you're really feeling a dash of bravado, try blending the bean-veggie mixture and serve as a bean paste over rice -- absolutely delicious and quite filling as well!

Yield: 6-7 cups.

Hira's Multi-Bean Soup

1 cup cooked mung beans
1 cup cooked aduki beans
1 cup cooked lima beans
2 cups cooked lentils
½-¾ cup tamari
1 Tbs. dill
2 Tbs. Spike

Soak the mungs, adukis and lima beans overnight. Cook all four varieties of beans in separate pots until well done. (See chart on p. 107 for cooking times.) The lentils will take the least amount of time. Add all the beans, including their cooking water and the remainder of the ingredients, and simmer for 15-20 minutes. Adjust tamari to your own preferred "saltiness." Remove from heat and serve.

Although admittedly this soup takes a lot of pots to prepare, we guarantee that once you've made it, you'll enjoy it and be glad you did. (And if not, you might talk Hira into coming down and washing your pots for you.)

Yield: 4-5 cups.

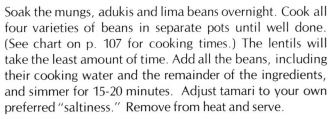

Split Pea Soup

2 Tbs. oil
1 tsp. basil
½ tsp. black pepper
1 tsp. cumin powder
½ tsp. ginger
2 tsp. salt
8 cups water
2 cups dried split peas
½ cup carrots
½ cup celery
½ cup green peppers
1 tsp. honey
1 Tbs. lemon juice
2 Tbs. soy sauce

Saute spices in oil, adding 8 cups of boiling water when all the spices are sauteed. Stir in the vegetables, split peas, honey and lemon juice, and bring to a second boil. Turn down the heat and simmer for 45 minutes to 1 hour, stirring frequently to avoid sticking. Add soy sauce and serve a thick, delicious pea soup. Just bring in your slices of bread and deep wooden bowls and you're ready for some good eating.

Yield: 7 cups.

Hearty Red Lentil Soup

1½ cups red lentils (dry)
4 cups water
4 Tbs. oil
½ tsp. mustard seed
½ tsp. cumin seed
2 tsp. coriander
1 tsp. curry powder
1 tsp. chili powder
2½ tsp. salt
½ cup chopped carrots
¾ cup chopped celery
¼ cup chopped green pepper
1 cup chopped tomato
2 cups additional water

Wash and drain the lentils. Cook with 4 cups of water until they're soft (or in a pressure cooker for 15-20 minutes). In a saucepan heat the oil and add the mustard and cumin seed. When the seeds begin to pop, add the other spices and vegetables and saute. Add the cooked lentils and additional water and cook another 10-15 minutes over a medium heat.

Yield: 7½ cups.

Soothing Broth

3 cups vegetables of your choice
5 cups water

Any vegetables may be used for a light, healthful broth. Boil water; prepare the vegetables by shredding (carrots, beets or potatoes) or finely dicing them (as in the case of broccoli, cauliflower, celery or cabbage). Place the vegetables in water and allow them to simmer on a very low flame for 20 to 30 minutes or longer. Then strain the broth mixture, and if you like, season with tamari or your favorite vegetable spices. (You can make a wonderful broth or soup stock by simmering vegetable peelings, carrot tops, string bean ends, etc.) This serves as an excellent base for embellishments; add rice, noodles or legumes, or enjoy simply as is.

Yield: 5-6 cups.

Golden Dream Soup

2 whole raw carrots
1½ cups cauliflower
1 small zucchini, chopped
1 cup greenbeans
3 cups water
1½ tsp. salt
¼ tsp. sage
1-2 Tbs. dill (depending on your taste-buds)
1/8 cup tamari
3/8 to 1/2 cup nutritional yeast

One of our chef, Narendra's, classics. On a low flame, simmer the vegetables, water, spices and tamari until medium cooked, but not mushy. Remove this mixture from the heat, and blend it up in your blender. Add the yeast, stirring it in completely, and serve with crackers or as an accompaniment to a rice dish. This is truly a "dream" soup -- it's either the dill or the yeast or both together which give it its distinctive flavor. For diversity you can add broccoli, spinach, celery or potatoes in quantities you like; adjust the seasonings accordingly.

Yield: 7-8 cups.

Barley-Tomato Soup

3 Tbs. oil
1 tsp. cumin powder
1 tsp. curry powder
¼ tsp. black pepper
1½ cups green peppers
1½ cups chopped carrots
3 cups water
1 cup cooked barley
1½ cups fresh tomatoes

Chop all the fresh vegetables. In a deep saucepan, heat the oil and add the spices. Stir for several minutes and then saute the green peppers lightly. Add the carrots and saute several minutes longer. Then add the water, barley (already cooked) and tomatoes. Cook over a medium heat for 15-20 minutes, and serve piping hot. Note: When you use whole barley grains, be sure to allow plenty of time for barley to cook thoroughly. (See section on cooking grains, pp. 114, for more specific directions.)

Yield: 8 cups.

Potato-Pea Soup

6 to 8 medium potatoes
3½ to 4½ cups milk
2 tsp. salt
¼ cup butter
1 cup shredded cheddar cheese
1 cup fresh or frozen peas

Here's a steamy hot soup -- or a meal -- whichever you prefer. Steam or boil the potatoes until tender. Then drain and mash them, blending mashed potates in with the milk. When fully blended, add the salt, butter, cheddar cheese and peas and cook over a low flame, stirring constantly. Heat for approximately 20 minutes and then serve.

Yield: 10 cups.

Hot Beet Borscht

8 cups diced beets
3-4 Tbs. lemon juice
3 Tbs. vinegar
3-4 Tbs. honey
1 tsp. dill weed
1 tsp. basil
10-12 cups water
1½ tsp. salt

Although we give you the ingredients, to make a good beet borscht, you'll have to be somewhat of a Jewish cook, adding a bit here, a bit there. No Jewish cook I know (or any other true gourmet) cooks by measuring; they all cook by taste.

Dice and cook the beets. Add smaller amounts of lemon juice, vinegar and honey, and "balance out" the sweetness and sourness of the borscht according to your taste. Add the spices, water and part of the salt (about 1 teaspoon) and allow the mixture to cook for 20 minutes. Turn off the stove and set aside the borscht mixture for ½ hour. Then retest borscht; by this time many of the flavors will have come together, and you can add the remainder of the salt and any other of the above ingredients which will help balance the sweetness and sourness. You can serve hot or cold. Cold beet borscht blended up with yogurt or sour cream is an excellent lunch or dinner appetizer.

Yield: 1 gallon plus one cup.

Raw Beet Borscht

8 cups shredded raw beets
3½ cups water
½ cup tamari
¼ cup lemon juice
¼ cup vinegar
¼ cup honey
1 tsp. dill weed
1 tsp. basil
½ tsp. salt
Yogurt or sour cream as desired

Grate the beets, place in a bowl and add remainder of the ingredients, mixing and tossing them together. Serve topped with sour cream or yogurt.

Yield: 8 cups.

12·Entrees:
Legumes, Grains, and Pastas

Evening time is here; you've had a pleasantly active day at work, can feel your "stomach clock" ticking, and your hunger alarm ready to go off any minute. What to serve for supper? Or perhaps, like us, you're approaching the noonday meal... the most plentiful one. (Since we arise and retire early, we prefer not to eat too much later in the day. Makes the next morning's jogging and yoga that much easier...)

At any rate, think of your options for the meal. Consider the ease of grain cooking: you measure your ingredients, allow the water to boil, and while the grain is gently simmering, you can be off on a number of errands -- putting groceries away, feeding the cat, or thinking of how you'll manage the laundry, supper for four, and the studying you need to do for your art course. The beauty of most of these meals is that they provide rich and hearty dining while requiring fewer cooking hours than you might imagine. The trick is to think ahead. Imagine the night before what you'd like to serve for tomorrow's supper, and then put the lentils or chickpeas up to soak, or prepare the rice or noodles in advance. Then, when your actual meal-prep day arrives, you have everything on hand, and the fun part -- spicing, testing and tasting -- is all yours.

When we recipe-tested for this cookbook, we were able to prepare 15 to 20 entrees all in one morning, mainly because we had evolved a system of organizing all phases of cooking. 7 am -- out came a cart with peas, lentils, carrots, spices, flour, all scrupulously measured. Kidneys, chickpeas and soybeans were bulging out of their jars, having been soaked the night before. Cooking was almost child's play, with everything in front of us, ready to be cooked. Of course, keeping track of everything required keen focusing. If someone happened to peer over our shoulders and wonder what it was we were cooking, we would be hard-pressed to answer, with seventeen pots on the stove!

Luckily for you, it won't be necessary to cook in quite this way (unless you're planning a large banquet one of these days...) Still, the same principles of organization apply on a smaller scale, and can free your energies, enabling you to cook in a fast yet creative, focused manner.

In the following sections, we present you with a wide array of main dish foods. Grains, pastas and legumes of all varieties are included with special charts and cooking instructions for each. Also see Chapter 10 for vegetable entrees and side-dishes to help coordinate your meal pleasingly. And don't forget the menu suggestions listed for you at the end of Chapter 8.

Legumes

Plants having edible seeds within a pod are considered "legumes" and include such dietary staples as lentils, mung, lima, soy and other beans, peas and chickpeas. Sprouting legumes increases their protein content and Vitamin C. A very inexpensive source of protein, legumes combine with grains to provide optimal nutritional requirements, complementing each other in their essential protein yield. Legumes also provide a variety of nutrients including iron, thiamin, niacin, and riboflavin and have been shown to lower blood fats and decrease hardening of the arteries. Therefore their addition, particularly to a meat-eater's diet, is beneficial to health and preventative in nature.

Have you heard the old refrain:

> "Beans, beans, that wonderful fruit
> The more you eat, the more you toot.
> The more you toot, the better you feel,
> So let's have beans at every meal."

For those unaccustomed to eating bean dishes, the problem of gas or discomfort is indeed a factor. However, adaptation is possible. Very few people cannot tolerate beans if they are properly prepared and eaten in the right combinations. A few helpful hints:

1) Soak the beans (especially kidney, soy, navy, or chickpeas) overnight.

2) Cook the beans from 4-6 hours at a medium to low temperature.

3) Begin eating the beans in smaller quantities, chew thoroughly, and be careful how you combine with other foods.

Cooking for long periods, as well as soaking overnight, helps break down some of the more stubborn starches in legumes so that they are more readily digested when eaten.

We use beans in entrees, soups, dips, spreads and sprouts. Their colors, shapes and textures add a pleasing variety to simple meals. We've enjoyed the delicate flavor of mung sprouts Oriental style, or the creamy spicy goodness of lentils in Indian dahl. Once in a while our residents go all out for the occasion; we've been known to dress up in sombreros and sarapes, bring out the tacos and refried beans and do a Mexican hat dance to warm up everyone's appetite. Have fun with your own inventions, but remember there's many a fine time to be had from a legume!

Legume Cooking Chart

LEGUME-1 CUP	COOKING WATER	COOKING TIME	YIELD
Aduki beans	4 cups	1¾ hrs.	3 cups
Black eyed peas	3 cups	1 hour	2¼ cups
Garbanzo beans	6 cups	3-4 hours	3 cups
Kidney beans	4 cups	1¾ hours	2¼ cups
Lentils*	3 cups	45 minutes	3 cups
Lima beans	4 cups	1¾ hours	2¼ cups
Mung beans	4 cups	1 hour	3 cups
Pinto beans	3 cups	2½ hours	2¼ cups
Split peas*	3 cups	45 min.	3 cups
Soybeans	4 cups	4-5 hours	2½ cups

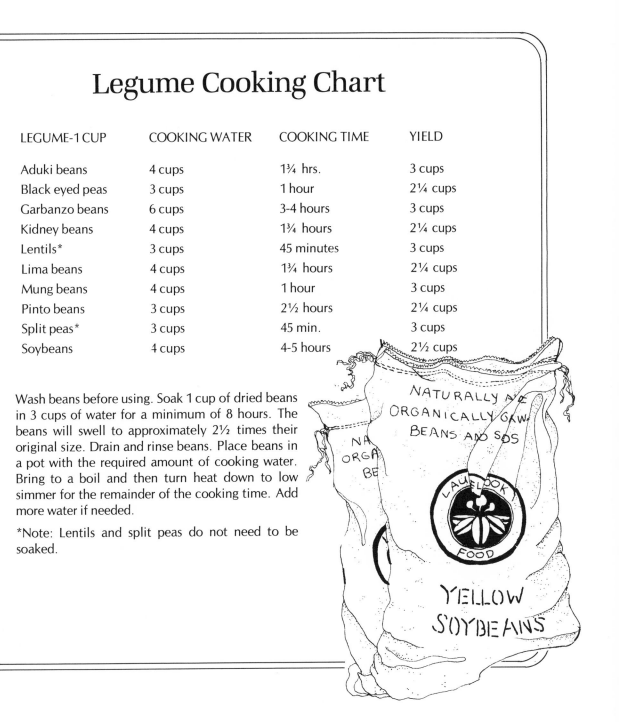

Wash beans before using. Soak 1 cup of dried beans in 3 cups of water for a minimum of 8 hours. The beans will swell to approximately 2½ times their original size. Drain and rinse beans. Place beans in a pot with the required amount of cooking water. Bring to a boil and then turn heat down to low simmer for the remainder of the cooking time. Add more water if needed.

*Note: Lentils and split peas do not need to be soaked.

Lentil Burgers

1 cup cooked lentils
2 Tbs. oil
⅓ cup whole wheat flour
½ Tbs. tamari
½ tsp. cumin
1/8 tsp. allspice
1/8 tsp. nutmeg
½ cup wheat germ
¼ tsp. salt
Bread crumbs as needed
¼ cup wheat germ (for rolling)

In a large bowl, add the first 9 ingredients, mixing in well with your hands, until the mixture sticks together. If the mixture feels too wet to form patties, add bread crumbs as needed. Roll the patties in wheat germ and place on an unoiled baking sheet. Bake at 350° for 20-30 minutes. Serve the burgers with Soy Sesame Sauce or Light and Easy Brown Gravy. (See p. 139 for these recipes.)

Yield: 4 patties.

Tomato Bean Bake

1 cup diced celery
1 cup diced green pepper
1 cup chopped tomatoes
3 cups cooked kidney beans
3 Tbs. oil
¼ tsp. cayenne
1 cup tomato paste
⅓ cup honey
¼ cup molasses

Wash and dice the celery and peppers, and chop the tomatoes. Saute the peppers, celery and cayenne in oil. Combine with the remaining ingredients in a baking dish, and bake at 350° for 1 hour.

Yield: 5 cups.

Refried Mexi-Beans

2 cups kidney or pinto beans
1 tsp. salt
2 cups grated cheese (Cheddar, longhorn, etc.)

An easy-to-make beany-cheese paste, Refried Mexi-beans go well in tacos, for filling burritos, or served by themselves. Soak the beans overnight. Cook them until tender, and then blend them up with salt at a low speed until almost smooth in consistency, adding a small amount of soak water as needed. Put the blended beans in a shallow oiled baking dish; sprinkle grated cheese on top and bake at 350° for 30 minutes.

Yield: 5½ cups.

Chickpea Casserole

4 cups cooked chickpeas
½ cup sliced green peppers
1/8 cup oil
½ tsp. turmeric
¼ - ½ tsp. curry
½ tsp. mustard powder
1 tsp. salt
½ tsp. coriander
¼ tsp. parsley
1/8 tsp. hing (optional)

Cook the chickpeas and set them aside. Wash and slice the peppers into thin strips. Saute the spices in oil, and then saute the peppers. Add the chickpeas, and cook 5 minutes longer, mixing well. Serve hot. This is a tasty dish evoking the Orient in a very simple easy-to-prepare cooking process.

Yield: 4 cups.

Millet Chickpea Casserole

3 cups cooked millet
1 cup cooked chickpeas
½ cup chopped green peppers
¾ tsp. salt
1/8 tsp hing (optional)
1 tsp. tamari
¾ tsp. curry
Pinch coriander
2 Tbs. butter

First cook the millet and chickpeas; then wash and chop the green peppers. Saute the spices and peppers in butter, add millet and chickpeas, and continue to stir over a medium flame for 5 minutes. Serve hot.

Chickpea Patties

½ cup uncooked chickpeas
1 cup uncooked bulgar
1½ cups water
2 Tbs. oil
1 tsp. salt
1 Tbs. Nutritional Yeast
1 cup cold water
½ cup rolled oats

Soak the chickpeas overnight. Boil 1½ cups water, stirring in bulgar, and cook for 15 minutes. Add the oil, salt and yeast. Blend the chickpeas with cold water until smooth, and add them to the bulgar mixture. If the mixture is too wet to form patties, add oats. Allow it to sit for a while, so the oats can absorb any extra moisture. Drop the mixture onto a greased baking sheet. The consistency of the mixture will be fairly wet. Bake at 350° for 10 minutes. Turn the patties over and bake another 15 minutes. Top with Tahini Sauce (see p. 140) and parsley, or serve with mustard.

Yield: 12 large-sized patties.

Chickpea Delight

1½ cup dry chickpeas
6 cups water
¼ cup chopped green pepper
3 Tbs. oil
1 tsp. mustard seed
1 tsp. turmeric
1 Tbs. tomato paste
1 Tbs. salt
½ tsp. curry powder
1 tsp. ground coriander
2 Tbs. lemon juice
3 Tbs. honey

Soak the chickpeas overnight in 6 cups water. Cook them in water until tender, adding additional water if needed. Once cooked, drain. Wash and chop the peppers. In a separate pan, heat the oil and add mustard seed. When the seeds begin to pop, add turmeric, tomato paste, all other spices, and the lemon, honey, green pepper and chickpeas. Cook the whole mixture for 7 to 10 minutes over medium heat. You'll be delighted by how special chickpeas can taste, especially in the company of tomato and green pepper.

Yield: 4 cups.

Hummus

3 cups cooked chickpeas
¼ cup water
⅛ cup tamari
¼ tsp. black pepper
¼ cup lemon juice
3 Tbs. tahini

"Hummus" is a tasty Middle Eastern spread made from mashed chickpeas and served with crackers or pita bread. It's surprisingly easy to prepare.

Cook the chickpeas thoroughly until they're almost mushy. Put the liquid ingredients in blender first, then chickpeas and spices. Sometimes a blender won't blend all the chickpeas, so you can stir them up with a spoon when you transfer the mixture to a bowl. Chill overnight for flavors to blend.

This makes a yummy cracker dip or sandwich spread. We like it on pita bread with sprouts or lettuce. You can also add cucumbers, tomatoes, green peppers, or your favorite vegetable.

Although we prefer this recipe without oil (since we've cut back on the amount of oil added to most of our cooked food), you can add 1/8 cup of oil to above recipe for a creamier consistency. This is the way it's traditionally prepared.

Yield: 2¾ cups.

Taco Bean Filling

3 cups cooked kidney beans
1/8 cup green peppers (optional)
2 Tbs. butter
1 tsp. cumin seed
½ tsp. salt
½ tsp. paprika
1 tsp. oregano
½ tsp. chili powder
¼ tsp. cayenne
¼ tsp. mustard powder
¼ cup tomato paste
½ cup crushed tomatoes
½ Tbs. molasses

Soak the kidney beans overnight. Cook them thoroughly, and drain off the water. Then wash and chop the green pepper. Saute all the spices and the green pepper in butter. Add the rest of the ingredients and stir together over a medium flame, for about 10 minutes.

You may wish to experiment either with lentils or aduki beans for a different flavor and texture; be our guest. This is a delicious filler for tacos or an alternate chili recipe.

Yield: 3½ cups.

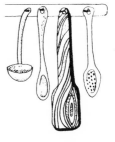

Chili Con Veggies

1½ cups uncooked kidney beans
¾ cup green peppers
¾ cup celery
¼ cup butter
¼ tsp. celery seed
1 tsp. chili powder
½ tsp. cumin
½ tsp. turmeric
1 Tbs. tamari
1½ tsp. lemon juice
1/8 tsp. salt
1 cup tomato paste
1 cup stewed tomatoes

This is a sure-fire winner among the chilis and a "sure-fire" taster too (if you make it hot...). Soak the beans overnight. Cook them until soft, and drain them. Wash and dice the green pepper and celery. Saute all the spices in butter, and then add the peppers, celery, and then the tomato products. Finally, add the beans. Simmer for 15 minutes. You may add more cayenne, but be careful...it can set your mouth on fire (in a manner of speaking...).

Yield: 3½ cups.

Grains and Pastas

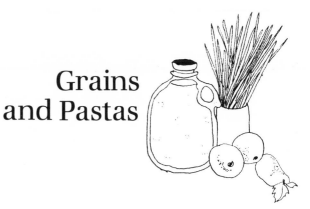

Grains form the staple of our diet, and along with vegetables and legumes can truly be considered our "staff of life."

A grain is actually the seed of different grasses, such as wheat, rye, rice or barley, and can either be sprouted or cooked to provide nourishment. High in carbohydrate, grains have the advantage that their starch converts to sugar much more slowly in digestion than simple or concentrated sugars; thus they provide energy and a satisfied feeling over a longer period of time. They all have protein, B-complex vitamins in varying degrees, and are mainly prepared in such forms as cereals, breads, pasta, puddings or baked goods. Sprouted grains form very tasty, incredibly nutritious breads as well!

Aside from serving the usual rice, oats or corn, at the Retreat we also use other less common but equally rich and nutritious grains; bulgar is similar to whole wheat, with a fantastic subtle flavor all its own. We enjoy it in a cheesey casserole, as a "pilaf" dish or mixed with nuts and raisins. It also makes a remarkably fine sweetened morning cereal. High in protein, phosphorous, calcium, and iron, bulgar is versatile in use.

Millet, although known to some only as an element in birdfood, feeds us "grown chickens" very well, and is a staple of the Retreat diet. It warms the body and is thus a good wintertime grain, and digests with more alkaline than acid residue, helping to ward off disease and prevent winter colds. We enjoy millet steamed plain or served with a brown gravy (see p. 139).

We have long been aficionados of brown rice, and consider it a staple of our diet. We use it in puddings, stuffed peppers or tomatoes, and best of all, served with tofu and sauteed Chinese vegetables. We prefer to eat the rice whole because it retains the outer kernel of the rice grain, supplying more of the protein, vitamins, and other minerals so important for our nutrition. It is important to thoroughly *wash* the rice both before and after cooking. This helps the grains be fluffy and not stick together, and cuts back considerably on extra starch content.

The manner of cooking rice, as well as other grains, is very important. We have found through experience that the secret of cooking grains well is to use less water than most cookbooks recommend and to cook them slightly longer at a lower heat. We use a ratio of only 1½ parts water to 1 part grain. Using this ratio, each grain comes out separated, light and fluffy, rather than soggy and stuck together. When cooking with this amount of water, the bottom layer of rice in the pot may be very slightly scorched at the end of the cooking. Don't throw it away! It's the tastiest part!

Enjoy whole grains as part of any meal. Whether you serve them individually or combined in a pilaf or seven-grain cereal, their taste and aroma lend themselves to a variety of enticing cooking and spicing techniques. Enhance their natural sweetness with cinnamon and allspice or emphasize their subtle heartiness with a touch of curry or Italian oregano and basil.

Also included in this section are pastas, which are cousins of the grain family and a very satisfying focus of any meal, particularly the extra special ones. Try our lasagna or yogi pierogi for an especially enjoyable eating experience.

Seclusion Special

½ Tbs. oil
¼ tsp. mustard seeds
½ tsp. tumeric
1 cup brown rice (dry)
1 cup mung beans (dry)
5½ cups water
1½ tsp. cumin
1 tsp. curry powder
¼ tsp. pepper
¼ tsp. ginger powder
1 tsp. salt
½ cup finely chopped cabbage
¼ cup chopped green pepper
½ cup finely shredded carrots
¼ cup raw peanuts (optional)

Marinade:

½ cup oil	1 Tbs. honey
⅓ cup lemon juice	1 tsp. basil
½ Tbs. salt	¼ tsp. oregano
½ Tbs. tamari	

In 1974, our spiritual teacher, Yogi Amrit Desai, spent an intensive period of seclusion in a small meditaiton home. During that time, his wife, whom residents affectionately call Mataji, prepared his daily meal and carried it up the hills to his retreat house in the woods. One of her special creations at that time was this light, high-protein dish. Retreat residents became enamored of this dish and dubbed it "Seclusion Special", in honor of Yogi Desai's special retreat. You need not enter seclusion to enjoy its flavorful goodness and nutritional benefits!

In a saucepan heat the oil, and add the mustard seeds. When the seeds begin to pop, add turmeric and stir the mixture. Fold in the rice and beans, coating them with the oil-spice mixture. Add water and the remainder of spices, mixing them thoroughly and letting them simmer until the grains and beans are well cooked (approximately 40 minutes). Combine the cabbage, peppers and carrots with the cooked rice and beans, and set aside. Prepare the marinade and pour it over the grain-bean-veggie mixture, blending it in thoroughly. This is a hearty dish which can go either hot or cold, depending upon your preferences and the time of year. It's nice to eat in "seclusion" but equally fun in a large gathering.

Grain Cooking Chart

GRAIN (1 CUP)	WATER	COOKING TIME	YIELD
Barley*	2½ cups	1¼ hours	3 cups
Brown rice	1½ cups	45 minutes	3 cups
Buckwheat groats	2 cups	20 minutes	2 cups
Bulgar	1¾ cups	15 minutes	2½ cups
Cornmeal	4 cups	25 minutes	3½ cups
Millet	1¾ cups	40 minutes	3½ cups
Rolled oats	2 cups	20-30 minutes	2 cups
Whole oats*	3 cups	1¼ hours	3 cups
Whole wheat berries*	3½ cups	2½ hours	2½ cups

Wash your grain thoroughly by placing it in a collander under running water. Place 1 cup of the grain in a saucepan. Add water, and bring to a boil, then turn the heat down to a simmer and continue to cook the grain until done (keeping covered all the time). Then rinse the cooked grain before serving.

*Note: Barley, whole oats and whole wheat berries may be soaked for a few hours or overnight to shorten cooking time.

For cooking pasta (macaroni, ziti, shells, spaghetti, etc.), follow these directions: for every one cup of pasta, use 3 to 4 cups of water. Boil the water and while it's boiling rinse off the pasta. Then add it to the saucepan and cook for a minimum of 15 minutes. (Lasagna or heavier noodles take longer.) Test a piece for softness, then drain and rinse the pasta carefully. The yield will be approximately 2½ times the dry measure.

Millet Stuffing

6 cups cooked millet
¼ cup melted butter
1 cup diced celery
Pinch pepper
1 tsp. celery seed
2 tsp. basil
1 tsp. thyme
1 tsp. dill
1/8 tsp. paprika
2 Tbs. water
¼ cup tamari

Here's an excellent and easy holiday stuffing to accompany your mock tofu turkey or other main dishes. Simply cook the millet and set it aside. Then saute the celery and spices in butter. Add a small amount of water, the cooked millet and tamari, stirring until all the ingredients are well-blended. You can place it in a casserole and heat for 10 minutes in a medium oven just before serving.

Yield: 7 cups.

Ginger Brown Rice

1½ cups cooked brown rice
2 Tbs. oil
½ tsp. mustard seed
1 small diced carrot
½ tsp. curry powder
¼ cup diced green pepper
½ tsp. salt
1 tsp. chopped ginger or ginger powder
1 cup yogurt

Cook the rice and set it aside. Heat the oil and add mustard seed, waiting until the seeds have "popped", then add the carrot and curry and saute over a low flame until the carrots are tender. Then add the cooked rice and all remaining ingredients except yogurt, allowing mixture to cool. After it's cool, mix with yogurt and serve. This is a flavorful adaptation of Indian cookery we hope you enjoy.

Yield: 2 cups.

Nutty Carrot-Rice Loaf

3 cups cooked rice
2½ cups grated carrots
¼ cup peanut butter
½ cup water
½ cup coarse bread crumbs
2 Tbs. fresh parsley
1 Tbs. thyme
½ tsp. salt

Cook the rice; grate the carrots, and then blend the peanut butter with water to a smooth consistency. In a large mixing bowl, combine all the ingredients, mixing well. Place in a lightly-oiled loaf pan. Bake at 350° for 30 to 35 minutes. (If a softer top is desired on your loaf, cover with foil while baking.)

Yield: 5 cups.

Horish (Curried Rice & Eggplant)

3 medium eggplants
Enough milk or salt water to cover eggplant when sliced
4½ cups water
3 cups brown rice
1 Tbs. curry powder
3½ cups green peppers
6 cups chopped fresh tomatoes
¼ cup butter or oil for sauteeing
¼ cup lemon juice
½ cup tamari
½ cup tomato paste
2 cups water

Prepare the eggplant by removing the stems and the skin. Slice it into long slices about ½ in. thick, and then soak them in cold milk or salt water to remove their bitterness. Boil the water, and add the rice and curry powder, simmering with the lid tightly closed until the rice is done. Wash and chop the green peppers and tomatoes into medium-size pieces and set them aside. Saute the eggplant and pat dry with paper toweling. Let it cool. Add the tomatoes and green pepper to a sauce made from lemon juice, tamari, tomato paste and water. Cook this mixture for 15 to 20 minutes. Add the eggplant and continue cooking over a low heat, stirring continuously, until the eggplant is hot.

Serve by heating the rice and pouring the hot tomato-eggplant mixture over it. This is a more complicated process; however, we think you'll find the results well worth it. Excellent repast for the holidays, or that gourmet supper you've been wanting to invite your close friends to enjoy…

Yield: 12 cups veggies, 5 cups rice.

Baked Mexicali Casserole

2 cups diced green peppers
2 Tbs. oil
5 cups diced tomatoes
1 cup cornmeal
3¾ cups cooked corn
1 tsp. cumin
1 tsp. salt
½ tsp. cayenne
8 cups shredded cheddar cheese
½ cup water

Prepare all your vegetables; saute the green pepper in oil until it's tender, then add the water and the remaining ingredients, with the exception of the cheddar cheese. Cover this mixture, and cook for one hour, stirring occasionally and adding water if it gets too thick. Place it in a casserole dish and sprinkle the cheese liberally on top. Place in your oven at 350° and bake for 15 minutes, or until the cheese melts. Served with sombrero and sarape, this will make your diners think they've relocated to sunny Mexico.

Yield: 8 cups.

Sunshine Millet

4 cups cooked millet
3 Tbs. oil
1½ tsp. mustard seed
1½ tsp. turmeric
1½ cups diced potatoes
½ cup chopped green peppers
1½ cups diced carrots
1 cup water
1 tsp. honey
1½ tsp. lemon juice
1 tsp. salt

Cook the millet and set it aside to cool. In a separate pan, heat the oil and add the mustard seed. When the seeds have popped, add the turmeric, chopped vegetables and water, and mix well. Cook over a low heat for 15 minutes or until the vegetables are tender. Then add the remaining ingredients and the millet and mix well. Combined with the spices, this millet dish has a very "sunshiney" look to it -- and hopefully it will wake up your taste buds as well.

Yield: 4 cups.

Spiced Barley

2 cups uncooked barley
5 cups water
¼ cup butter
¼ Tbs. tarragon
½ tsp. thyme
½ tsp. salt
¾ tsp. caraway seeds
1 crushed bay leaf
¼ cup sesame seeds
1½ Tbs. tamari

Cook the barley in water, then add the remainder of the ingredients after the barley has cooked completely (at least an hour). Steam over low heat, remove from heat, and serve. (Remove bay leaf before serving.)

Yield: 6 cups.

Barley Rice Pilaf

1¼ cups uncooked brown rice
½ cup uncooked barley
¼ cup sesame seeds
3 cups water or soup stock
½ cup chopped green peppers
1 tsp. oil
¼ small bunch parsley
½ tsp. thyme
½ tsp. crushed rosemary
¼ tsp. salt
½-1 Tbs. tamari

Toast the rice, barley and sesame seeds dry in a pan for several minutes, stirring continuously. (This gives them added flavor.) Then add water (or soup stock if you have it on hand). Cook on a low flame once the water has reached a boil. After the grain has cooked and only a little water remains, add the peppers, oil, spices and tamari. Cook a few minutes, then turn off the flame and steam the mixture until done. A hearty dish bringing you the combined value of the rice and barley -- it's almost a meal in itself.

Yield: 5-6 cups.

Spanish Rice

6 cups cooked brown rice
½ cup diced carrots
1 cup diced green peppers
3 cups diced tomatoes
2 Tbs. oil
½ tsp. salt
Dash hing (optional)
½ tsp. chili powder
Pinch cayenne
½ tsp. oregano
½ tsp. basil
1 tsp. dill
2 Tbs. fresh parsley
3 cups water
1 cup tomato paste
¼ cup tamari
1 tsp. lemon juice
1 cup peas

Cook the rice and set it aside. Wash and dice the carrots, peppers, and tomatoes. In a large skillet, saute the spices, parsley, green pepper and carrot in oil, plus 2 Tbs. of water. Add small amounts of water as needed. Add the tomato paste and 1 cup water, stirring frequently. Mix in the tamari, lemon juice, and tomatoes, and let them cook thoroughly, stirring constantly. Stir in the cooked rice and peas, and cook on a low flame 15-20 minutes, and serve.

Yield: 12 cups.

Rice Pulau

2 cups raw brown rice
1 cup diced carrots
¼ cup butter
2 Tbs. honey
½ tsp. salt
½ Tbs. cumin
¼ tsp. cayenne
¾ tsp. ginger
1 Tbs. turmeric
3 cups water
¼ cup roasted peanuts
¾ cup raisins
1 cup green peas

A "Pulau" is an East Indian casserole dish which contains a particular grain as its base -- either rice, wheat or bulgar.

Wash the rice until the water is clear. Dice the carrots, then melt the butter in a skillet, and stir in the honey. Saute the washed rice, carrots and spices in sweetened butter, until golden. Add the water and bring it to a boil. Let it boil for 5 minutes, then turn down the heat and simmer for 25 minutes. Turn the heat off and let the rice steam until the water is gone and the rice is cooked. Gently stir in peanuts, raisins and peas. Cook over a low flame until hot. Do not overcook the peas -- their fresh green color adds a colorful touch to this Indian dish.

Yield: 5 cups.

Pizza Bulgar

8 cups cooked bulgar
6 cups thick pizza sauce
(see pp. 120-121)
1½ pounds shredded hard cheese
1½ red peppers, sliced into rings
½ Tbs. poppy seeds

Here's an interesting and nutritious variant on pizza which will satisfy your pizza appetite as well as providing the positive benefits of a cooked whole grain. Cook the bulgar and set it aside. Prepare the pizza sauce, shred cheese, and chop all the vegetables. In a large 9 x 13 in. casserole tray layer the ingredients in the following order: 4 cups of bulgar, 3 cups sauce, ⅓ of the cheese; then, again, 4 cups of bulgar, 3 cups sauce, ⅓ of the cheese. Finally, place all the pepper rings on top followed by the remains of the shredded cheese, and sprinkle on poppy seeds. Bake at 375° for one hour, and serve. An option in preparation is to mix the tomato sauce with the bulgar and then make your layers with bulgar-sauce and cheese in between. Either way, hearty appetite!

Yield: 9 x 13 in. casserole pan.

Anandi's Bulgar

⅓ cup butter
1 bay leaf
1½ tsp. basil
½ tsp. oregano
1 tsp. cumin
¼ tsp. fennel seed
¼ tsp. salt
Dash pepper
2¾ cups dry bulgar
3 Tbs. tamari
3½ cups boiling water

The creation of one of our pioneering residents, Anandi's bulgar has endured to the present generation of Retreat bulgar afficionados. To make, melt the butter in a large saucepan and saute all of the spices plus bay leaf for several minutes. Wash and strain the dry bulgar, being careful not to let the bulgar sit in cold water too long, as this causes it to expand. Add the washed bulgar to butter-spice mixture and saute it for five minutes. Add tamari and boiling water and turn the heat down. Steam over a low flame with the lid on tight until it's ready. You can test the grain for doneness, but try not to mix or stir the bulgar until it's thoroughly cooked. The fennel seed gives a pleasant aromatic flavor to this dish.

Yield: 6 cups.

Narendra's Knockout Pizza

Sauce:
4½ cups crushed tomatoes
2 cups water
1½ tsp. salt
1½ Tbs. oregano
1 Tbs. basil
2 whole bay leaves
Pinch hot pepper (optional)
1 tsp. cumin
1 6 oz. can tomato paste
4 to 5 cups grated cheese
5 to 6 cups assorted veggies of your choice

Dough:
½ tsp. yeast
3 Tbs. honey
2 cups comfortably tepid water
water)
1½ Tbs. oil
1½ Tbs. salt
6 cups (total) flour; either all whole wheat, or ½ whole wheat, ½ unbleached flour for a lighter dough

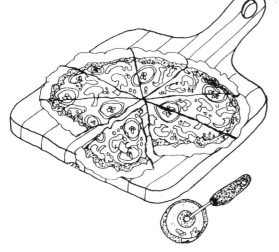

We bring you these directions from a seasoned Neapolitan pizza maker. Narendra worked many years as an Italian chef, and herewith shares his inner secrets of pizza-making.

First prepare your pizza sauce. Combine all the ingredients listed for this sauce with the exception of the grated cheese and the assorted vegetables. Cook this mixture over a low flame, stirring frequently for approximately 30 minutes. Add extra water if needed. (Approximate yield: 5-6 cups.) Cover and set aside, or refrigerate if you're using the next day.

To prepare the dough, begin by putting the yeast, honey and water together in a bowl. Let them sit no longer than two minutes, so that the yeast does not get overly activated. Then add the oil and salt and sift in the flour gradually. Knead this mixture for 5 minutes or until it is thoroughly mixed. (You can even use an electric mixer, it you like.) If it's sticky, sprinkle on a little extra flour, then put it into a well-oiled bowl or container, set it aside and let it rise for 45 minutes. Then cut the dough into as many pizzas as you'd like to have (2 to 4 pieces) and form them into balls. Put them on an oiled tray, oiling the tops of the balls as well. Cover with plastic wrap, and refrigerate for at least 1½ hours. Narendra recommends using them the following day if possible, as this gives the yeast a chance to fully activate and work its way into the dough. Either way, remove 4 hours prior to use. For each 16 in. pie, use 8 ounces of sauce between ½ and 1 pound of grated cheese (try all mild Cheddar, or a combination of either sharp Cheddar and mozarella or muenster and mozarella).

With a rolling pin, roll out each ball of dough to a rectangular shape, fitting a baking sheet with low sides. Use a little extra flour on the rolling pin and rolling surface so the dough doesn't stick. At this point, if you feel a little brave, flip it in the air. If not, just roll it to the desired thickness (from paper thin to ¼ in. -- or whatever you prefer). Then you're ready for the final stage. At last, it's time to layer your sauce, cheese and veggies!

Narendra suggests placing the raw vegetables on top (not underneath the cheese) so that the cheese can rise up as it melts and cover them well around the edges. Use any of your favorite vegetables -- green pepper, mushrooms, squash, broccoli, etc. In the layered approach, your dough is on the very bottom, then comes the sauce, next the cheese, and on the very top, the veggies. If you like a crispier crust, first bake the dough alone for about five minutes at 500° on a cookie sheet or until light brown on top of the crust. Take it out of the oven, arrange the layers as mentioned, and put it back in for 20 minutes at 500°, depending on whether you like it soft or crunchy. Enjoy!

Incidentally, Narendra is willing to take registrations for private pizza lessons, if any of you are interested. Offer good in the continental U.S., Alaska, Hawaii, etc.

Yield: 2 pizzas.

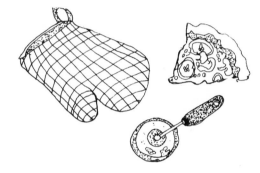

Macaroni & Cheese

1½ gallons water
1 tsp. salt
1 tsp. oil
5 cups uncooked whole wheat macaroni
½ cup butter
½ cup flour
4 cups milk
8 cups grated Cheddar cheese (2 lbs.)
1 tsp. salt
½ tsp. pepper
½ tsp. cayenne
4 cups grated cheese (mozzarella)
½ tsp. poppy seed

Boil 1½ gallons of water with 1 tsp. salt and 1 tsp. oil. When the water boils, add the macaroni. Continue to boil for 15 minutes more. Then drain the noodles in a collander when completely cooked. Meanwhile, melt the butter in a saucepan, and stir in the flour to make a smooth paste. Slowly add the milk, whisking thoroughly. Cook until the mixture reaches a boil, stirring constantly. Gently add in 8 cups of grated cheese, stirring until the cheese melts. Add the spices. Mix the drained noodles with the cheese sauce. Pour the mixture into a 9 x 11 in. baking dish, topped with 4 cups of grated mozzarella cheese. Sprinkle with poppy seeds. Bake at 350° for 30 minutes, or until the cheese turns a light brown on top. If a salty cheese is used, use less salt in the sauce. You can also use less milk, if a thicker sauce is desired.

Yield: 9 x 11 in. pan.

Hira's Yogi Pierogies

Dough:
1 cup whole wheat flour
½ cup whole wheat pastry flour
½ tsp. salt
2 Tbs. liquid lecithin
6-7 Tbs. water

Filling:
4 Tbs. mashed potatoes
4 Tbs. shredded cheese

1½ Tbs. butter
Salt and pepper to taste

Handed down to our kitchen herbalist Hira from her Ukrainian ancestry, these hot "potato-in-a-pie" turnovers are worth every minute of preparation. First, prepare your filling. It's handy to have some leftover mashed potatoes stored in your refrigerator, but in case you don't, make a small batch. Add the grated cheese.

Place the flour in a mixing bowl, and add salt. Add the lecithin, and add enough water to form a flexible dough. Divide the dough into 5 parts, and roll into 4-5 inch circles, 1/8 inch thick. Place 1½ Tbs. filling into the circle. Fold over and pinch together with a wet fork. Trim to a triangle shape. Boil in water, 2 at a time, for 5 minutes. Poke the top with a fork, 2 to 3 times. In a heavy skillet, melt the butter and add salt and pepper. Fry the pierogies for about 7 minutes on each side with the pan covered, until they are brown and crispy. Watch the heat of the pan carefully, so the butter doesn't burn. And be careful when turning them over -- hot oil can really burn. Serve when just barely cooled down.

Yield: 5 pierogies.

Lasagna

1½ gallons water
½ tsp. salt
½ Tbs. oil
10 oz. artichoke noodles
2½ cups thick lasagna sauce (see p. 142)
1½ cups cottage or ricotta cheese
4 cups or 1 lb. grated mozzarella cheese

Boil the water with salt and oil. When the water's boiling, add the noodles, and cook at a rolling boil for 20 minutes. Drain the noodles and cover them with cold water to prevent them from sticking together while you prepare the rest of the lasagna. Pour a thin layer of sauce in the bottom of your pan; next, a layer, of noodles, another of sauce, then ricotta cheese, mozzarella cheese; more noodles, sauce, ricotta cheese, mozzarella cheese, etc., layering in that order and finishing with a layer of mozzarella on top. Bake at 350° for 40 minutes. Unearth your Italian accent and serve.

Yield: 9 x 9 in. pan.

13
Dressings, Dips, and Sandwiches

Italian herb

Tahini Dip

Sukanya

Perhaps nowhere in the culinary world is the sensitive blending of just the right herbs, spices, oils and flavorings as apparent as in a simple, well-made dressing or dip. Complementing the fresh and wholesome goodness of raw vegetables, garden salads, whole grain crackers and other vegetable goodness, an artfully created dip or dressing will bring forth and harmonize with the natural flavor of its "carrier" without overwhelming it.

Complementing the flavors and textures of your dish, dips and dressings are akin; they differ mainly in their water or liquid content. However, some types of ingredients do lend themselves more easily to dressings than dips (i.e. cucumbers, beets, celery, tomatoes), and others more to dips than dressings (cream cheese, tofu, peanut); still, no hard and fast rule applies. You will notice in the following pages that all of the above ingredients plus many more have been combined both for dressings and for dips in varying quantities.

We have experimented, through failures and successes, with innumerable ingenious ways to utilize raw and cooked vegetables and blend superb spreads and dips. Hence, our weekly "raw banquet" day, featuring an eye-catching arrangement of various raw vegetables and sprouts and an assortment of raw dips, has become a favorite among Retreat residents. Easy to digest, light and cooling to the body for hot summery days, and balancing the nutritional benefits of the raw vegetables with high-protein tofu, cottage cheese or nut spreads, such meals provide an enjoyable and taste-pleasing meal.

A word on oil -- we prefer to use a light safflower, sunflower or corn oil in our dressings. Soybean oil is somewhat heavy, overwhelming the delicate herbal flavors. Sesame and olive oils, though a bit expensive, are also delicious choices. And on herbs and spices -- unless specified, all ingredients refer to ground or crushed herbs and spices. If you have access to fresh herbs, so much the better. We sometimes use Spike seasoning, available at most grocery stores.

Try your own dips and dressings. With artfulness and a bit of daring, you may find them gaining prominence in your meals.

Cucumber, Lemon & Dill Dressing

2 cups cucumbers
1 cup lemon juice
2 Tbs. honey
3 Tbs. oil
1 tsp. kelp
1 Tbs. dill weed
¾ cup sunflower seeds

Chop the cucumbers, making sure all the outer skins are first peeled off, and add them to the blender along with the other ingredients. Prior to adding the sunflower seeds, blend the mixture once so that it becomes liquid in consistency; then slowly add sun seeds, making sure these get thoroughly blended.

Yield: 3 cups.

Beetnut Dressing

1 cup chopped beets
1 cup carrot juice
1 cup sunflower seeds
½ cup rejuvelac or water
½ cup oil
¼ cup lemon juice
½ tsp. kelp
1 Tbs. dill
2 tsp. tamari
1 tsp. caraway seed

Use the beets raw or cooked and combine them with the freshly-juiced carrot juice, sun seeds and other ingredients. Make sure you blend the mixture adequately. For a more flavorful taste, grind caraway seed in the seed grinder before blending it in with the other ingredients.

Yield: 3 cups.

Greeny-Tahini Dressing

1½ cup peas
½ cup carrot juice
½ cup tahini
1 tsp. tamari
A vegetable juicer

Cook the peas, drain them and let them cool. Cut the carrots and juice them in your juicer, combining them with the remaining ingredients and the peas. Blend in well for a thick dressing which can also double as a dip.

Yield: 2 cups.

Green Bean Cream

1 cup string beans
2 Tbs. fresh parsley
1½ cups fresh tomatoes
1 Tbs. oil
1 Tbs. lemon juice
Choice of 1 whole avocado or ¾ cup tahini
½ cup celery juice
½ cup carrot juice

Chop up the green beans, parsley and tomatoes in amounts specified and place in your blender, along with the oil, lemon juice and either avocado or tahini. Have the carrots and celery already prepared for juicing and process through the juice extractor. Add to the mixture in your blender and blend well; be sure to serve as soon as possible so that you gain the full value of the enzymes and nutrients in the freshly juiced carrots and celery.

Yield: 3½ cups.

Kukatahini

¾ cup sesame seeds, toasted and finely ground
1½ cups cucumber
1 cup tahini
½ cup lemon juice
½ cup oil
1/8 cup tamari
1/8 cup honey
¼ Tbs. cumin
3/8 tsp. paprika

Toast the sesame seeds in your oven on medium heat (approximately 15-20 minutes); remove them and allow them to cool. Grind them in a seed or coffee grinder. Then peel and cut the cucumber into small pieces. Blend all wet ingredients first, then add spices and finally blend in the sesame seeds gradually. Blend for quite some time so that all the seeds and other ingredients are well-absorbed. This dressing is also good poured over cooked vegetables or grains.

Yield: 4 cups.

Apple Butter

4 cups sliced apples
1 cup water
⅛ tsp. cinnamon
⅛ tsp. coriander
¼ cup dates

Wash, core, and slice apples. Cook down over medium flame with 1 cup water, dates, and spices until water is consumed and apples are thick and mushy. Blend until smooth and chill.

Yield: 1 cup.

Guacamole

3 cups avocado
½ cup tomatoes
½ cup green pepper
1 tsp. fresh parsley
1/8 tsp. chili powder
½ tsp. salt
2 Tbs. lemon juice
2 pinches cayenne
1 pinch cumin
1 pinch celery seed

Mash the avocado with a fork until it has a creamy consistency. Chop the tomatoes and green pepper and add to the avocado mixture in a bowl. Chop the parsley very fine, and along with the remaining seasonings, add to the avocado mixture. (Try lime juice instead of lemon if you have it available.) Adjust saltiness to your own taste -- also add a bit more chili or cayenne, if you like. Mexicans use a wonderful spice called "cilantro" -- try a few chopped leaves if you can find it. This is an excellent dip for accompaniment to a Mexican meal (great with tacos or cheese crackers), or for a raw food meal, served with other spreads and raw vegetables.

Yield: 3½ cups.

Walnut Cream Sandwich

Cream cheese
Avocado
¼ cup walnuts
4 tomato slices
Sprouts
2 slices whole wheat bread (see p. 157-159)

Cream the cream cheese until smooth, adding milk if necessary. Spread both slices of bread with creamed cream cheese. Put the tomato and avocado on 1 slice and walnut halves on the other, with the sprouts sandwiched in between. Even your favorite "health food" skeptic will love this sandwich.

Creamy-Spice Dressing

1½ cups cottage cheese
1¼ cups yogurt
½ cup oil
½ cup water
¾ Tbs. fresh or dried parsley
¼ tsp. dry mustard
½ tsp. paprika
½ tsp. coriander
1/8 tsp. pepper
1 Tbs. tamari

Add all the ingredients in the blender and blend to a creamy consistency. You can reduce the water if you'd like to use it for a dip; otherwise it makes a good salad dressing with zest.

Yield: 3 cups.

Carrotbeet Dressing

1½ cups cooked beets
1½ cups cooked carrots
¼ cup oil
¼ cup lemon juice
½ cup water
1 tsp. tamari
1 tsp. kelp
2 Tbs. dill weed

Cook the beets and carrots and allow them to cool. Blend them when sufficiently cool with the remaining ingredients. Make sure you allow enough time for blending so that the mixture has a creamy consistency. Options to add to the dressing are: ½ cup fresh parsley and/or ½ cup alfalfa sprouts.

Yield: 3 cups.

Spi-cu-nut

1¼ cups peanut butter
1 cup water
1-2 cucumbers
½ Tbs. Spike seasoning

Blend water and cucumbers, then blend in peanut butter. Add Spike in the final blending

Yield: 3-4 cups

Creamy Olive Sandwich

Cream cheese
Green olives with pimiento (add 1 Tbs. per sandwich)
Sprouts
Dark pumpernickel bread

Simple but sweet. Blend the cream cheese in a food processor till creamy but still thick. Add a little milk if necessary. Finely chop up the green olives with pimiento. Spread the cream cheese on Bali's Rye Bread (see p. 165) and sprinkle evenly with the green olives and pimiento. Serve with a generous amount of alfalfa sprouts.

Parsley-Tahini Dressing

¾ cup parsley
½ cup tahini
1 Tbs. lemon juice
½ cup water
1 tsp. tamari
Dash cayenne

Chop the parsley, add the other ingredients and blend together well. The tahini gives this dressing a rounded, nutty flavor, and the cayenne and parsley add "zip."

Yield: 1½ cups.

Mala-Bean Dip

4 cups dry beans (you can use pinto, aduki, kidney beans, or a combination)
¼ cup oil
1½ Tbs. chili powder
½ Tbs. cumin
1 tsp. oregano
½ Tbs. salt

Rinse the beans before soaking; then soak them overnight. Cook the beans until soft in their soak water; drain the water and preserve. In the oil, saute all the spices and add the spice mixture in with the beans, blending up to a creamy consistency. If you'd like the mixture a little more watery, add more of the soak water. This is a delicious bean mixture, which now that we know the secret for, even our children absolutely adore. The secret in brief was this: one day the bean dip was served for lunch and all the children said, "Oh yuk -- beans. Who likes beans?" Then our chef had the savvy to rename the dish after Mala, one of the biggest bean dissenters. Naturally, when Mala appreciated the beany taste, all the children followed suit. Nice ending! (Now if you serve up "Stanley Spinach," or "Christina's Carrots," and the children still won't eat them, please don't blame us. It was just an experiment.)

Yield: 8 cups.

Tahini-Miso Sandwich

½ cup tahini
2 Tbs. miso

For simple tastes. Mix well together. Serve on crackers with sprouts or spinach. This spread is great to keep while traveling, as it's light, keeps well and is satisfying.

Yield: ¾ cups.

Date Nut Cream Sandwich

Chopped walnuts
Chopped dates
Cream cheese/milk (as needed)

Cream the cheese adding a little milk if necessary. This is best done in a food processor if you have one, or it can be done with an electric mixer. For a wonderful sandwich, spread 2 slices of bread with the cream cheese, add a layer of walnuts (slightly chopped), and chopped dates. Wonderful!

Mellow Mayo

1 cup milk (regular or soy)
½ tsp. mustard
¼ cup vinegar
1 tsp. salt
1 Tbs. honey
1½-2 cups oil (cold-pressed is best)

Add the first five ingredients together. Place them in your blender and blend together well. Remove the lid of the blender, then slowly add oil as you blend once again. Continue to add the oil until the mixture becomes thick and won't blend anymore. Chill and serve. This forms a base for practically anything you'd use regular mayonnaise for -- from Russian dressing to Hollandaise sauce.

Yield: 3-3½ cups.

Pleasing Pea-Tomato Dip

2 cups peas
2 cups fresh tomatoes
¼ Tbs. kelp
1 Tbs. tamari
¾ Tbs. Spike

Lightly cook fresh or frozen peas. Chop all the tomatoes and blend in with the cooled peas and other ingredients. The consistency is thick, making an excellent dip for crackers or fresh-cut raw vegetables, and the taste is pleasing -- we can all testify. (P.S. It almost has the flavor and feel of avocado, at more reasonable prices...)

Yield: 4 cups.

Tomato Sun Spread

2 cups chopped tomatoes
½ cup oil
1 Tbs. kelp
1 Tbs. honey
½ tsp. tamari
1 cup sunflower seeds

Here's a tempting tomatoey spread, good with crackers or freshly cut vegetables. Chop the tomatoes and place in your blender, adding all the seasonings except the sunflower seeds. Blend first to a liquid consistency, then add the sun seeds, blending to a thicker consistency and making sure all the seeds are well blended.

Yield: 3 cups.

Herb Butter

¼ lb. butter
1 Tbs. tomato paste
½ tsp. marjoram
½ tsp. oregano
½ tsp. basil
½ tsp. savory

Cream the butter with tomato paste. Add herbs. Wonderful on any bread or cracker with a bowl of good soup.

Yield: ½ cup.

Harmony Hero (a Vegetarian Hoagie)

3 Provolone or Cheddar Cheese slices
4 tomato slices
4 cucumber slices
2 romaine lettuce leaves
1 cup of various veggie mixtures
1 cup alfalfa sprouts
3-4 Tbs. Tahini Dressing (see p. 126-127)
1 pita bread (see p. 163), or 2 slices Bali's
Rye Bread, (see p. 165)
Avocado slices (in season)

1. Take a whole pita and slice in a half moon across the top (i.e., cut the pita into 2 halves).

2. Line both inside sides of the pita with romaine lettuce leaves.

3. Put your protein food next (slice of cheese, fried tofu, feta cheese crumbled, tofu salad -- whatever).

4. Place 4 slices of tomato, making sure it reaches to the bottom of pita. You may also use cucumber, zucchini, mushrooms, and/or onions.

5. Half way done! Then squirt evenly any dressing, again reaching into bottom of pita.

6. Next stuff in a generous amount of various raw veggies: basically a salad mixture containing small chunks of zucchini, avocado, cauliflower, carrots, red cabbage, green peppers, or whatever you have on hand.

7. Squirt again with dressing.

8. Add sprouts, stuffing them down inside the pita and across the top.

9. Finishing touch: Bang bottom of sandwich on table top so ingredients "settle in".

There you have it: a scrumptious hero even Dagwood would find impressive!

Peanana Butter

Natural peanut butter
Banana
Honey or fruit butter -- apple or date --
your favorite (see pp. 127, 130)
Coconut
Raisin bread (see p. 160)

Spread both slices of bread with peanut butter. Put about 1 tsp. of honey on each slice (don't get too much near the edges or it'll drip). Slice the bananas and cover 1 slice completely with banana slices. Sprinkle coconut on top. Toast the bread for an added treat.

Carrot Chutney

2 Tbs. oil
½ tsp. mustard seeds
½ tsp. fenugreek seed
1 grated carrot
2 cloves
3 tsp. lemon juice
¼ cup honey
¼ tsp. salt
Pinch ground cloves
Pinch cinnamon

A chutney is an Indian relish or side dish that enhances the rest of the meal and can be served either warm or chilled. Serve it with rice dishes, curried vegetables or chappatis (see p. 148). For carrot chutney, heat the oil, add the mustard and fenugreek seeds. When the seeds have popped, add the carrot and cloves and cook on a low flame for 2 to 3 minutes, then cool the mixture. Add the salt, ground cloves and cinnamon and serve. You can experiment with different types of chutneys, according to your inclination -- the main ingredients are salt, sweetener, lemon juice and something pungent or bitter such as cumin, ginger and pepper. Try chutneys with dates, apples, pumpkin, or any of your favorite fruits or vegetables.

Yield: 1½ cups.

Peanut Butter Tahini Spread

¾ cup tahini
¼ cup peanut butter
1 Tbs. miso
1 Tbs. honey

Mix all ingredients together. This is delicious served on crackers with plenty of sprouts or spinach.

Yield: 1¼ cups.

Italian Broccoli Dressing

6 cups cooked broccoli

Tomato sauce:

3/8 cup tomato paste
1½ cups water
1/8 cup lemon juice
½ Tbs. tamari
1 tsp. basil
1 tsp. dill
½ tsp. black pepper
¼ cup oil

Cook the broccoli thoroughly; drain and allow it to cool. While the broccoli is cooking, you can prepare the tomato sauce by mixing the tomato paste and water or by using already prepared sauce. Add the broccoli, sauce and remaining ingredients, making sure to blend well so that the dressing has a creamy consistency.

You may find you need to prepare more salad because everyone's lapping up the dressing. (Perhaps you can foresee this event and set some extra aside to begin with…)

Yield: 5 cups.

Garden Fresh Carrot Dressing

1 cup parsley
1 cup carrot juice
2 Tbs. and 2 tsp. lemon juice
2 Tbs. tamari
1 Tbs. oil

Chop the parsley and set aside. Make the carrot juice using a vegetable juicer, or juice from cooked carrots. Blend all the ingredients together in a blender and you have a light, summery dressing which doubles as a cold soup. A variation is to add ¼ cup of tahini to the dressing before blending; this makes it thicker in consistency.

Yield: 1½ cups.

Romaine Rollups

Romaine lettuce leaf
Tofu Spread (see p. 177)
Harmony Hero ingredients (see p. 132)
Hummus (see p. 110)
Peanut Butter Tahini Spread (see p. 133)

A simple alternative to sandwiches made with bread, Romaine Roll-ups are a lighter, lower-calorie and more easily digested option. Simply place sandwich fillings lengthwise, and secure them closed with a toothpick. You may add extra sprouts, diced or grated raw vegetables, dressings, sprouted sunflower seeds, or whatever suits your fancy.

14·
Sauces
and
Gravies

Gravy. The very thought evokes memories of sumptuous Thanksgiving banquets: hot turkey platters, mounds of whipped potatoes, and plenty of hot buttered biscuits to dunk into pools of smooth brown gravy. For health-seeking souls intent on nutritious fare, such memories need not be altogether discarded. Savory, hot gravies can be made without the use of beef or meat stock -- gravies which offer vitamins, and protein and lend themselves happily to our Country Mashed Potatoes (see p. 83) or whole wheat biscuits (see p. 159). (The secret in many cases is using the good-tasting nutritional yeast heretofore described.)

Gravies and sauces, unlike the usual bottled-with-sugar-and-preservatives-variety which comes off the grocery shelf, or the kind made from the baked drippings of a local turkey or cow can (and historically were, we are certain) be wholesome, delightfully edible additions to a steamed grain, a vegetable dish, or a legume "burger" for a main course meal. Try ours -- we think you'll be happily surprised at how easy, and fine, making your own vegetarian-style gravies and sauces can be, and how wonderfully they complement an already superb meal.

In Chapter 20, "Sweet Things and Snacks", you'll find a selection of sweet sauces, toppings, and icings to serve with pies and cakes (or to simply stick a finger into -- who can resist?)

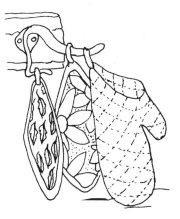

Basic White Sauce

1'/8 cup butter
¼ cup flour
1 cup milk
3/8 tsp. salt
Pinch pepper
¼ tsp. thyme
Pinch nutmeg

Melt the butter. Turn off the flame and whisk in flour to make a smooth paste, then whisk in the milk. Heat again, stirring constantly until thickened, and add spices. This is excellent over vegetable pie, or as the cream base for creamed potatoes, asparagus, or whatever vegetables you prefer.

Yield: 1 cup.

White Poppy Sauce

½ cup oat flour
1 tsp. butter
½ cup cold milk
1 cup cold water
½ tsp. salt
1¼ tsp. marjoram
Pinch nutmeg
1 tsp. poppy seeds

Toast the flour in a dry griddle until you get a nutty odor (about 10 minutes). Add the butter and stir to form a smooth paste. Turn off the heat. Very slowly add the cold milk and water, whisking in thoroughly. Whisk in the remaining spices and poppy seeds. Over a low flame, heat until the desired consistency is reached. Use this sauce the same as you would the Basic White Sauce Recipe (see p. 138).

Yield: 1 cup.

Runamuck Gravy

½ cup butter
1 Tbs. marjoram
½ Tbs. basil
¼ tsp. black pepper
1 cup oat flour
3 cups *cold* water
3 Tbs. tamari

Melt the butter, add spices and saute them in your pan with butter. Add the flour and water intermittently, mixing together as you add, whisking well. Add the tamari, and continue to cook over a low flame, whisking continuously until it reaches desired consistency. This title gives you some options, especially if you're an inexperienced gravy maker.

Yield: 3½ cups.

Soy Sesame Sauce

½ cup toasted sesame seeds
½ cup toasted sunflower seeds
3 cups soymilk
¼ cup whole wheat flour
¾ tsp. salt
¾ tsp. tamari
1/8 tsp. black pepper
¾ tsp. oregano

Toast the seeds in your oven or in a dry skillet. Then coarsely grind them in a blender or food grinder. Heat the soymilk in a pan. Whisk in flour, salt, spices, tamari and seeds. Cook until thickened, stirring constantly. Goes nicely on vegetable patties and nut loaves.

Yield: 3¼ cups.

Barbecue Sauce

2 cups tomato paste
½ cup water
¾ Tbs. oil
¼ cup honey
½ Tbs. molasses
¼ cup prepared mustard
1 Tbs. tamari
5 Tbs. lemon juice
¼ Tbs. fresh chopped parsley
½ tsp. allspice
1 tsp. salt
½ tsp. cayenne
½ tsp. mustard powder

Blend all the ingredients. Ready to use on soyburgers, tofu steaks, etc, this sauce is so easy to prepare.

Yield: 3 cups.

Light and Easy Brown Gravy

2½ cups cold water
¼ cup arrowroot
¼ cup tamari
Pepper to taste

In a saucepan, whisk the arrowroot into cold water. Heat the water, then add tamari. Over a medium flame, cook to a thick consistency, and add pepper to taste.

Yield: 2¼ cups.

Tahini Sauce (for Chick Pea Patties)

½ cup sesame seeds
1 cup water
½ cup tahini
1/8 cup lemon juice
¼ tsp. salt
1/8 cup oil

Blend all the ingredients together in your blender. Depending on your taste, add more or less salt. Also, be aware that the mixture gets fairly thick and may sometimes not blend completely. In that case add a little more water and blend once more. Serve over the chick pea patties (see p. 109) for a rich, satisfying meal.

Yield: 2 cups.

Ginger-Soy Sauce

2¼ cups water
¼ tsp. ginger
1/8 tsp. black pepper
¼ tsp. dry mustard
6 Tbs. tamari
4 Tbs. arrowroot

Heat 2 cups water, with spices and tamari. Dissolve the arrowroot in ¼ cup cold water. Slowly add the dissolved arrowroot into the heating water, whisking vigorously. Continue to cook, stirring frequently, until the sauce thickens. Serve with sauteed vegetables, over Barbecued Tofu (see p. 180) or to accompany a rice dish. This is a versatile, piquant sauce you'll enjoy.

Yield: 4 cups.

Country Style Gravy

2 Tbs. butter
4 Tbs. whole wheat pastry flour
1 cup milk
1 cup water
1 tsp. salt
½ ground black pepper

In a skillet, melt the butter. Add the pastry flour, stirring until it turns brown. Slowly add the milk, stirring to dissolve lumps. Then add water, salt and pepper, and continue to cook over a medium heat, stirring constantly, until the desired consistency is reached.

Then pull up your rice dish, or potatoes and peas, or anything in the world you'd like Country Style Gravy on. However, we'd hesitate to put it on cheesecake.

Yield: 1½ cups.

"Tapas" Taco Sauce

1 cup diced or crushed tomatoes
1/8 cup tomato paste
½ Tbs. vinegar
¼ cup water
1/8 tsp. mustard powder
1/8 tsp. cinnamon
¾ Tbs. chili peppers
¼ tsp. black pepper
½ tsp. salt
¼ tsp. cumin
½ cup diced green pepper
1 Tbs. butter

Wash and dice the green pepper, and saute it in butter until it's soft. Blend all the other ingredients together, add the green peppers, and serve.

"Tapas" refers to the heat generated through spiritual disciplines, but there's potential "heat" in a chili pepper as well: so be aware!

Yield: 1½ cups.

Jashoda's Spaghetti Sauce

1⅓ cups tomato paste
1⅓ cups chopped tomatoes
1 cup water
½ Tbs. tamari
¼ Tbs. honey
½ Tbs. lemon juice
½ Tbs. oregano
½ Tbs. basil
2 bay leaves
¾ tsp. salt
1/8 tsp. cinnamon
¼ Tbs. parsley
1/8 tsp. cayenne
1/8 tsp. cumin

Blend all the ingredients together, and stir over medium heat for 30 minutes. This is delicious served hot over spaghetti, leftover whole grains, or steamed vegetables.

Yield: 3 cups.

Cheese Sauce

1 cup milk
2 cups grated cheese (preferably Cheddar, and *not* mozzarella)
1 Tbs. arrowroot flour
½ tsp. mustard powder

Mix the ingredients together in a blender at high speed. In a saucepan, heat the mixture over a low flame until the sauce becomes thick, stirring constantly. Very tasty over steamed broccoli or cauliflower.

Yield: 1¼ cups.

Thick Lasagna Sauce

3¼ cups tomato paste
1½ cups crushed tomatoes
3 Tbs. molasses
1½ tsp. lemon juice
1 Tbs. tamari
½ tsp. cumin
¼ tsp. cinnamon
¼ tsp. kelp
1 Tbs. + 1 tsp. parsley
1 Tbs. + 1 tsp. basil
1 tsp. celery seed
¼ tsp. cayenne
⅓ tsp. ginger
1 Tbs. + 1 tsp. oregano
1 bay leaf

Blend all the ingredients together and your sauce is ready to go. See lasagna recipe (p. 122) for steps of preparation.

Yield: 5 cups.

Mustard Sauce

½ cup prepared mustard
4 tsp. dry mustard
½ tsp. ginger
½ tsp. tamari
¼ tsp. cayenne

Combine the above ingredients together in a bowl, mixing them well. This will give you approximately ½ cup of hot mustard to use over veggie burgers, along with tofu or sandwich spreads or in our highly recommended Chinese Eggroll recipe (see p. 84-85). Add more cayenne if you like -- but taste as you go!

Yield: ½ cup.

Orange Ginger Sauce

1 tsp. grated orange rind
1½ Tbs. grated fresh ginger
⅓ cup butter
⅓ cup whole wheat flour
1 cup soy milk
1 cup orange juice
1 Tbs. tamari
Black pepper to taste

Grate the orange rind and ginger root. Melt the butter in a sauce pan, and whisk in the flour, continuing to whisk for 3 to 4 minutes. Slowly add the milk, while continuing to whisk. Cool 5 minutes over a low flame. Add the orange juice, tamari, orange rind, ginger, and pepper. Cook another 10 minutes, stirring occasionally. A sweet variation on ginger soy, you may find it tasteful poured over cooked veggies, beans or to top a taco or crepe!

Yield: 2 cups.

Sweet & Sour Sauce

1⅓ cups orange juice
½ cup tamari
½ cup vinegar
3/8 cup barley malt (or honey-¼ cup)
2 tsp. dry mustard
1/8 Tbs. coriander
3/8 tsp. ginger
¼ cup arrowroot flour
½ cup cold water

In a mixing bowl combine the orange juice, tamari and remaining seasonings with the exception of the arrowroot flour and water. Mix together well, and set aside. Then combine the arrowroot flour with cold water and stir together. When the mixture is smooth, fold it into the orange juice mixture, then pour it into a saucepan and heat over a medium flame, stirring constantly. When the mixture reaches the boiling point, turn it down to simmer, still stirring constantly. The mixture will become thick and syrupy in texture, then you can remove it from the heat and set it aside to cool -- or serve immediately over Chinese vegetables and rice or as an added treat along with Chinese Eggrolls (see pp. 84-85).

Yield: 2½ cups.

15·
Breadmaking

It will help, at this point, if you can quietly conjure up the last time you were in a bakery, or sat patiently in Grandma's kitchen as the loaves rose in the oven, or worked with oats and wheat yourself, kneading and forming them into a variety of shapes and tastes. How can we not extol the flavor and aroma of ready-fresh bread? Nothing quite compares to it.

Now if you haven't baked your own yeasted or quick breads, it is very fitting that your glance fell upon this chapter. In the pages that follow we offer you step-by-step tips and information on breadmaking. Even though we're unable to be with you hand-in-hand to help you with the process, or test your loaves when they're fresh out of the oven, imagine, by the nature of these instructions and the faith we have in you, that we're right by your side. For veteran breadbakers, we simply offer you more samples to add to your repertoire.

We've given you grains for entrees and suppers in Chapter 12. Here now are grains you may choose for your breakfast meal, though, in truth, a hot hearty cereal, a muesli, or Malti's melty muffins will go well any time of day. Enjoy all the recipes contained herein -- the crackers and quickbreads, Bali's rye, and any of the yeast breads that happen to catch your eye (we got hooked by the nostrils a long time ago)!

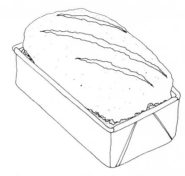

Quick Breads

Herewith, a sampling of our best-loved quick breads -- crackers, muffins and crepes and pancakes. Most of these can be created in very little time, and be out on the table within a couple of hours from start to finish. They make wonderful breakfasting, hearty soupside fare, or for the unscrupulous snacker, rewarding late-night projects by the oven.

Bali's Herbed Crepes

2 cups milk
1½ cups whole wheat flour
¼ cup whole wheat pastry flour
2 Tbs. arrowroot flour
1½ tsp. dill
½ tsp. basil
½ tsp. salt
Pinch pepper

From "Bali" (Balaram), resident chef and Retreat purchasing agent. Mix all dry ingredients well; add milk and stir with a whisk until well-blended. Heat a crepe pan over a medium-high flame until evenly hot. If you don't have a crepe pan, a flipped-over cast-iron skillet serves nicely; just clean the bottom, flip upside-down over your flame and heat. Lightly butter the pan when hot. Pour on about ½ cup batter per crepe and quickly tilt the pan all around so that the batter is very thin and forms a nice round shape, spreading out over the pan. Cook until lightly browned; then flip over with spatula and brown on the other side, using a medium-high heat. Crepes can be reheated later in the oven or frozen until ready for use. For filling, use Ratatouille (see p. 81), Tofu Sunshine Spread (see p. 179), or fresh butter and grated cheese with thin tomato slices.

Who would have thought that an eggless crepe would "work" and taste so wonderful? These are very light and fluffy and wrap well around the filling of your choice...or simply spread with some creamy butter. Bon Appetit!

Yield: 10-12 crepes.

Raisin Puffs

1 cup milk
1 Tbs. melted butter
⅓ cup honey
½ cup raisins
1½ cups whole wheat pastry flour
¼ tsp. salt
1 cup wheat germ
2 tsp. baking powder

Preheat oven to 350°. Combine all the dry ingredients in one bowl and the wet ingredients in another bowl. Sift the dry into the wet ingredients, stirring just enough to moisten them. Do not overmix. Spoon into an oiled muffin tin and bake at 350° for 20 to 30 minutes. These are delicious for your breakfast tray or to accompany any meal and make it special.

Yield: 12 muffins.

Happy Apple Muffins

1 cup finely chopped apples
2 cups whole wheat pastry flour
3 tsp. baking powder
2 tsp. cinnamon
½ cup milk
¼ cup oil
½ cup honey
¼ cup yogurt

Preheat your oven to 400°. Wash and finely chop the apples. Sift together dry ingredients, then combine all wet ingredients. With a minimum of stirring, combine wet and dry ingredients, and gently fold in apples. Pour into well greased muffin tins, and bake at 400° for 20 to 25 minutes. These are simply scrumptious!

Yield: 12 large muffins.

Little Miss "Bran" Muffins

1 cup whole wheat flour
1 cup bran
2 tsp. baking powder
¼ tsp. salt
¼ cup yogurt
¼ cup oil
¼ cup molasses
¼ cup honey
¼ cup milk
½ cup raisins

Preheat your oven to 400°. Mix the dry ingredients together, and then combine the wet ingredients. Add the wet to dry ingredients, stirring as little as possible. Pour into a greased muffin tin, and bake at 400° for 20 to 25 minutes.

Yield: 8 muffins.

Honey Wheat Muffins

3 cups whole wheat pastry flour
¾ tsp. salt
2 tsp. baking powder
¼ cup oil
¼ cup honey
1½ cups milk

Preheat your oven to 350°. Combine the dry ingredients, and then combine wet ingredients. Add both together, folding gently and quickly until just moistened. Spoon the mixture into a greased muffin tin and bake at 350° for 30 minutes.

For variation, add 1 tsp. allspice, cinnamon and ½ tsp. nutmeg or ginger, or ½ cup raisins, chopped dates, walnuts, pecans, or almonds.

Yield: 12 muffins.

Chappatis

2¼ cups whole wheat flour
2 tsp. butter
¼ tsp. salt
1 cup warm water
¾ cup whole wheat flour (in separate bowl)
¼-½ cup melted butter
1 tsp. oil

Chappatis are Indian pan-bread, crispy brown (flatter than pita but similar in appearance). They make an excellent accompaniment to any meal as a variation on the bread theme and are particularly "at home" with Indian fare. The nice thing about chappatis is that you can ladle different foods, curried veggies or rice or chutneys onto the chappati, roll them up and munch them! To make them, mix your first batch of flour, butter and salt together. Add the warm water and mix the dough. Cover and allow it to sit for one hour. Then add 1 tsp. oil to the dough and mix in thoroughly. Roll the dough into 20 to 25 small balls about 1 inch in diameter. Flatten the balls between your palms with dry flour and roll to form 3 in. to 4 in. circles. Sprinkle with flour once more and roll the dough into 6 in. circles. Put the rolled dough on pre-heated skillets and turn over after 30 seconds, or when you see small bubbles. Let the chappatis cook 30 more seconds. Hold the chappati at the edge with tongs over the direct flame of the stove. Then place the cooked chappatis in a dish and spread with melted butter. Absolutely delicious!

Yield: 20-25 chappatis.

Malti's Melty Muffins

½ cup grated cheese
3⅔ cups whole wheat pastry flour
½ tsp. salt
½ tsp. baking soda
2 tsp. baking powder
½ cup butter
2 cups sour milk

Preheat your oven to 450°. Grate the cheese, then mix the dry ingredients together. Cut in butter until the mixture is crumbly and uniform. Fold in milk, being careful not to overstir, and gently and quickly fold in cheese. Pour into oiled muffin tins and bake at 450° for 20 to 30 minutes. These muffins (along with the "Piece de Resistance" batch) undoubtedly comprise the most popular and best remembered breakfasts at the Retreat. Immortalized through Malti's efforts, they derive from her one-time job as a cook on an Australian cattle ranch.

Yield: 8 muffins.

Whole Wheat Sesame Crackers

2¼ cups flour
1 cup sesame seeds
1 tsp. salt
2 Tbs. + 2 tsp. oil
1 cup water
2 tsp. tamari

Preheat your oven to 350°. Mix, then knead all the ingredients well. On an oiled baking sheet, roll the dough out very thin, and cut it into squares, 2½ in. by 4 in. Sprinkle lightly with salt. Bake at 350° for 10 to 15 minutes or until brown on the edges.

Yield: 2 dozen crackers.

Country Style Cornbread

2¼ cups whole wheat pastry flour
3½ cups cornmeal
½ tsp. baking powder
½ tsp. baking soda
1 tsp. salt
¾ cup butter
1 cup honey
3 cups milk or soymilk

Preheat your oven to 325°. Sift together the dry ingredients. Cream butter, add the honey and mix together well. Alternately add the milk and then the flour mixture to the butter. Batter should be wet and fall off spoon easily. Pour into a greased 9 x 12 in. pan, and bake at 325° for 1¼ hours. Tastes delicious with Split Pea (see p. 99) or Hearty Red Lentil Soup (see p. 100) and makes a complete protein source, combined with either soup.

Yield: One 9 x 12 in. pan.

Piece de Resistance Muffins

3⅔ cups whole wheat pastry flour
Pinch salt
½ tsp. baking soda
2 tsp. baking powder
1 tsp. cinnamon
½ cup butter
1½ cups milk
½ cup honey
½ cup raisins

Preheat the oven to 450°. Mix your dry ingredients together, and then cut in butter, until the mixture is crumbly and uniform. Combine together the milk and honey. Fold these into the dry ingredients, being careful not to overstir. Gently fold in raisins. Pour whole mixture into a greased muffin tin, and bake at 450° for 20 to 30 minutes. These muffins ooze honey and sweet raisins and are delicious alternatives to cinnamon buns. If your creative urge happens to strike at 3 o'clock in the morning or 10 o'clock at night, you'll enjoy the results of puttering at the stove, and there won't be a "piece" of your "resistance" muffins left as telltale evidence...(unless you care to save some...they're so good).

Yield: 14 muffins.

Sukanya's Truckstop Pancakes

1½ cups whole wheat pastry flour
⅔ cups whole wheat flour
3 tsp. baking powder
1 tsp. salt
1 Tbs. egg replacer
1 Tbs. cinnamon
2 cups milk
½ cup safflower oil
2 Tbs. honey

Sift all the dry ingredients together, including egg replacer and any bran left from sifting. Sifting will add extra lightness to the pancakes, even though you add the bran back in. Mix all wet ingredients with whisk until well-blended. Using the whisk, mix wet and dry ingredients together with a few strokes -- do not beat-- until barely mixed. Overstirring the batter will make for tough, heavy pancakes. Lightly grease a skillet or heavy frying pan, and heat until water drops "dance" in it. Ladle pancakes onto the pan. Cook over a medium flame until the top surface is bubbly. Carefully flip them over and cook until browned. Once the pancake is flipped over, do not flip it back -- this makes them tough. Do not pat the top with the spatula; this also will make them tough. Serve piping hot with butter, maple syrup, strawberry glaze, or your favorite topping.

Yield: 12 pancakes.

Golden Brown Biscuits

6 cups whole wheat pastry flour
1½ tsp. salt
3½ tsp. baking powder
1½ tsp. baking soda
2¼ cups sour milk
¼ cup oil

Sift together the dry ingredients. Make a well in the middle of them and pour in the milk, then the oil. Stir just enough to moisten the dry ingredients. Place the dough on a well-floured board and knead it briefly. Then roll the dough ¼-½ in. thick, and cut into 2 in. circles. (If you cut them bigger, they'll rise less.) Place on an ungreased baking sheet, closely together, and bake at 450° for 10-15 minutes, or until the bottoms are golden brown. For a crustier biscuit, you can butter the pan before placing biscuits on it.

Yield: 20 biscuits.

Crunchy Cheese Crackers

1½ cups rolled oats
1½ cups whole wheat flour
4 Tbs. poppy seeds
2 cups grated cheese
½ cup softened butter
1 tsp. salt
½-¾ cup water

Preheat your oven to 325°. Mix all the ingredients together into a dough. Add just enough water so that the dough is not too dry and crumbly or too wet and sticky. Roll onto a greased cookie sheet, ¼ in. thick, and sprinkle with kelp and cayenne. Slice into squares, 4 x 6 in. Prick each cracker two or three times with a fork to keep from bubbling up while baking. Bake at 325° for 30 to 45 minutes, and store them out of reach. (Otherwise they'll disappear rapidly!)

Yield: 25 crackers.

Cinnamon Oat Cakes

1 cup oat flour
½ + 1/8 cup whole wheat pastry flour
1 tsp. cinnamon
2 tsp. baking powder
¼ tsp. salt
½ cup butter
1 Tbs. honey

Preheat the oven to 350°. Stir the dry ingredients together. Cut in butter until mixture is crumbly, and add the honey. Roll the dough out ¼ in thick and cut into 3 in. circles. Place it on a greased cookie sheet and bake at 350° for 15 to 20 minutes. These are great with honey butter spread on top, when they're hot out of the oven! Or you can use cookie cutters and roll out rabbit shapes for Easter, hearts for Valentine's day, or turkeys for Thanksgiving, as we do.

Yield: 1½ dozen.

Taco Shells

1 1/8 cups boiling water
2½ Tbs. butter
1 cup cornmeal
¼ tsp. chili powder
¼ tsp. black pepper
3/8 tsp. salt
1½ cups whole wheat flour

Boil the water. Add the butter, and allow it to melt. In a large mixing bowl, pour this liquid over the cornmeal. Allow it to stand for 10 minutes. Knead in spices and enough flour until the dough is very dry, then roll it into 9 small balls. On a floured board, roll each ball out with a rolling pin or wooden dowel, forming circles. Heat a skillet until the water "dances" on it. Place a taco shell in the skillet. When browned on one side, flip it over and cook it until browned on the other side. Roll the sides of the shell up into a taco shape while it's cooking. If you wait too long, it will be too hard and will crack. Cook the remaining shells in this way. Then stuff with your favorite taco fillings, and top with Tapas Taco Sauce (see p. 141).

Yield: 9 shells.

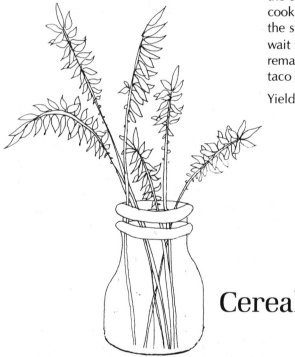

Cereals

Children of a super-civilized society, most of us, sadly, missed growing up on true whole-grain cereals in all their natural glory. Whole grain breakfast cereals have made a flashy comeback over the past 10-15 years, but many of the pre-packaged types in the grocery stores still have sugar (which competes with whatever B-vitamins might come through) and even preservatives. With a little imagination and experimenting, and a trip to your local food co-op or health food store, you can create endless superb whole-grain breakfasts that will provide your body bulk, protein, B-vitamins and the highest quality nourishment for pennies per serving. Rediscover the soul-satisfying experience of a hot whole grain cereal on a chilly morning. You may never reach for the Frosted Flakes again.

Fond-of-Farina

4 cups water (or 2 cups water and 2 cups milk)
¾ tsp. cinnamon
1 tsp. vanilla
Pinch salt
¾ cup farina
¼ cup chopped dates
¼ cup honey

Boil the water, adding cinnamon, vanilla and salt to the water. Slowly whisk in the farina and allow the mixture to come to a boil once again, stirring continuously. Add the dates and turn it down to simmer for 3 or 4 minutes. Then add honey and serve.

Yield: 4 cups.

Wheat or Rice Flakes

1-2 cups flakes (any variety)

By making your own breakfast cereal flakes, you can be sure no sugar or additives have been added to your cereal, and can save money as well. Most health food stores carry wheat, rice or oat flakes. On cookie pans or other flat trays, toast the flakes until lightly browned in a 350° oven. Cool and then serve with soymilk, cream or a mixture of milk and honey.

Yield: 1-2 cups.

Crunchy Granola

2½ cups oats
½ cup wheat germ
½ cup bran
¼ cup coconut
¼ cup cashews
½ cup raisins
1/8 cup sunny seeds
1/8 cup sesame seeds
½ cup honey
¼ cup oil

Mix all the ingredients together and toast the mix on large cookie sheets at 325°, turning every few minutes with a spatula until lightly browned (approximately 15 minutes). Then remove and allow it to cool before serving. A versatile food with many uses, we've applied granola liberally to apple crisp toppings, cookies, and used it as a banana cream pie crust, or in puff balls for children's Christmas stockings. Add any other ingredients your heart desires such as nuts, dried fruits, or spices.

Yield: 1¼ lbs.

Millet Breakfast Pudding

4 cups cooked millet
½ cup grated coconut
½ cup raisins or chopped dates
1 cup ground sunny seeds
2 cups water
4 Tbs. honey
1 tsp. vanilla
1 tsp. lemon juice

Place the cooked millet in a baking dish with the coconut and raisins. Blend the remaining ingredients in a blender to make a delicious seed milk. Pour this seed milk over the millet mixture and mix in well. Bake at 350° for approximately 20-30 minutes and then let it sit for an additional 10 minutes before serving, if needed, to absorb any extra liquid. This is an easy, flavorful breakfast (or dessert for that matter). The next time you're cooking millet, save some extra for this dish.

Yield: 8 cups.

Hot Raisin Bran Cereal

3 cups water
½ tsp. salt
⅓ cup wheat germ
⅔ cup bran
¼ cup dry milk powder
2 Tbs. raisins or dates

Bring water to boil. Stir in all ingredients and cook gently for 10 minutes.

Yield: 4 cups.

Muesli

2 cups oats
2½ cups water
1½ Tbs. honey
½ tsp. vanilla
¼ cup chopped dates
¼ cup wheat germ
¼ cup raisins
½ cup sunny seeds
½ to 1 tsp. cinnamon or cardamom
Optional: slivered almonds or cashews

Muesli provides you all the necessary nutrients with a festive touch. A delightful breakfast, muesli can easily be prepared the night before by combining all the ingredients in a large mixing bowl or container. Then the next day you can wake up to an "instant breakfast". Or, simply add all the ingredients together on that same day, allowing the dates and raisins to soak a good while in the honey-oats mixture. For an extra special dessert, just cut back on the water (use only 1½ cups) and place the mixture on top of some homemade ice cream! Sprinkle with almonds or peanuts, and serve -- a true delight!

Yield: 3 1/8 cups.

Oatmeal Awakener

4 cups water
Pinch salt
¾ tsp. cinnamon
2 cups rolled oats
½ cup raisins
4-5 Tbs. honey

Boil the water, adding salt and then the cinnamon. Stir in your rolled oats and raisins and cook only 5-10 minutes. Add the honey and serve hot. Another method of preparation is to soak the oats overnight and simply heat the mixture in the morning. This allows for a lighter, less gummy texture. Either way, a must for a cold winter's morning!

Yield: 4 cups.

Rice Cream

1 cup cooked rice
¾ cup milk or soymilk
½ tsp. vanilla
2 Tbs. honey
¼ tsp. cinnamon

Blend all the ingredients and serve in mugs or custard dishes. This is a recipe we stumbled upon in an attempt to provide a tasty more "familiar" morning meal for children unused to vegetarian cooking. Rice cream is simple to digest, so the "old" folks like it as well. It makes a nice dessert, as well as breakfast food, and can be served hot or cold. Add milk to chosen consistency.

Yield: 1¾ cups.

Bulgar-Sesame Porridge

1 Tbs. oil
1 cup bulgar
¼ cup sesame seeds
¼ cup wheat germ
¼ cup coconut
¼ tsp. salt
2-3 Tbs. honey
3 cups water

A pleasant alternative to oatmeal, this cereal is prepared by sauteeing all the ingredients except the water in oil. Add water to the mixture and then steam for 25 minutes. This has a pleasant, sweet and nutty flavor -- helps you off to an energetic day.

Yield: 3 cups.

Raisinberry Cereal

1 cup wheatberries
3 cups water
½ cup raisins
¼ tsp. cinnamon
1 Tbs. honey

This old-time country dish can be easily prepared. Simmer the wheatberries in water until thoroughly cooked, approximately 45 minutes or more. Add the raisins, honey and cinnamon for the final 10 minutes of cooking, and serve hot.

Yield: 3 cups.

Yeasted Breads

More than any act of cooking, yeasted breadmaking is a communion of you with the gift of food. With every knead and fold and push, your energy becomes part of the bread you prepare, creating loaves that not only provide protein, B-vitamins, and bulk, and leave satisfied friends in their wake, but which nourish spirit and heart as well. Experiment with adding loving, warm and gentle feelings to the bread you prepare —and see if the compliments don't increase.

Yeasted breads are unparalleled in their texture, beauty, and taste. Like most good things in life, they take more time to make. They are worth the energy expended, however. The varieties are endless -- as numerous as the leftovers in your refrigerator and the horizons of your imagination. Some of our best breads have been made by throwing in leftover soups or breakfast porridges. Herbs and leftover vegetables make a hearty lunchtime bread to serve alongside a bowl of chunky vegetable soup. Grated cheese can be added. Or, savory herbs. And the shapes of the bread are just as numerous -- fun-to-peel-apart cinnamon rolls, elegant rolled cheese croissants, braided strudels (not as complicated as they look), cloverleaf rolls, French Knot rolls, and your fundamentally earthy and uncomplicated loaf. Once you've mastered the basics, many adventurous hours lie in wait for you. We've included basic yeasted-dough instructions here, as well as some well-loved varieties.

Basic Whole Wheat Bread

6-8 c. whole wheat flour
1½ c. milk
¼ cup honey

1½ c. water
¼ c. oil

1 Tbs. yeast
1 Tbs. salt

1. Heat the water (and milk, if using) in a saucepan to a comfortably warm temperature of about 100° . Do not overheat; the heat will kill the yeast and that's the end of your bread. Test it on your wrist -- about bathtub temperature is right. Turn off heat.

2. Stir in the honey, oil, and yeast. Let sit a good 8 minutes while yeast wakes up and begins growing.

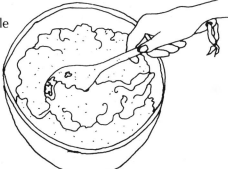

3. Sift your flour and salt together. Sifting makes a lighter, nicely textured bread. Salt is important -- without it the bread tastes flat. But never add salt to the yeasting water -- salt stops yeast action if added too soon.

4. Pour the liquid mixture into your bowl. Slowly begin to stir in the flour mixture, stirring well after each addition of about 2 cups flour (See Fig. 1).

5. As you add more flour the dough will begin to pull away slightly from the sides of the bowl. At this point, forget your spoon, flour up your hands, and begin mixing with flourey hands, right in the bowl.

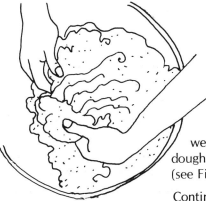

Continue adding flour and working it with your hands, pushing the flour into the dough and beginning to form a lump of dough in the bowl. When you have a fairly solid (i.e., not liquid) mound of dough, lightly flour the table and scoop the dough out onto the table.

6. Kneading: Use the heels of your hands to push against the dough, pushing it away from your body. Then, use your fingers to pull the dough back towards you, in a folding-it-over motion, as if you were trying to knead as much air into the dough as possible. Turn the dough in quarter-turns about every ½ minute, so you are kneading evenly (see Fig. 2)

Continue adding flour until the dough is not sticking to your hands or to the table. You will need to keep adding a little flour to your hands as you work, just dusting them to keep the dough from sticking. You may also need to flour the table periodically—again, lightly—as you work. Too much flour in the dough will make the bread dry; too little will make it too sticky to knead. Stop adding flour when the dough is firm and nonsticky.

7. Knead until the dough is a nice firm shape. Kneading releases the gluten in the flour -- the sticky stuff that makes it all hold together and provides good texture. Develop a rhythm as you knead. Let yourself be absorbed in the kneading and in the bread forming under your hands (see Fig. 3).

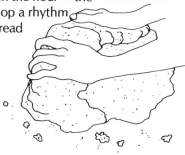

8. When nice and firm, the bread is ready to rise. Check by pressing the dough about ½ inch with your thumb; if dough bounces back, it is ready.

Lightly oil your mixing bowl (don't worry about the little bits of dough left in there -- but do remove what you can), put in the dough -- this leaves you with the now-oiled side up and prevents a crusty top from forming on the dough after the first rising. Cover with a towel, and place dough in a warm place (not hot), such as near a radiator, in an oven that has a gas pilot and is turned off, on top of a gas stove that is turned off, etc. Let rise for 1½ hours, or until the dough doubles in bulk.

9. While dough rises, oil your bread pans lightly and thoroughly. You may also use saucepans (for nice, round loaves), old coffee cans, square cake pans (for flatter square bread), or just about anything that strikes your fancy. Preheat oven at 350°.

10. *Punching down:* When dough has doubled in bulk, push down into the center with your fist ("punching down"). The dough will deflate, as gas, created by growing yeast, escapes from the dough. Remove from bowl and reknead dough for several minutes.

11. *Forming the loaves:* Divide dough in half. Knead each loaf-dough with right hand while turning and folding dough with left hand. Turn the dough at quarter-turns as you work, turning the dough into the center until you have a compact ball.

Then, roll the dough into a log-shape. Pinch the seam tightly to close, and flip your loaf over so the seam is on the bottom. Square off the sides somewhat with your hands and flatten the loaf a bit. Place into oiled loaf pans, seams down, brush the top with oil, and let rise an additional 20 minutes in a warm place until the dough rises just above the edge of the bread pan (see Fig. 4).

12. Make three diagonal slashes ½-inch deep across the top of the loaf and bake at 350° for 50-70 minutes. (Duration depends on your oven, dough, the weather, and other unpredictable factors.)

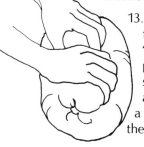

13. To Tell When Bread Is Done: Remove from oven. Knock pan gently on counter, flip over and let bread fall out of pan. Crust should be a nice even, brown color. "Knock" on the loaf -- it should sound hollow if done. If not, pop it back into the pan and into the oven for 5-15 more minutes -- every batch and every oven are slightly different. If really unsure, cut a slice and take a look. You can put slice and loaf together in the pan and right back into the oven -- no problem. Or, stick a toothpick into the bottom of the loaf and if it comes out sticky, put it back into the oven. Cool by laying on the lengthwise sides (to avoid overly moist bottoms), or

on cake racks. Do not package or wrap up in plastic until fully cool or bread will become damp and possibly moldy.

Spread with butter, honey, jam or what-have-you and serve with a mug of herbal tea. Share with your friends, enjoy and give thanks!

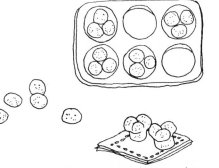

Variations
Clover leaf Rolls

Perfect for elegant dinners.

1 loaf recipe yields 18 rolls.

Grease a muffin tin. Form the dough, in the last stage before the final rising, into small 1 in. diameter balls. Place 3 balls side-by-side in each muffin cup. Let rise. Bake 25-40 minutes at 350°, depending on size of rolls (watch carefully).

Buns

Suitable for a bean burger or sandwich. A 1 loaf recipe yields 6 buns.

Divide the dough into 6 equal pieces, and knead into small, round bun-shapes. Place on oiled baking sheet and let rise; bake as usual (may take slightly less time -- check after 40 minutes).

Knotted Rolls

Fun to make and eat as well. A 1 loaf dough yields 8-10 "knots", depending on size. Brush with oil and sprinkle with poppy or sesame seeds. Roll dough into long strands, about 10-12 in. long and 1 in. in diameter. Simply "tie" the dough into a knot, tucking the leftover end underneath and pinching. Let rise; bake at 350° about 30-40 minutes.

# Braided Loaves

A bit of the old country. Form dough into three long strands by rolling with hands on the table. Pinch all three ends together at one end; braid the strands and then pinch to complete the final end. Place braid on an oiled pan, brush top with oil and sprinkle with poppy or sesame seeds. Let rise; bake as usual.

Herb Bread

Make Basic Whole Wheat Bread, increasing the honey to 2/3 cup, and add to the wet mixture before adding flour: You may choose to substitute molasses in place of honey, or omit the sweetener altogether.

½ tsp. thyme
½ tsp. rosemary

1 tsp. oregano
1 tsp. dill

1 tsp. basil
1 tsp. parsley

Raisin-Nut Bread

Make Basic Whole Wheat Bread, and add to the wet mixture before adding flour:

1 cup raisins
1 tsp. cinnamon

½ tsp. cloves

1 cup chopped walnuts

High-Protein Bread

Make Basic Whole Wheat Bread, and substitute in place of the regular flour:

1 cup soy flour

⅓ cup wheat germ

1 cup powdered milk

Prepare as usual.

Whole Wheat Sweet Bread

2 cups milk
⅓ cup honey
1 Tbs. yeast
½ cup oil
1 tsp. lemon juice

4 cups whole wheat flour
1½ cups - 2 cups whole wheat pastry flour
2 tsp. salt
1 Tbs. cinnamon

½ tsp. nutmeg
1 Tbs. orange rind
¾ cup raisins
¾ cup walnuts

Heat the milk until it's lukewarm. Pour into a large mixing bowl and stir in the honey. Sprinkle yeast on top and let it dissolve. Let it sit for 5 minutes. Add the oil and lemon juice and mix well. Sift in the flour, salt, and spices. While still stirrable, beat well to develop the gluten and mix in the orange rind, nuts and raisins. Knead until springy -- the dough should be on the wet side -- stiff or dry. Oil the bowl and roll dough in it. Cover with a damp towel and place it in a warm place to rise until doubled, about 1½ to 2 hours. Punch down, and shape the loaves. This is an excellent bread to experiment with -- create fancy shapes, twists, and rings, or whatever your creativity leads you to. Place loaves in oiled bread pans or cookie sheets. Let it rise for 30-50 minutes, until doubled. Bake at 350° for 1-1¼ hours. Remove from the pans and allow it to cool. An excellent holiday and special occasions bread.

Yield: 2 loaves.

Whole Wheat Bagels

1½ cups warm water	¼ cup honey	5-6 cups whole wheat flour
½ cup lukewarm milk	3 Tbs. oil	5 quarts water
2 Tbs. yeast	1½ tsp. salt	2 Tbs. honey

Heat milk and water until lukewarm. Temperature is important so that yeast is not killed. Dissolve yeast in the milk and water mixture and let sit 4-5 minutes. Then add honey, oil and salt, mixing in well. Beat in flour until dough forms into a ball and is too stiff to beat. Turn onto a floured board and knead and work in more flour until it is elastic and fairly heavy. You'll want the dough heavier than regular bread for a more "bagel" texture. Oil a large bowl and roll dough around until coated with oil. Let sit in bowl, covered with a wet towel, in a warm draft-free place. Let rise until doubled in bulk -- about 1½ hours. Punch down and divide into 16-18 pieces. Begin boiling the water, and add 2 Tbs. honey. While the water is heating, form dough into bagels. Knead each piece of dough into a smooth round ball, flatten it a little and stick your finger through the center, forming a hole.

Drop the bagels, 4 or 5 at a time, into the boiling water. The bagels will drop and then rise to the surface, and will expand in size. After 3-4 minutes boiling on one side, flip over to the other side and boil another 3 minutes. Remove bagels from water with a slotted spoon, draining off excess water. Place bagels on greased cookie sheets and sprinkle with poppy seeds or sesame seeds. Bake at 375° for 30-35 minutes, or until golden brown. Slice and serve toasted or plain with butter, cream cheese, and sliced olives, or your favorite sandwich spread.

Yield: 16-18 bagels.

Cinnamon Rolls

1⅓ cups butter
¾ cup honey

Cream Together and set aside until ready to roll out the rolls.

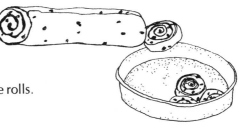

DOUGH

Prepare as instructed for Whole Wheat Sweet Bread, omitting the lemon juice, nutmeg and orange rind, and increasing cinnamon to 2 Tbs., and the honey to ½ cup. When dough has risen and been punched down, roll out a rectangle with a rolling pin about ½ in. thick. Using your fingers, "smear" the smear over the surface of the dough about ¼ in. thick. Sprinkle with raisins, walnuts, and a generous shaking of cinnamon over the surface. Roll the rectangle into a long roll. (If your original rectangle is more than 10 in. wide, you may make two separate rectangles by cutting it lengthwise. The wider your rectangle south-to-north, the fatter your rolls. However, you can overdo it.)

Take an 8 x 8 in. square baking tin, 1 loaf pan (for the ½-dozen), and cover the bottoms and sides with the remaining smear, about 3/8 in. thick or so. Over this, sprinkle still more raisins, walnuts, and some cinnamon. Place the cut rolls flat into the pans, leaving about 3/8 in. between each, so that they have some room to rise and expand without getting too squashed. Let rise until almost doubled. Bake at 350° for 40 minutes.

When done, immediately place a serving dish or plate on top of the pan, and quickly flip over while rolls are very hot. The smear will be a gooey, sweet glaze and will run down into the rolls. Serve immediately with fresh butter, and savor the sweet results of your efforts.

Yield: 1½ dozen.

Croissants

Sweet, melt-in-your mouth, flakey light crescent rolls -- a veritable taste of old France.

Prepare Basic Whole Wheat dough as usual. After punching down, roll out the dough on a floured board or tabletop into one large rectangular piece. Smear the top surface with butter. Fold this in half, then quarters, then eighths, until you cannot fold the dough anymore. This gives the layered texture to croissants, which provides their characteristic flakey lightness. Now you're ready to again roll out into a rectangular shape, 1/8 in. to 1/4 in. thick. Again smear the top surface with butter.

Cut the rectangle of dough in half lengthwise; then cut each long half into triangles (see diagram). Roll up each triangle from wide end to pointed, small end, rolling tight so that many layers are created. Pinch at the end to hold the dough in place. Place the rolled up triangle on an oiled baking sheet, and curve and pinch into a crescent shape, pressing the end tips of the crescent down somewhat. Allow to rise as usual for 25-30 minutes. Bake at 350° for 30-40 minutes, or until golden brown.

One loaf dough recipe makes 12-16 croissants.

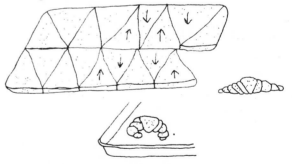

Cheese Croissants

Incredible—an even more delectable variation of our croissants. Prepare croissant dough as usual, and set aside 3 cups of your favorite grated cheese. After the final butter smear, but before cutting the dough into triangles, sprinkle generously with grated cheese. Roll, allow to rise, and bake as usual.

Hot Cross Buns

These were made one year at the Retreat in traditional observance of Good Friday. Who knows, perhaps they'll become another Retreat custom . . .

Make the Basic Whole Wheat Sweet Bread recipe, p. 160. Add to recipe:

2 Tbs. lemon peel, freshly grated or dried   Poppy seeds
1½ Tbs. allspice

Prepare sweet bread as directed, omitting orange rinds and walnuts. After dough is punched down, form into small buns (p. 159) about 2½ in. across, before rising. Brush each bun with oil and sprinkle generously with poppy seeds. Let rise, and bake at 350° for 35-45 minutes.

While the buns are baking, prepare the Cream Cheese Frosting, p.215. Thin with enough milk to make a creamy-soft consistency. If you do not have a fancy cake decorator, you can prepare an "icer" to make your crosses by cutting the corner of a plastic bag diagonally, making a hole about 3/8 in. wide. Place icing into bag, and knot or twist-tie the top very securely.

As your buns come out of the oven, squeeze a fat cream-cheese cross onto the top of each. (Go on, make them big!) We found that the hot buns can be iced without any runny "crosses". Serve immediately with fresh butter and sweet tea.

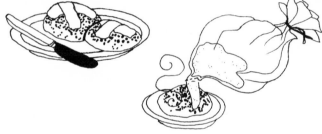

Pita Bread

1 Tbs. yeast   1 tsp. salt
1½ - 2 cups lukewarm water   3-4 cups whole wheat flour

Dissolve the yeast in lukewarm water and let it sit for 10 minutes or until bubbly. Stir in 1 cup of flour, then sprinkle in the salt and gradually work in the rest of the flour. Dough should be springey -- firm but not overstiff. Knead for 15 minutes. Oil a bowl, and roll your ball of dough in it; cover it with a damp cloth and let it rise until doubled, in a warm place -- about 2 hours. Preheat your oven to 450°-500°. Punch down the dough and knead it into 2 even logs; cut into 12 equal pieces. On a floured surface, roll out each ball into a round circle, no less than ¼ in. thick. If any thinner they won't puff up as well. Place the pitas on lightly-floured cookie sheets. Let them rise at least 45 minutes until slightly puffy: this is crucial -- you can tell by the puffiness which ones will pocket and which ones won't (some may need to sit a few minutes longer).

Pre-heat the cookie sheets in your hot oven and when the pitas are ready to be put in the oven, remove the hot cookie sheets and transfer the pitas to them quickly. If you have a problem with them sticking, sprinkle the hot cookie sheet lightly with cornmeal. Be careful not to deflate the pitas while transferring. Place the cookie sheet in the hottest part of your oven and do not open the oven door during the first 6 minutes. (The high heat is causing the pocket to develop and you don't want it to fall.) Check the pitas at 6 minutes, and if necessary brown 2 or 3 more minutes. To prevent drying out, place the still hot pitas in foil-wrap -- this makes a real difference as to whether you have a dried-out pita or a soft, supple and easy-to-handle pita. After they are cool, you may freeze or refrigerate them, or use them right away.

Yield: 12 pitas.

Sourdough Bread

STARTER

1 cup yogurt	1 cup whole wheat flour
½ cup powdered milk	1 cup lukewarm water

Mix all the ingredients in a bowl (not metal -- the acid will react with it). Cover with a tea towel and set in a warm, draft-free spot. Stir the starter twice a day. When it begins to bubble, that means it's working. This will take 3 to 5 days, depending on the temperature. If it begins to smell foul or moldy, throw it out and start again.

PREPARING BASIC BATTER OR SPONGE:

To each cup of starter, add 2 cups water and 2½ cups flour. Beat together well. Let it sit overnight in a warm, draft-free place. In the morning, replace whatever amount of starter you took -- e.g. if you took 1 cup, replenish it by adding 1 cup of batter to your starter.

MAKING THE BREAD:

3 cups basic batter, or sponge	2 Tbs. honey	¼ cup water
½ tsp. salt	2 tsp. oil	3-4 cups flour

Put the starter in a wooden bowl, adding the ingredients listed, and the flour last. Knead the flour in until it forms a ball, is elastic, and no longer sticky (about 10 minutes). Oil a bowl, place the ball of dough in it, and roll it around until the ball is lightly coated in oil. Let it rise until doubled in bulk -- this may take several hours. Shape it into a loaf and let it rise until doubled in pan. This may take 2 to 3 hours. Bake at 350° for 1-1½ hours. Remove from pan and cool.

Yield: 1 loaf.

Bali's Rye Bread

½ cup water	½ cup molasses	2 tsp. salt
1½ Tbs. yeast	3 cups dark rye flour	2 Tbs. caraway seeds
2½ cups lukewarm water	4½-5 cups whole wheat flour	1 Tbs. anise seeds

Outrageously good rye bread from Bali. Sprinkle yeast on top of ½ cup lukewarm water. Barely mix it in and let it sit for 10 minutes, or until it's puffy. Stir molasses into the second amount of water. Then stir in the rye flour with a whisk. Add the yeast, mix in thoroughly, and then add the whole wheat flour until thick but still stirrable. Beat vigorously with a wooden spoon to develop the gluten. Then mix in the caraway and anise. Sprinkle salt over the mixture and stir. Add the rest of the flour until it's necessary to start kneading with your hands. When the dough forms a ball, remove it from the bowl and place it on a floured board. Knead 10 to 15 minutes. Oil a large bowl and place the ball of dough in it. Roll the ball around until it is lightly coated with oil, then cover it with a damp towel and set it in a warm place to rise. Let it rise until it's doubled in bulk, punch down and let it rise again until double. Divide the dough in half and form 2 loaves. Place it in oiled bread pans, and let it rise. Bake at 350° for about 1 to 1¼ hours. Remove the bread from the pans and allow it to cool.

Yield: 2 loaves.

16·
Dairy
Products

At Kripalu Retreat we enjoy all kinds of dairy products, deriving a certain amount of our protein, fat, carbohydrate and calcium needs through the inclusion of milk drinks, smoothies, cheeses and yogurt. As with all aspects of our diet, we have gradually undergone change and experimentation, and some residents in each of our ashrams are experimenting with a reduced or wholly dairy-free diet to discover its effects. Many have found soy products to be a satisfying alternative. Dairy used in moderation, balanced with other types of foods, is an excellent supplement to a vegetarian diet. Yet it is well to ponder some of the effects of milk and milk products. It has been shown that calcium from cow's milk is in excess (about 3 times) of what humans can absorb; also, the protein to carbohydrate ratio is greater in cow's milk, and such milk is not as easily digestible as for instance, human milk.[1] This factor, however, changes dramatically when the milk is processed through the use of cultures into yogurt or cheese -- then the cultures themselves take over some of the digestion and breakdown of the milk substances to make them more easily tolerated by humans. That is one reason why we lean so heavily on our homemade yogurts and cheeses.

As in all things, we favor moderation and balance. Our diet provides a very rich and rounded eating experience; certain dairy dishes, such as a cucumber and yogurt salad, an herbed cottage cheese with raw veggies for lunch, or a maple walnut ice cream dessert, harmonize beautifully with the remainder of our diet. Use of all natural, homemade ingredients, such as raw as opposed to homogenized milk, and preparation of foods with a joyful, pleasant attitude, are the most important factors in making eating into a meditative, fun experience. In this chapter we'd like to introduce you to our favorite dairy companions: yogurt, yogurt cheeses, and ice cream. Please also see Chapter 17 on Soy Products for corresponding products using soy milk. With most recipes, we use soy milk interchangeably and derive the same or greater proportions of protein and minerals with fewer calories, offering both dairy and soy versions at each meal to suit the needs of all.

Yogurt

Have you ever glanced at those rich, creamy yogurt cultures in health food stores and sighed at the expensive prices, wondering how you might come up with a suitable alternative? Try yogurt -- Kripalu style! Our method is nearly flawless, for we've been experimenting for many years now. The following items will be needed for you to get started:

A dairy thermometer   3½ cups milk   ½ cup milk powder
3-4 Tbs. plain yogurt (the "culture")

Here are the steps to follow for making your own delicious homemade yogurt:

1. In a blender, blend ¼ to ½ cup milk powder with regular milk. Be sure to use non-instant milk powder. Adding the milk powder yields a thicker, sweeter-tasting yogurt in our experience.

2. Heat the milk mixture in a saucepan, stirring constantly. Heating kills bacteria in milk which might inhibit the growth of the yogurt culture. Use a dairy thermometer to measure the heat of the milk. When it reaches 180°, promptly remove from heat.

3. Place the saucepan in a sink of cold water and cool the milk to 125°. Then stir in the yogurt culture (either from a previously made batch of yogurt, or any store bought variety without flavoring or additives. We recommend Dannon plain yogurt.) We prefer adding the culture at higher temperatures, as it yields a sweeter yogurt. Once the culture is added, pour the yogurt into a quart jar, or individual dishes or cups if you prefer.

4. Place the mixture in a warm place (110°-120° F) for mixture to fully "yog". This takes about 6 to 8 hours. You can use your oven, with just the pilot light on, or some other warm and suitable place.

5. At the end of "yogging" time, place the yogurt in the refrigerator. Your homemade yogurt is ready to be eaten. Once cooled, sweetener, fruit slices or any combinations of spices or other ingredients can be added to the yogurt. Use in sauces, smoothies, salad dressings, baked dishes, soups or stews. Its uses are as limitless as your imagination. Yogurt is a superior dairy product, providing you pre-digested milk protein, more accessible calcium stores, and a good synthesizer for B-vitamins.

Yogurt Cheese

Here is another versatile product which you can easily make and which can be used in a variety of ways, depending on how long you allow it to "cheese". You can have a softened version of pot cheese, or let it sit longer and have creamy cream cheese. Let it sit a little longer still and you have a thicker, denser cheese product. So experiment with these different forms if you like. Here's the process:

1. Pour completed yogurt into a cheesecloth bag or into a piece of cheesecloth which you have fastened from all sides.

2. Tie a string around the top of the bag, and suspend it from a hook or nail over an empty bowl. The whey or liquid matter of the yogurt will drip out. The longer it drips, the firmer the cheese. Generally it will require 4 to 6 hours.

3. At the end of the "dripping" time, you can use the cheese. If you prefer it in a thicker, more condensed form, then place the cheese in a colander, cover with a cloth and place in your refrigerator with a bowl underneath so that the drip process can continue.

4. Use whenever you desire. Yogurt cheese can be made into icings and toppings, used in dips and spreads, or served as an addition to salads, sandwiches, casseroles, etc. And don't forget to use the whey! Whey is a wonderfully robust, wholesome by-product of the yogurt, and has a lot of healthful enzymes, B-vitamins, and minerals for your body to rejoice in. Drink up!

Homemade Ice Cream

There is nothing quite like homemade ice cream for a hot summer reviver. We list below a variety of ingredients you can use, hoping, of course, that with such a sparkling snack you'll be able to come up with other ingenious combinations.

For the most part these recipes are straightforward -- that's why few directions are given. Simply blend ingredients in a blender, making sure they are uniform in consistency. Then pour the mixture into an ice cream freezer (electric or human powered) and crank it as needed. Remember to stock up on crushed ice, rock salt, and some *Winnie the Pooh* stories to read while you're cranking.

Homemade ice cream tends to melt much more quickly than store-bought, so be sure your family and friends are gathered around when the ice cream is done. Friends and relations also come in very handy if you're hand-cranking the ice cream.

If you have no ice cream maker available, then combine ingredients, blend and freeze in long baking pans. Take out trays and re-blend mixture while *partially* frozen and return to freezer.

These ice creams have a satisfying flavor with something more akin to a sherbert consistency. However you make them, enjoy your frozen dessert and experiment with favorite flavors of your own. Also try out soy ice creams (see Chapter 17) for recipes which for the most part can be used interchangeably with the dairy ice creams.

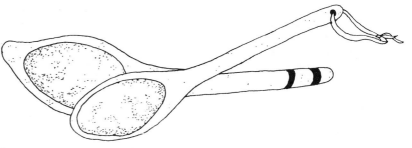

Apple Spice Ice Cream

½ cup milk
3 cups apple juice
1 cup milk powder
⅔ cup honey
1 Tbs. oil
½ Tbs. lecithin
1 tsp. cinnamon
½ tsp. ginger
1 tsp. coriander

Follow the original ice-cream directions, blending in all ingredients listed. Serve this tasty blend on top of some yummy apple or orange cake or any other variety!

Yield: 1 quart.

Old Fashioned Vanilla Ice Cream

3 cups milk
1 cup milk powder
⅔ cup honey
2 Tbs. oil
2 Tbs. vanilla
1 Tbs. lecithin

For carob: add ½ cup carob powder, one less Tbs. of vanilla, ½ tsp. almond extract, and change proportions of milk to 3½ cups and milk powder to ⅔ cups. Makes the same amount.

For carob mint, add ½ cup carob powder, ½ cup milk powder; reduce 1 Tbs. vanilla and ½ Tbs. lecithin, and add ¼ tsp. peppermint extract.

Yield: 1 quart.

Banana Nut Ice Cream

1½ cups milk or yogurt
4 medium *ripe* bananas
½ cup honey
¾ cup milk powder
1 Tbs. vanilla
1 Tbs. liquid lecithin
½ cup cashews or your favorite nuts

Blend all ingredients with the exception of the nuts. Add these after blending other ingredients, and then blend only a short time (several seconds is enough). This makes a rich, nutty ice cream you can bet your bananas everyone will love!

Yield: 1 quart.

17·
Soymaking and Soyfoods

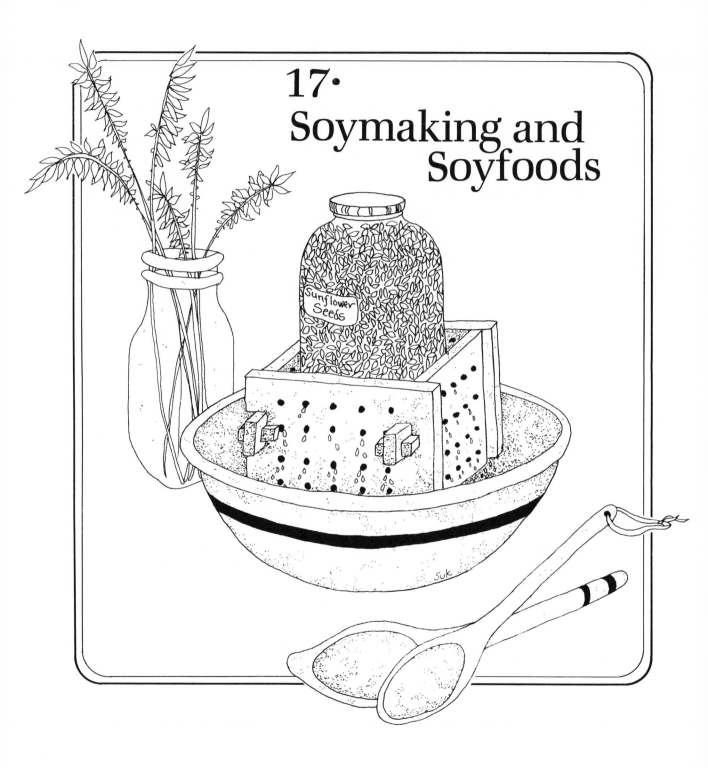

One of the most versatile foods available, soybeans can be used to create a wide variety of culinary delights, from sweet date soymilk to sauteed tofu, to one of our favorite flavors of "ice bean" (soy ice cream).

A non-mucous forming, high-protein food, soybeans are an excellent diet choice for vegetarians as well as for those with milk allergies, low-cholesterol, low-carbohydrate and low-fat diets, and those striving to eliminate dairy products from their diets. The rest of us eat it because it tastes so good! Low in cost, soybeans are an economic boon in these days of steadily rising food prices.

At the Retreat, we derive most of our soy products from raw soybeans. Soy flour can also be used for some products while soy powder, available from health food stores, can be used to make many soy foods.

Most soy products are made from a "slurry", which is a puree of soybeans or soy flour and water. The consistency of the slurry varies according to the desired consistency of the soymilk. After the soymilk is made, it can be used in the same way as cow's milk, made into yogurt, or curdled to make tofu (see below).

Soymilk

1. Soak 9⅓ cups beans in triple the amount of water for 12 hours.
2. Throw away the soak water and rinse the beans in a colander. (This helps eliminate the flatulence causing agent in the beans called oliosacharides, which will have been leached in the water.)
3. In a blender, blend the beans with 3½ gallons of boiling water using an equal amount of water for each blenderful of beans. Keep the water boiling continually. (This helps give the milk a milder, less beany taste.) As soon as you blend the beans and water into slurry, pour it into a heated pot and continue blending the rest of the beans. Blend on low for 5 seconds and then turn to high for 1-2 minutes.
4. Cook the slurry at a gentle rolling boil for 20 minutes.
5. Line the colander with a coarse pressing cloth, like cheesecloth. Pour the hot slurry into the cloth, then draw up the corners and twist shut.
6. Push down with a heavy jar or pot. Press out as much soymilk as possible. (Make sure the colander is sitting in a pot big enough to hold all the milk.)
7. Untwist the bag. For a little extra though thinner milk, you may stir a little boiling water into the remaining pulp and press again.
8. The milk may now be cooled quickly for drinking. (We suggest adding molasses or honey to sweeten.) Make into yogurt or curdle to make tofu.
9. The pulp which has remained behind in your pressing cloth is called okara, and can be used in making granola and other recipes.

Yield: 12 cups soymilk.

Tofu (in blocks)

Tofu, the traditional high-protein bean curd of Japan, is an appealing soy "cheese" which lends itself to many recipes. To make tofu, follow the instructions above for soymilk with the following variations: in step #1, soak 1½ cups dry beans and blend with 12 cups water. The water need not be kept boiling.

1. Once the milk has been made, and is still quite hot, combine 1 Tbs. dry nigari (a solidifying agent available through health food stores) or 3 Tbs. vinegar or ¼ cup lemon juice with ¾ cup water as the solidifying solution.
2. Agitate the soymilk by stirring in a circular motion with a wooden spoon. Reverse directions often. Slowly, as you stir, pour ⅓ of the solidifying solution into the milk.
3. Stop stirring and pour another ⅓ of the solidifier on top of the milk. Cover and let sit for 5-7 minutes.
4. Uncover the milk and note if white curds are beginning to form. Very slowly and carefully, so that you don't break up the curds, pour in the remaining solidifier while stirring. Cover and let sit for another 3 minutes.
5. If white curds have formed in a clear yellow liquid, the curdling process is complete. If not, mix up a little more solidifier (too much will make the tofu bitter) and as you stir, slowly add it to the milk.
6. If you have a tofu press (available through our shop; write us for information), line it with a fine mesh nylon cloth and ladle in the curds and whey. If a pressing box is not available, use a colander. Fold and twist the cloth as before, and covering the cloth with a plate, place a clean brick or jar filled with water on top of it as a weight.
7. Allow the whey to drain for 1-2 hours.
8. Uncover the tofu, slice it and saute or make a salad with it and enjoy.

Yield: 2 cups or 1 lb. tofu.

Soy Flour Tofu

Making tofu out of soy flour is a quick and easy method that yields a crumbly tofu good for spreads, dips, pies and mayonnaise. It has a somewhat different consistency than the tofu made from beans and doesn't press as well into a cake. When pressed, the tofu has a drier consistency.

1. Bring 1½ gallons of water to a boil.
2. Slowly whisk into the water 4 cups of soy flour.
3. Cook at a gentle boil for 20 minutes.
4. Carefully stir in ¼ cup nigari solution (the solution is made by mixing ½ cup nigari with 2 cups water. One-third cup lemon juice or one-quarter cup vinegar may be used in place of the nigari.) Follow the same curdling procedure as that described in the making of pressed tofu from beans.

5. Observe the mixture. The curds should begin to separate from the whey. If the separation is not complete, gently stir in another 2 Tbs. nigari solution, lemon juice, or vinegar.

6. Begin to ladle off the whey.

7. Prepare a colander lined with cheesecloth in a sink. Ladle the curds into the colander. Let sit for one hour so that the remaining whey can drip out of the tofu.

8. The tofu is now ready to be used in any recipe or refrigerated for later use.

TIPS ON TOFU PRODUCTION

1. Block tofu should be stored in the refrigerator in water. Changing the water daily will allow the tofu to stay fresh longer. It can be stored up to 1 week in this manner, covered of course.

2. Nigari should never be used in its dry form to curdle the tofu. A nigari solution should always be made in the proportion of one-half cup dry nigari to 2 cups water.

Soy Recipes

Now that you've learned the art of basic soymilk and tofu making, you're ready to go on to some of the amazingly versatile recipes soy foods provide. The greatest quality of soy and tofu products is their adaptability. Having a slightly nutty but unremarkable taste in raw form, tofu, for example, lends itself to any type of preparation and tastes as delicious barbecued, curried or served up "chicken salad" style as it does whipped up with fruit and sweet flavors and served out as banana tofu cream pie. We defy you to come up with recipes that will make your tofu taste like: (1) scrambled eggs (brewer's yeast is the magic ingredient), (2) chopped liver (tamari helps...) or (3) pizza (this is a secret never-to-be-divulged recipe . . . except within these pages.) You can do just about anything you want with tofu products -- just use the same ingredients for whatever you'd like to produce and work around the different textures and possibilities the tofu provides.

Also included in this section are other soy recipes: recipes for soy ice cream (see Chapter 16 for general instructions on ice cream making), okara products, soyburgers, stews and the like. You could probably make an entire meal wholly from soy products (though we haven't yet been able to produce soy lettuce or carrots). Still, imagine these delicacies -- all part of our Soy cuisine:

Soybean Stew with Barbecued Tofu
Tofu Salad with Tofu Mayo Dressing
Curry Tofu Dip and Crackers
Tofu Cheesecake with Okara Crust Supreme
Soy Mocha Coffee with Whipped Soy Cream on top

Now, of course, we're not recommending an entire meal of soy foods -- that might be somewhat excessive -- but this is just to show you how versatile that tiny soybean really is. Enjoy your sojourn in the world of soy -- we ourselves are frequent travelers!

Tofu Salad

1/8 cup toasted sesame seeds
1 cup diced celery
1/8 cup fresh parsley
3 cups flour tofu
½ cup eggless mayo
¾ Tbs. tamari
1/8 cup nutritional yeast
1 tsp. cumin seed (or cumin powder if unavailable)
½ tsp. black pepper
1 tsp. dill
½ cup alfalfa sprouts

Toast the sesame seeds. Chop the celery and parsley and mix in with the tofu, mayo, tamari, and spices. Add sesame seeds and sprouts, mix well and serve. This can be used as a salad or a sandwich spread.

Yield: 4-5 cups.

Tofu Curry Dip

1 cup tofu
2½ tsp. lemon juice
2 Tbs. oil
1 Tbs. miso
½ tsp. curry powder
¼ tsp. chili powder
¼ cup fresh parsley
½ cup water

Break the block tofu into smaller pieces and combine it with lemon juice, oil, miso and the remaining spices in your blender, adding water a little at a time. You may find you need more or less water, depending upon the water content of the tofu itself. This is excellent on a cheese tray or served up with condiments and crackers.

Yield: 1½ cups.

Tofu-Yeastey Pizza

¼ cup butter
2 cups nutritional yeast
¼ cup arrowroot
1 tsp. salt
½ tsp. pepper
2 tsp. oregano
2 cups cold water
½-1 lb. block tofu
Pizza dough & sauce (see p. 120)

Melt butter, whisk in yeast and arrowroot and spices. Heat, whisking constantly until thick. Add crumbled up block tofu to mixture. Spread on prepared pizza dough, with or without sauce, and bake at 500° for 20-25 minutes.

Yield: One pizza.

Tofu Spread

¾ cup soy mayo (see recipe)
1 cup finely chopped celery
4 cups flour tofu
¾ cup nutritional yeast
½ tsp. salt
½ tsp. paprika
1 tsp. chili powder
½ tsp. cumin powder
¼ tsp. cinnamon
¼ tsp. ginger

Sprouts - as desired.

Prepare the soy mayo according to recipe (see p. 182), and set aside. Combine the celery with the remaining ingredients, including soy mayo, blending together well. Garnish the spread with parsley and serve on sandwiches or as a dip.

Yield: 4-5 cups.

Eden Salad

1 lb. block tofu
4 cups lentil sprouts
2 cups diced pepper
2 cups chopped tomatoes

Marinade:
¼ cup lemon juice
¼ cup vinegar
⅓ cup honey
1 cup soymilk
2 Tbs. sesame seeds
½ Tbs. poppy seeds
¾ Tbs. salt
½ tsp. mustard powder
Pinch cayenne
½ Tbs. "Spike" seasonings
1 cup water
½ cup tamari

Dice the tofu in small ½ in. cubes. Add the lentil sprouts, chopped tomatoes and diced peppers. Combine all marinade ingredients and pour over the tofu and vegetables. Marinade in your refrigerator for at least 2-3 hours before serving.

Yield: 10 cups.

Soybean Stew

2 cups dry soybeans
8 cups cold water
1 cup chopped tomatoes
1 cup chopped green pepper
3 Tbs. butter
6 Tbs. whole wheat flour
½ cup miso
½ cup tomato paste
2 tsp. honey
5 cups water
1/8 tsp. sage
¼ tsp. rosemary
1 tsp. thyme
½ tsp. salt
Pinch cayenne
½ tsp. marjoram

Soak 2 cups of soybeans overnight or for at least 10 hours. Cook the soybeans in a saucepan; they will need to cook at least 8 hours so that they soften adequately. Watch them and add water when necessary. Prepare the vegetables, steaming them separately, with the exception of the tomatoes which can be added last. Melt the butter, whisk in the flour and then the miso, tomato paste, honey and water. Mix so all ingredients are smoothly absorbed and then add spices. Stir in vegetables and drained soybeans. Cook for 20-30 minutes over low flame, stirring frequently.

Yield: 8 cups.

Soyburgers

2 cups dry soybeans
½ cup diced celery
½ cup diced green peppers
½ cup diced carrots
¼ cup chopped parsley
¼ cup peanut butter
1 cup toasted wheat germ
1 Tbs. tamari
½ Tbs. sage
¾ tsp. kelp
1 tsp. cumin
½ Tbs. salt
¾ tsp. chili powder
1/8 tsp. cayenne
½ tsp. thyme
¾ tsp. celery seed
Whole wheat flour for coating patties

Soak your soybeans overnight. Cook them until soft, about 6 hours. Then finely dice the celery, green peppers, and carrots. Chop the parsley. When the beans are soft, mash them and add the peanut butter, wheat germ and tamari. Mix together well, continuing to mash the beans. Your hands work well for this process, better than a spoon or masher. Add the spices and mix thoroughly. Form patties, and dip them in flour. Bake on a lightly-oiled baking sheet at 350° for 30 minutes, or pan fry them.

These provide better than average protein needs without the fat of a regular hamburger. Dress them up with tomato and lettuce, relish, or a Russian dressing, or hot sauce. They're delicious! Don't forget pita bread or whole wheat from our bread section (see p. 163, 157-159) as an accompaniment.

Yield: 12 burgers.

Sauteed Tofu

¾ cup water
½ cup tamari
½ tsp. tahini
½ tsp. ginger
¼ cup oil or butter
8 cups cubed tofu

In a saucepan, combine the first 4 ingredients, heating up for 5 to 10 minutes, until hot. While this sauce is cooking, saute tofu in a hot oiled frying pan. Cook until the tofu soaks up the oil and starts to get "dryish", *stirring as little as possible*. Add the sauce over the tofu and gently stir. Continue to cook for 10 to 15 minutes, allowing the tofu to absorb the flavor of the sauce.

This is the basic tofu, you can then adjust to your own tastes -- add rice, wok-fried Chinese veggies, or prepare in a soup, or in a casserole. There's no end to creativity when tofu is your topic.

Yield: 5½ cups.

Okara Burgers

¼ cup green peppers
¾ cup chopped celery
½ cup finely grated carrots
1 Tbs. miso paste
¼ cup water
1½ cups okara or cooked soybeans
Pinch sage
1 tsp. parsley flakes
Pinch thyme
Pinch cayenne
Pinch curry
¼ tsp. pepper
1 Tbs. tamari
2 Tbs. sesame seeds
1 cup toasted wheat germ
¼ cup whole wheat flour
Flour for coating patties

Finely chop the peppers and celery, and grate the carrots. Dissolve the miso paste in water. At a low speed, blend the vegetables, miso, okara, or cooked soybeans and spices. Add the rest of the ingredients to this mixture in a mixing bowl. Form it into patties, and coat them with flour. Pan fry them over moderate heat. You'll see they're done when they're nicely golden-brown. This is good use for okara, the by-product of tofu making.

Yield: 7 burgers.

Tofu Sunshine Spread

¼ cup butter
1 cup nutritional yeast
¼ cup whole wheat flour
2 Tbs. arrowroot in ½ cup cold water
1 Tbs. prepared mustard
½ tsp. salt
¼ tsp. pepper
1 tsp. Spike
1 cup water
1 lb. crumbled block tofu
½ cup chopped green pepper
¼ cup lentil sprouts (optional)

Melt butter. Add yeast, arrowroot, and flour. Mix well. Add mustard, salt, pepper, Spike, and water. Whisk well. Heat and continue to whisk until mixture thickens. Turn off heat -- add tofu, green peppers, and lentil sprouts. The spread can be served warm on toast with lettuce, tomato, etc., or can be chilled and used for cold sandwiches.

Yield: 3 cups.

Barbecued Tofu

1 lb. (2 cups) tofu
5 Tbs. Barbecue Sauce (see p. 139)

Slice tofu into rectangular patties ¼ in. - ½ in. thick. Lay the patties in a baking dish, and top each with 1 Tbs. barbecue sauce. Spread the sauce over the patties. Bake in the oven at 350° for 20 minutes.

The Fourth of July or Memorial Day never seemed quite so sparkly as when you brought out the tofu barbecue. Add some corn on the cob cooked over charcoal and a fresh salad and you have a new "all-American" rendition of good holiday eating. Don't forget the carrot sticks and the potato salad!

Yield: 5 patties.

Szechuan Eggplant Tofu

2 cups cubed tofu
3 cups diced eggplant
½ tsp. fresh ginger root
1 cup stock
2 Tbs. tamari
¼ cup oil
2½ Tbs. honey
1 tsp. salt
1/8 tsp. pepper

Cut the tofu into ½ in. cubes. Peel and cut eggplant into ½ in. cubes. Mince some fresh ginger root. Saute the tofu until it's crispy on all sides. Combine the stock, ginger and tamari and set aside. Fry the eggplant in oil heated to 340° for about 1 minute or until golden. Meanwhile heat ¼ cup oil in a wok on a high heat. Add the eggplant, tofu and stock mixture. Simmer until only a small amount of liquid remains, and add honey, salt and pepper to taste.

This is a delectable Eastern dish we hope you'll enjoy. Two suggestions: add another ½ tsp. ginger and a pinch of cayenne if you like it very hot; also try a pinch of hing to enhance the flavors as well.

Yield: 3 cups.

Tofu Hero

These are several variations you can try for a delicious Tofu Hero sandwich. Use the same ingredients and process as the Harmony Hero, (see p. 132), substituting tofu in place of cheese. Variations:

1. Fry slices of tofu in oil and a little tamari.

2. Cut up chunks of block tofu.

3. Use Tofu Spread (see p. 180).

Tofu Cheesecake

3 cups tofu
⅓ cup oil
¾ cup honey
½ tsp. salt
1 tsp. vanilla
¼ cup soymilk
⅓ cup lemon juice

Blend together all the ingredients. Pour into an 8 in. pie crust which has been pre-baked for 15 minutes. Bake at 350° for 45 minutes. Chill and serve. This is another tofu taste wonder. Good for anyone with allergies, dairy digestion difficulties, or simply wanting some good nutrition in a tasteful package!

Yield: One 8 in. pie.

Spinach Tofu Casserole

6 cups packed raw spinach
1 Tbs. caraway seeds
2 tsp. Spike
½ tsp. salt
¼ tsp. pepper
2 Tbs. tamari
4 cups flour tofu
3 Tbs. oil
¼ cup wheat germ to sprinkle on top

Pack down 6 cups spinach to measure. Saute spinach in oil, tamari and spices. Add in tofu and saute all together. Place in a small baking pan. Top with wheat germ and bake the casserole for 10 minutes at 350°.

Yield: 4 cups.

Tofu Burgers

1 bun
One 4 oz. slice of block tofu
Oil
Tamari
Gomazio
Tofu mayo
Mustard or relish
Tomatoes
Lettuce
Sprouts

Fry the tofu in oil on a medium flame until crispy, adding 1 Tbs. tamari. Spread mayo, mustard or relish on a bun. Assemble your tofu, tomatoes, lettuce and sprouts, adding gomazio for added flavor, and you have the tastiest burger imaginable. "Gino's" has nothing to compare to the mild, unfatty, highly digestible tofu from which we make our meals.

Yield: 1 tofu burger.

Tofu Mayo Dressing

1 cup tofu
2½ tsp. lemon juice
2 Tbs. oil
1 Tbs. miso
1/8 tsp. salt
Dash pepper
¼ cup water

Break the tofu in smaller pieces (use block tofu) and place in your blender with other seasonings. Depending upon the moisture content of the tofu (and your own taste) add more or less water as you blend. Use as a regular mayonnaise or as a base for Russian, Bleu Cheese, or other dressings. This has a wonderful flavor and consistency and you may enjoy serving it plain for salad lovers and tofu fanciers.

Yield: 1½ cups.

Spanakopita
(Greek Tofu Spinach Pie)

1 recipe phyllo pastry—see Baklava
(p. 231)
¾ lb. spinach
½ lb. tofu
Salt and pepper to taste
2 Tbs. melted butter

Roll phyllo dough out paper thin. Cut into rectangular strips about 5½ in. x 10 in. Brush with melted butter. Chop spinach and steam. Saute diced tofu with salt and pepper until crisp. Mix spinach with tofu. Place 3 Tbs. spinach mixture in right hand corner of pastry. Fold in a triangle form using all of pastry strip. Bake at 400° for 25-30 minutes.

Yield: 5 pies.

Soy Vanilla Ice Bean

3½ cups soymilk
⅔ cups honey
1 Tbs. oil
3 Tbs. vanilla
1 Tbs. lecithin

Please refer to the ice cream introduction under the dairy section (p. 169) for general instructions on ice cream making. Follow these same instructions, substituting soy products for dairy.

1. For soy carob use the above recipe, add ½ Tbs. oil, ⅔ cups carob powder, and reduce both the vanilla flavoring (use only 1 Tbs.) and the lecithin (use ½ Tbs.) and add 1 tsp. almond extract.

2. For soy carob mint use the soy carob recipe proportions: increase the honey to ¾ cup and replace the almond extract with ¼ tsp. peppermint extract.

3. For soy cardamon, use the soy vanilla recipe, reducing the vanilla and lecithin (use 1 Tbs. vanilla, ½ tbs. lecithin), increase the honey to one cup, and add ½ Tbs. coriander and 1 tsp. cardamon.

Yield: 1 quart.

Carob-Tofu Cream Pie

½ cup oil
4 cups tofu
1 cup honey
¼ tsp. salt
1 tsp. vanilla
½ cup carob powder
⅔ cup soy milk

For an even richer pie, add:

¼ cup carob powder
½ tsp. vanilla
½ cup honey

Here is an excellent pie for the unsuspecting. Why not surprise your relatives and friends with this lush dessert; only don't whisper a word of the tofu within. No one will suspect from the crumbs on their chin!

Blend together all the ingredients. Pour into a pre-baked and cooled 9 in. pie crust. Chill in your refrigerator for at least 3 hours.

An alternative method is to pour into an unbaked crust, bake at 350° for 30 minutes and let cool. Top with sliced bananas, coconut, or Whipped Soy Cream. (See p. 185).

Yield: One 9 in. pie.

Soy Mocha Ice Bean

3 Tbs. chicory root
1½ cups water
2½ cups soymilk
1 cup honey
2 Tbs. oil
1 Tbs. carob powder
½ Tbs. lecithin

Simmer the chicory root in water for 7-10 minutes, and then set aside, allowing to cool. Strain and add to the remaining ingredients. Blend and prepare as with other ice cream recipes.

Yield: 1 quart.

Soy Maple Walnut Ice Bean

3 cups soy yogurt
¾ cup honey
2 Tbs. oil
½ Tbs. lecithin
2½ tsp. maple flavoring
1½ tsp. walnut flavoring
½ cup walnuts, crushed or chopped

Blend all the ingredients except the walnuts. Stir in the walnuts before pouring the mixture into freezer. Prepare as with remaining ice cream recipes and freeze.

Yield: 1 quart.

Whipped Soy Cream

½ cup soymilk
¾ -1 cup oil
2 Tbs. honey
¾ tsp. vanilla

Pour soymilk and ¼ cup oil into your blender. Blend them at high speed. Slowly pour in another ¼ cup oil. Add the honey and vanilla. Slowly add the remainder of the oil as the mixture thickens. Chill before serving. This is an excellent thick topping -- good for pies, cakes and puddings, or dash a dollop into your favorite grain coffee.

Yield: 1½ cups.

Okara Crust Supreme

1¼ cups okara
½ cup butter
¼ cup honey
½ cup coconut
½ cup wheat germ

Toast the okara in your oven or in a dry skillet until it's brown, and allow it to cool. Melt the butter. Add honey. Stir in all the other ingredients. Press into two 8 in. or 9 in. pie pans. This makes an excellent crust for pudding pies, fruit pies, or any of your special desserts.

Yield: Two bottom crusts.

Soy Coffee

¾ cup soybeans
3 cups soaking water
4½ cups cooking water
Honey, maple syrup, or light molasses to taste
Milk or soymilk to taste

Soak beans overnight (or for at least 8 hours). Strain the water and spread beans thinly over an unoiled baking sheet. Roast in the oven for 2½ hours at 350°, stirring occasionally, until dark brown.

Grind roasted soybeans in a grain grinder. (Sometimes a blender will work, depending on the model.) Place ground roasted soybeans in 4½ cups boiling water and simmer for 20-30 minutes to make coffee. Strain the Soy Coffee, sweeten with honey, maple syrup or light molasses, and add milk or soymilk to taste.

Yield: 2½ cups.

18·
Fruits

"Chitra, do you have all the crates and boxes we need?"

"I hope so. The step van's all loaded and it's time we're on the road. We've got a long list today."

"Okay, I've got everything -- the money, purchase order, and our lunches. Let's go..."

"Shubhie" (as we call her), climbs into the van dressed in her very best marketing shirt and jeans, hair neatly braided. We're on our way to Ontelaunee Orchard in Leesport, sailing down the road with visions of "sugar plums" dancing in our heads. Or should I say, winesap apples?

As soon as we arrive, we find our friend George, who takes us on a produce inspection tour, smiling all the way. We smell, feel and taste samples of apples and pears and choose for those at home our favorite Stamens, Delicious and Winesap apples, and Bartlett pears as well. Around back we watch the spotted, not-so-perfect fruits come rolling down the chute into a truck parked below, and choose what we want. Though these apples may be bruised and "second class", when we get done they'll make first class sauces, pies, and fruit butters.

Then back in the truck again, we're on our way to Zern's, a large farmer's market near Boyerstown, Pa. Hiking up and down the colorful aisles, we pass up clothing, antiques, books and sweet confections (sometimes . . .) to find the plump produce we've been looking for. Then on the road again, we finally arrive back home, tired and happy, with our faithful kitchen van flooded with fruit crates and produce. While we unload and store them all, the apples, pears and grapes silently smile at us, letting us know we indeed have received the "fruits of our labor".

This chapter presents you fruits in all their variety -- fruits which can be steamed, blended, baked, chopped, sliced or served whole with equal enjoyment. We change them as the seasons change, finding sweet strawberries in June, mouth-watering melons in July and August and rosy apples and pears in the fall. They're good as breakfasts and equally good for dinner, lunch or dessert. Try the recipes that suit your "fruity" fancy!

Melon Basket

1 watermelon
1 cantaloupe
1 honeydew
1 cranshaw (a honeydew-like melon)

Cut all melons in half. Using a melon baller, scoop out all of the fruit. Combine the melon balls together with their own juice and return to the empty watermelon halves. Serve from the basket halves with an extra bowl of melon on one side. A simple yet festive treat for a hot summer day.

Yield: 2½ gallons.

Apple Boats

3 apples
¾ cup Walnut Cream (see p. 128)
¼ cup raisins
¼ tsp. cinnamon

Cut off top of apples and core, sparing as much of the fruit as possible. Scoop out the center, leaving a ½ inch shell. Chop up the centers, and add the nut cream and raisins and mix well. Re-stuff your apple boats with the filling and garnish the tops with a sprinkling of cinnamon.

Apples, by the way, are a wholesome, complete food, providing enzymes, fruit sugar, vitamins and minerals, not to mention the beneficial effects of pectin and cellulose, which gently aid digestion.

Yield: 3 servings.

Apple-Oat Greeting

½ cup oats
1 cup water
¼ cup lemon juice
½ cup yogurt
6 cups shredded apples
3 Tbs. honey
⅓ cup chopped nuts (optional)

Soak your oats in water overnight. The following day combine the oats with all other ingredients; mix together well and serve. A lovely, light way you can start your morning.

Yield: 5 cups.

Ambrosia

5 oranges
1 cup pineapple chunks
1 cup strawberries
1 cup yogurt
1 Tbs. honey
½ cup coconut

Peel the oranges and pineapple and slice them into chunks, then slice the strawberries in half. Whisk honey into the yogurt. Add the fruit and coconut to the yogurt mixture and stir. Tastes like the nectar of the gods!

Yield: 5 cups.

Apple Date Mate

4 apples
¼ cup dates
¼ tsp. cinnamon

Grate apples and slice the dates into small pieces. Toss together with cinnamon and serve. This tastes delicious with a generous hunk of cream cheese on the side or some homemade yogurt or pot cheese.

Yield: 3 cups.

Nisha's Natural Fruit Jello

4 Tbs. agar-agar
2 cups cold water
2 cups hot water
1½ cups fresh strawberries
1½ cups fresh pineapple or other tropical or exotic fruits -- mangoes, papaya, etc.
¼ cup fresh lemon juice
2 cups orange juice
¾ cup honey

Add agar-agar to cold water and allow to sit for a minute. Then add hot water and boil for 2 minutes. Meanwhile, slice strawberry and chunk pineapple; squeeze lemon juice and set aside. Mix orange juice, honey and lemon juice. Add fruit to orange juice mix and fold into bowl or casserole dish with agar-agar. Let jel for 8 hours and then serve. This is one of the most delicious breakfasts imaginable—makes a nice easy dessert too. (Agar-agar comes in different forms and strengths. Check package for proportion agar-agar to liquid.)

Yield: 8 cups.

Sweetly Light Fruit Salad

2 apples
2 pears
2 bananas
¼ cup dates
1 cup grapes
¼ tsp. cinnamon

Slice apples, pears, bananas and dates. Add grapes and cinnamon. Toss the fruit salad and serve with a sweet sauce (see nut sauce toppings, pp. 128, 130, 216).

For a simpler variant of the above, slice 2 bananas, 1/8 cup of dates and toss in 1/8 cup of coconut. This makes a tasty banana-date salad.

Or if you're leaning toward citrus, slice 5 oranges and add in ⅓ cup of shredded coconut. Easy, light and yet a little bit more than just orange!

Yield: 5-6 cups.

Baked Bananas

2 bananas
2 Tbs. honey
¼ tsp. cinnamon

Slice bananas in half and arrange sliced side-up on an oiled baking sheet. Mix honey and cinnamon, and drizzle lightly over bananas. Bake for 20 minutes at 350°.

Yield: 2 servings.

Baked Apples

3 apples
¼ cup dates or raisins
1/8 cup chopped nuts
¼ cup honey
1 tsp. butter
1 tsp. lemon juice
½ tsp. cinnamon
½ cup water

Core the apples. Chop the dates and nuts, and stuff your apples with the date-nut mixture. Place apples on an oiled baking pan. Combine the remaining ingredients in a saucepan and simmer for five minutes. Pour the heated mixture over apples and bake at 350° for forty minutes.

For a simpler version of above, using 3 apples, core them and stuff with two dates each. Place 1 cup water on bottom of casserole tray, add the apples and bake at 350° for one hour.

Yield: 3 servings.

Cinn-apple Sauce

3 apples
¼ cup water
¼ tsp. cinnamon

Chop the apples and blend with water and cinnamon. The applesauce can be served lightly warmed, if you desire, or blended with pears or bananas for a different flavor combination that can be served hot or cold.

To make bann-apple sauce, use only 2 apples with above recipe, and add 2 bananas before blending. Blend all ingredients, adding ¼ cup additional water if you prefer a more liquidy consistency. If you like, you can experiment with other spices, adding ½ tsp. vanilla and a pinch of cloves and ginger besides.

Blending these fruits and serving them raw provides you all of their nutrients in the most optimum state: just as Ma Nature made them!

Yield: 1½-2 cups.

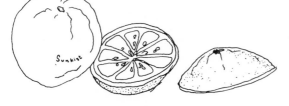

Citrus Celebration

4 oranges
1 cup grapefruit
1 cup pineapple
1 cup strawberries
½ cup coconut (optional)

Peel and slice the oranges and grapefruit into chunks. Chunk the pineapple, halve the strawberries, and toss all the ingredients together in a large serving bowl.

Consider how healthfully you've chosen to eat, with a large natural boost of Vitamin C, plus all the wondrous accompanying ingredients -- the bioflavanoids, potassium and other minerals, the digestive enzymes of the pineapple, and the cleansing properties of orange and grapefruit. While you were just thinking of the fruit itself, we imagined its potential for your health and called it a "Citrus Celebration."

Yield: 5 cups.

Fruit Compotes

Fruit compotes are a wonderful invention, giving you an opportunity to experience new blends, fruity flavors and aromas, and brightening your breakfast (or any meal for that matter...)

Most of our recipes call for on-the-stove preparation; however, you can just as easily bake these fruity dishes in the oven and serve up a sumptuous compote treat.

1. For a simple *Mixed Compote* slice two each of apples, pears, plums, and peaches; add ½ cup dates and cinnamon sticks. Cook over a medium flame until soft but not mushy, then serve hot or cold.

2. For *Fruity Prune Compote* use same ingredients as above, adding ½ cup each of dried prunes and apricots to replace dates (and a sprinkle of lemon juice). Add a small amount (1/8 to 1/4 cup of water) as needed to keep mixture from sticking. Prepare as in above recipe.

3. For *Apple-Banana Compote,* add 3 cups chunked apples, ½ cup water, ¼ cup dates, and ¼ cup raisins together. Cook them until the apples are soft, then add ¼ tsp. cinnamon. Allow the mixture to cool to room temperature, then add one sliced banana. Serve warm or chilled.

4. For *Apple-Nut Delight* slice 3 apples thinly and place in a saucepan with ¼ cup water. Simmer the apples for ten minutes, then add ¼ cup toasted sesame seeds, 1/8 cup chopped walnuts, and the following ingredients: 1¼ tsp. cinnamon, ½ Tbs. lemon juice, and 2 Tbs. honey. Cook this mixture until the apples are soft and then serve . . . a pleasing variation for a fruit compote!

Several compote recipes using other ingredients are also included—see Baked Bananas (p. 190), Peachy-Plum Compote (p. 192), and of course, good old fashioned Baked Apples (p. 190), not to be forgotten!

Peachey-Plum Compote

1½ cups water
3 cups peach slices
2 cups plum slices
¼ cup honey
2 Tbs. arrowroot
½ cup water
1 Tbs. lemon juice
½ tsp. vanilla

Combine water and peach and plum slices in a saucepan. Bring the slices to boil and then gently simmer for 15 minutes. Stir in the honey. Mix the arrowroot with ½ cup water and then slowly stir into the fruit mixture. By mixing the arrowroot with water you remove any lumps from the flour. Then adding it slowly (and patiently) you will discover it going through the thickening process. This happens after you bring it to a boil, then lower flame and cook another 5 minutes, stirring all the while. Remove from heat, add the lemon juice and vanilla and chill.

Yield: 4 cups.

19·
Beverages

Roastaroma

Sukanya

When it's time for something cold, wet, and thirst-quenching, here's a number of fine alternatives to the nutritionless, sugary sodas and overstimulating black teas and coffees so in abundance today. A beverage can be anything from a meal in a glass or rich dessert to a simple pick-me-up or thirst quencher. Quick and easy-to-prepare, beverages are particularly good on days when you're just too rushed to eat but want to keep your nutrition quota stable.

Here are a few tips: as much as possible use *fresh* ingredients in your beverages. In recipes calling for nuts or seeds, use fresh, untoasted varieties for the highest nutritive value, and if you wish, feel free to soak these before blending; soaking brings out their flavors and nutrients even more. (You can also soak dates or dried fruit for beverages including them.)

POWDERED MILK

For smoothies or milk drinks calling for prepared powdered milk, here is a simple means of preparation:

Blend in a blender or whisk together 1¼ cups powdered milk and 1 cup water until you have a smooth consistency, then blend in an additional 3¼ cups water. This can be used as a regular milk substitute in many recipes.

The magic kitchen helper in this chapter is your blender. With a blender you can come up with just about anything under the sun -- all you need are some fruits and seeds, yogurt or milk, carob, honey and seasonings. If you have a food processor, then you're one step further, for you can make excellent fresh vegetable juices, each of which has different cleansing and healthful properties. Try a mixture of apple-carrot, carrot-beet, or celery and parsley. 1 In this section we've included everything from citrus to protein drinks to soothing herbal teas. Each beverage has its special moment for you. While your children may enjoy a frozen banana drink, you can sit back and inhale the mellow flavor of a cup of roastaroma, blended and prepared in your own kitchen.

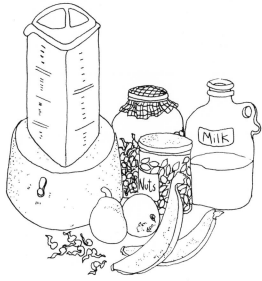

Orange Mint Cooler

1 cup orange juice
1 tsp. peppermint leaves

Fresh mint from your garden makes this drink a definite plus. Mix mint and juice together and if possible, let sit overnight in your refrigerator so the flavors seep in. Or else, blend and serve up right then and there. Very refreshing!

Another tasty, easy to prepare drink is *Spicey Orange Surprise:* to 4 cups of orange juice add 2 pinches nutmeg and ½ tsp. vanilla; blend and serve.

Try another variation: to ½ cup pineapple juice, add ¼ cup orange juice, 1 Tbs. honey, 3 or 4 strawberries, and some crushed ice. Blend and serve -- an excellent thirst-quencher.

Yield: 1 cup.

Carob Banana Froth

4 cups milk
4 bananas
2 tsp. vanilla
¼ cup carob
½ tsp. cinnamon
Dash salt
Mint leaves (optional)

Blend milk and vanilla; then blend in carob, cinnamon, mint and salt.

Yield: 6 cups.

Apple-Honey Wake Up

1 cup sunny seed sprouts
¼ cup lemon juice
1½ Tbs. honey
¼ cup powdered milk
3 grated apples
¼ cup wheat germ
1 cup water

Blend all the ingredients and serve. Makes a hearty wake-up "meal-in-a-cup".

Yield: 4½ cups.

Citrus Health Drink

8 soaked dates
⅓ cup fresh parsley
⅓ cup raisins
¼ cup lemon juice
1 cup orange or pineapple juice
1 cup water

Soak the dates for several hours. Chop the parsley, add all ingredients together along with dates and blend in blender. Serve garnished with parsley or a sprig of mint.

Yield: 2½ cups.

Hi-Protein Drink

5 raw almonds
⅓ cup dates or raisins
2 Tbs. sesame seeds
2 Tbs. sunflower seeds
½ Tbs. raw peanuts

Soak all the ingredients in 1 cup water overnight. In the morning blend up and serve. Add up to 1 extra cup water if you like a thinner drink. This is sweet and substantial—full of nourishment that's straight from Mother Nature!

Yield: 1½-2 cups.

Almond Milk

5 raw almonds
1/8 tsp. cardamon
1 cup milk
1/8 cup raisins or dates

Blend all the ingredients and serve. You can use regular or soymilk in this recipe and any of the beverages where milk is called for. See Soy section (Chapter 17) for instructions on making soymilk.

Yield: 1¼ cups.

For date milk add 5 dates and 1/8 tsp. vanilla to one cup of milk, blend and serve. One of our children's favorites, this drink needs no added sweeteners. Serve hot or cold.

Yield: 1¼ cups.

For Sunny Hunny Milk, add 1 tsp. vanilla, ¾ cup sunflower seeds, 1/8 tsp. cardamon and 2 Tbs. honey to 4 cups milk (you can use ½ milk; ½ yogurt) for a total 5½ cup yield.

Yield: 5½ cups.

Strawberry Milkshake

2½ cups yogurt
½ cup milk powder
¼ cup water
½ cup milk
1 tsp. vanilla
1 cup strawberries
2 Tbs. honey

Better than any store-bought milkshake, this has a freshness all its own. Combine all ingredients in blender, blend and serve.

Yield: 4 cups.

Ginger-Banana Smoothie

1 cup yogurt
1 banana
¼ cup honey
½ tsp. ginger powder
¼ tsp. cardamon
½ cup milk

Blend and serve. This makes a spicey, tangy yogurt drink which is practically a breakfast in itself . . . also a light and refreshing dessert.

You can make a tantalizing Orange Smoothie by blending ¾ cup orange juice with 2 cups yogurt, 1 tsp. vanilla, 1½ Tbs. honey and a pinch of nutmeg. This is an excellent drink or topping for citrus salad as well.

Yield: 2 cups.

Yog Nog

3¾ cups milk
1 tsp. vanilla
½ tsp. cinnamon
½ tsp. allspice
½ cup honey
1 drop almond extract
½ cup milk powder
½ tsp. nutmeg

Combine all the ingredients together, blend and serve. This provides a lighter "egg" nog without the eggs and has the same satisfying flavor. We drink it at Christmas and year-round!

Yield: 5 cups.

Carob Cream

2 frozen bananas
2 cups milk
2 Tbs. carob
1 Tbs. honey
1 tsp. vanilla

Thick and creamy, with a chocolatey-carob milkshake flavor. Freeze bananas the day before blending up shake. Combine all ingredients together and blend in blender. This is a very satisfying snack, almost a meal in itself!

Yield: 3 cups.

Yogi "Wheaties" Milk

1 cup milk
1 tsp. nutritional yeast
1 Tbs. wheat germ
½ Tbs. molasses
½ Tbs. honey

Blend all the ingredients together for a very nutritious morning breakfast drink. An option is to cut out the wheat germ and increase molasses to 1 tablespoon, decrease honey to one teaspoon. Then serve as molasses milk. Either way you receive ample carbohydrate, protein, minerals and B-vitamins to get a good start on your day.

Yield: 1¼ cups.

Banana-Seed Smoothie

¼ cup ground raw sunflower seeds
2 cups water
3 bananas
¼ tsp. cinnamon or cardamom

Grind sunflower seeds in a seed or coffee mill. Combine with remaining ingredients and blend up. This is a highly nutritious and tasty morning smoothie! For even better results, soak the sunflower seeds overnight (or for a minimum of 4 hours). Soaking the seeds helps make them more digestible as well as bringing out their flavors. Follow same directions as above. This is such a rich and full drink that with an extra banana or two and a hint of carob, it wouldn't be difficult to imagine this as a raw pudding or filler for a homemade pie crust.

Yield: 3½ cups.

Lassi Drink

3½ cups yogurt
½ cup milk
3 Tbs. honey
1 tsp. cardamon
½ tsp. coriander
1 tsp. cinnamon

Lassi is an Indian beverage, a pleasant breakfast drink served with fruits or cereals, or a nice alternative to dessert, served with cookies or baked goods. Blend all the ingredients together, chill and serve.

Yield: 4½ cups.

Cream of Almond Drink is a pleasing variation: to 1½ cups yogurt add 1/8 tsp. cardamon, 1 tsp. coriander, ½ tsp. lemon juice, ¼ cup honey and 1/8 tsp. almond extract. Blend and serve for two cups of divine drinking pleasure!

Yield: 2 cups.

Lemon Quencher

½ cup fresh lemon juice
⅓ cup honey
3½ cups water
Small bunch fresh parsley (optional)

A year-round excellent thirst-quencher, fresh lemonade is a snap to make and very satisfying. Blend all items at high speed, add parsley and serve. You may wish to add some cracked ice and blend to chill the drink more thoroughly, or add in a sprig of mint fresh from your garden.

One more tempting touch: prepare the drink as above, and add ice and Perrier or mineral water and you have a sparkling lemon quencher, one of the most satisfying drinks for quenching thirsts.

Yield: 4 cups.

Banana-Peanut Froth

1 large frozen banana
1½ cups milk
¼ cup peanut butter
¼ cup raisins
1/8 tsp. almond extract (optional)

Concocted by some of the brothers working in the kitchen one morning, this was the drink they came up with "accidentally" on a day when milk was served at breakfast and peanut butter sandwiches provided for lunchtakers. The drink has a milkshake consistency; simply combine all the ingredients, including the banana you froze yesterday (or the same day -- a minimum of 3 hours), blend and serve.

Yield: 2 cups.

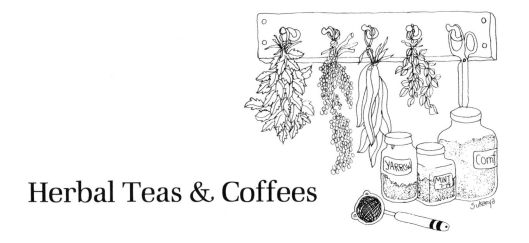

Herbal Teas & Coffees

"A weed is simply a plant whose gifts man has not yet discovered." So expressed Ralph Waldo Emerson, lover of the outdoors and respecter of God's natural bounty. Growing everywhere in wild profusion, herbs of all colors and healing qualities grace roadsides, garbage dumps, and meadows alike with cheerful and subtle beauty and fragrance. Peoples of all cultures and ages have known the lore and fine taste of herbs in creating delicate or robust teas (with healing and regenerative qualities to match). Yet for "civilized" man of the twentieth century, it is only within recent years that herbal teas have agiain found popularity, both for good taste, and for healthful effects.

Black teas and coffee, we all know, contain large amounts of caffeine which create an energetic feeling by stimulating or speeding up the circulatory and nervous systems. Like all else, such beverages taken in moderation by a healthy person will not have a strongly adverse effect. However, if consumed frequently and often, caffeinated drinks can create energy imbalances in our bodies and minds. Cycles of overwork, overeating, late night hours and early morning exhaustion are born; to accommodate, we consume even more stimulating drinks and then wonder why we lack vibrancy and health. Caffeine is addicting, and used indiscriminately, can be deleterious to a sound and healthy state of being.

A gentler and more self-attuned alternative exists within the pleasant world of herbal drinks, sweetened with honey or maple syrup (if at all) in place of the white sugar used in tea and coffee. Herbal teas in general have a soothing, relaxing effect on the body-mind, and help stimulate digestion and tone the general system. Different herbs have different subtle qualities. A mint tea soothes pain and is stimulating, increasing circulation naturally and gently. Tummy aches are comforted by ginger tea; jumpy nerves soothed with a cup of chamomile. A comfrey tea will help strained muscles and broken bones, and promote healing (used, of course, in conjunction with practical health care). For in-depth reading on herbology, we highly suggest *Herbs and Things*, by Jeanne Rose, and *The Herb Book*, by John Lust.

BREWING AN HERBAL TEA

1. Bring one cup water per serving to a boil.

2. For most herbs, turn off heat before adding tea to avoid a bitter taste.* Add the loose or tea-bagged herbs to the water and cover. Steep 5 minutes minimum to draw out the full flavor and oils of the herbs. Uncovered, the healing and flavorful oils of the herbs escape in the steam.

3. Strain, if necessary, and sweeten with honey or maple syrup. Give thanks for the simple and life-giving plants provided so abundantly in the natural world surrounding us.

Herewith, some fine herbal blends consumed with pleasant abandon in Kripalu Kitchen, and concocted by our master herbalist and good-cheer spreader, Hira. Also included are soy and toasted grain "coffees" we have come up with through patient testing, grinding and roasting . . . just waiting to accompany some Truck Stop Pancakes or hot cinnamon rolls on a wintertime morn. Experiment with your own blends and let us hear of your successes. Or your failures. We are a very sympathetic lot.

Chai (Spicy Indian Tea)

2 cups water
5 cups milk
20 cloves
2-3 cinnamon sticks
1 tsp. cardamom
2 Tbs. ginger (fresh grated if possible)
3 black peppercorns
1 Tbs. peppermint tea
½ cup honey

A traditional Indian favorite, customarily made with sugar and black tea, but just as good and more soothing to the body made with herbal tea and honey. Place water and all spices in saucepan and heat to boiling. Boil 3 minutes, reduce heat and add milk, honey, peppermint and black peppercorns. Heat until it almost boils, turn off the heat before boiling point, cover and steep 10 minutes. Strain and serve.

Yield: 6-7 cups.

*There are exceptions: most roots and barks, like sassafrass, and some other types of herbs (like wintergreen) require boiling or simmering to draw out their properties fully.

Whole Grain Roastaroma

2 gallons water
6 cups roasted ground wheat berries
6 cups roasted ground barley
2 Tbs. cinnamon (or 6-8 sticks)
1 Tbs. nutmeg
1½ Tbs. cardamom
2 Tbs. cloves, fresh ground
1 Tbs. ginger
2 Tbs. fresh ground anise
2 tsp. vanilla
1½ cups honey

Bring 2 gallons of water to a boil. Add roasted, ground grains and all spices. Boil gently, covered, for 15-20 minutes to bring out the full flavor of grains and spices. Strain well and sweeten to taste -- 1½-2 cups honey suits us. The grain will absorb some water in brewing.

To make roasted grains: you will need a food mill or grinder. Plan to do this ahead, and make plenty for future brewings. Spread whole wheat berries and barley over baking or cookie sheets. Toast at 450° for 30-40 minutes, stirring several times while toasting. Cool the grains and run them through a food mill or grinder, grinding to a medium-fine consistency (it may take 2-3 grinds.) Store in a covered jar until ready to use. For really superb flavor, nutmeg, cinnamon sticks, anise seeds, cloves, and/or cardamom pods can be ground and used in place of pre-ground spices.

Yield: 1½ gallons.

Cafe-au-Lait

1-2 cups milk
4 Tbs. Roastaroma (p. 203) or Soy Coffee (p. 185)
Honey or maple syrup
Dash Ginger or cinnamon

This wonderful variation on our Roastaroma grain coffee (or our Soy Coffee) evokes pleasant thoughts of French inns or European cuisine. Heat 1 cup water and 1 cup milk (or use milk only for a richer drink, as desired). Do not boil; stir constantly so milk does not scald. Add 4 Tbs. Roastaroma or Soy Coffee blend and simmer gently for 10 minutes, stirring frequently. Sweeten with honey or maple syrup to taste and serve in mugs with a dash of ginger or nutmeg on top. Pero or Cafix herbal coffee substitutes may also be used in place of Roastaroma and Soy Coffee blends.

Mocha Cafe-au-Lait: For a richer and sweeter variation, add 1 Tbs. carob powder and stir well before serving.

Yield: 2 servings.

Christmas Tea

7 cinnamon sticks
2 tsp. cloves
Pinch of nutmeg
4 cups water
Honey to taste

Boil water; add cinnamon sticks and cloves, simmer 3-4 minutes. Sweeten with honey. A wonderfully fragrant and simple holiday tea!

Yield: 4 cups.

Blue Mountain Tea

4 cups water
3 Tbs. peppermint tea
4 tsp. anise seed
1 Tbs. red raspberry leaf tea
Pinch nutmeg

Brew 1 Tbs. of the above mixture for every 1 cup of tea you prepare. Steep for 3-5 minutes, then strain and serve.

Yield: 4 cups.

20•
Sweet
Things
and
Snacks

"Pooh always liked a little something at 11 o'clock in the morning, and he was glad to see Rabbit getting out plates and mugs, and when Rabbit said, 'Honey or condensed milk with your bread?' he was so excited that he said, 'Both,' and then, so as not to seem greedy, he added, 'But don't bother about the bread please . . . '"[1]

For those of us who like "a little something" every once in a while, here are some tasty treats, pies and cakes -- all to please your sweet tooth, vegetarian or otherwise. Working with other cookbooks, we have encountered a dearth of good dessert recipes using natural products. We have therefore opted to supply a sturdy amount of dessert-type recipes, as this is often the area hardest to adjust to for nouveau healthy vegetarian cooks (and one of the most fun to experiment with, we might add).

Cooking with unprocessed, wholesome ingredients requires some industry on your part, as learning to work with whole wheat flours, and using honey instead of granulated sugars and yogurt or lecithin in place of eggs requires some experience for the uninitiated. However, the "proof is in the pudding," as the maxim says. Nothing tastes quite as satisfying as a cookie or crunchy treat you can bite into, knowing all the ingredients are natural, digestible and even salutary to your health!

Try your hand with some of our easy delectable pies, cakes and treats. Many of these recipes are simple enough that with minimal supervision you can let your children take over the preparation process. Or allow the "bigger" children (i.e., your friends and relatives) to have a try at making a Turkish delight or a Peanut Butter Swirl Bar. You may have trouble getting them out of the kitchen.

Cakes

There was a time when the thought of trying to bake a cake without eggs left me feeling bewildered. Like most of us, I had learned to bake using eggs as the essential binding ingredient. After many sunken disasters and, happily, more and more "rising" successes, I have finally learned some eggless secrets to baking. The following hints will help your cake rise and stay risen to peaks of scrumptious success.

1. Each egg can be replaced with either 2 Tbs. yogurt, a commercial egg replacer or a combination of liquid lecithin and water. I have used all three with success, although yogurt is my favorite binder.

2. Baking powder works best in the presence of both milk and a sweetener such as honey.

3. Whole wheat pastry flour gives a lighter texture than regular whole wheat flour.

4. Soy flour, although very nutritious, has a heavy effect on cakes, as do rye and buckwheat flour. You'll want to use these sparingly and in combination with a lighter flour.

5. Rice flour, chestnut flour, millet flour and oat flour can all be used in combination with whole wheat pastry for nice flavor and texture variations.

6. When substituting in a recipe, use 3/4-7/8 cup honey for 1 cup sugar, and increase the flour or decrease the liquid content by 1/2 to 3/4 cup.

7. Substituting fruit juice for water adds a nice flavor to cakes and cookies and allows you to cut back on other sweeteners.

8. Adding dates, raisins, and chopped fruits to cake batters also allows you to cut back on other sweeteners without losing natural flavor.

9. Carefully choose the kind of unrefined oil you use. We find soy oil to be too heavy and prefer a lighter safflower or occasionally corn oil.

10. Flavoring such as nut extracts are a nice alternative to vanilla and can create a whole different tone and flavor in an old recipe.

11. Be creative with icings and decorations. The possibilities are as endless as your imagination. I've served the same basic cake over and over with additions and subtractions of flavorings, fillings and frostings without being discovered yet.

The recipes that follow have all been tried and declared scrumptious countless times. Our only problem with them is getting enough batter in the pan after everybody's had a spoon in the bowl for a little taste. There just seems to be something warm and homey about uncooked cake and cookie batter that never leaves us with a problem finding someone to "clean the bowl".

Applesauce Cake

¾ cup butter
1 cup honey
½ cup yogurt
1 cup applesauce
2 tsp. vanilla
2½ cups whole wheat pastry flour
½ tsp. salt
1 Tbs. baking powder
2 tsp. cinnamon
1½ tsp. allspice
½ cup raisins
1 tsp. baking soda

Cream the butter and honey, and stir in all the wet ingredients. Sift the dry ingredients into the wet. Gently stir in the raisins, being careful not to overbeat the mixture. Pour into an oiled 9 x 9 in. cake pan, and bake at 325° for 45 minutes to an hour.

Yield: One 9 in. cake.

Carob-Almond Cake

¾ cup melted butter
1 cup honey
1 cup yogurt or sour milk
¼ cup apple juice
½ cup water
1 tsp. vanilla
½ tsp. almond extract
2½ cups whole wheat pastry flour
1 cup carob powder
1 Tbs. baking powder

Mix all the wet ingredients together. Sift the dry ingredients into the wet, and mix well. Pour into an oiled 9 x 9 in. pan. Bake at 325° for 1 hour.

Yield: One 9 x 9 in. cake.

Gingerbread Cake

1 cup melted butter
½ cup honey
¾ cup molasses
1 tsp. vanilla
½ cup yogurt
¼ cup milk
3 cups whole wheat pastry flour
¼ cup soy flour
1 Tbs. baking powder
½ tsp. salt
1 tsp. cinnamon
½ tsp. cloves
1½ tsp. ginger
½ tsp. nutmeg
2 cups raisins

Preheat your oven to 325°. Cream the butter, honey, molasses and vanilla together. Stir in the yogurt and milk. Sift the dry ingredients into the wet, and gently stir in the raisins. Pour into a greased 9 in. cake pan, and bake at 325° for one hour. Here's an all-around spicey, lush cake that's been high on our dessert list for years. Try it with a cream cheese frosting.

Yield: One 9 in. cake.

Crumbly Coffee Cake

½ cup melted butter
¾ cup honey
½ cup yogurt or sour milk
¼ cup milk
1 tsp. vanilla
2¼ cups whole wheat pastry flour
2 tsp. baking powder
¼ tsp. salt
1 tsp. cinnamon

Topping:
½ cup wheat germ
½ cup whole wheat pastry flour
1 Tbs. melted butter
3 Tbs. honey

Preheat oven to 325°. Cream the honey and butter together. Stir in yogurt or sour milk, milk and vanilla. Sift in the dry ingredients, and stir to a uniform consistency, but do not overbeat. Pour into a greased 9 in. cake pan. Mix together the wheat germ and flour. Add the butter and honey. Mix with fingers until mixture is in small crumbles. Sprinkle over the cake batter. Bake at 325° for 45 minutes.

Yield: One 9 in. cake.

Date 'n Carrot Cake

3 cups grated carrots
1 cup chopped dates
¾ cup melted butter
1 cup honey
1 tsp. vanilla
¼ cup yogurt
2¾ cups whole wheat pastry flour
1 Tbs. baking powder
½ tsp. salt
2 tsp. cinnamon

Preheat your oven to 325°. Grate the carrots and chop the dates; then cream the honey, butter and vanilla together. Stir in the yogurt. Sift the dry ingredients into the wet ingredients and gently stir in the carrots and dates, being careful not to overbeat the mixture. Pour into a greased 9 in. cake pan, and bake at 325° for 45 minutes to an hour.

This is a Retreat favorite. A very healthful dessert nevertheless having that rich "cakey" flavor, try it topped with a cream cheese icing. Also, add 1 cup of walnuts to the recipe as a pleasant variation.

Yield: One 9 in. cake.

Peach (or Pineapply) Upside-Down Cake

3 cups sliced peaches (or pineapple chunks)
½ cup melted butter
1 cup honey
1 cup water
2 tsp. vanilla
½ cup yogurt
2½ cups whole wheat pastry flour
1 Tbs. baking powder
½ tsp. salt
3 Tbs. wheat germ
¼ cup honey

Wash and slice the peaches (or, if using pineapple, cut the fruit into small chunks). Set aside. Beat together the wet ingredients; sift the dry ingredients into the wet, and stir gently. Place the sliced fruit on the bottom of a greased 9 x 13 in. pan. Be sure to drain all liquid off the fruit. Pour the cake batter over the fruit, and bake at 325° for 1 hour. Let the cake cool for 5 minutes, then invert the pan onto the plate. Drizzle with 1/8 - 1/4 cup honey.

This is a very nice, surprisingly easy cake to make and fits all your requirements for a special "something" at the end of the meal. Try it with a tiny bit of clove sprinkled on top, once you've inverted the cake.

Yield: One 9 x 13 in. cake.

Holiday Apple Walnut Cake

¾ cup oil or melted butter
1½ cups honey
½ cup yogurt
2 tsp. vanilla
3 cups whole wheat pastry flour
½ tsp. salt
2 tsp. baking powder
2 tsp. cinnamon
3½ cups chopped apples
1 cup chopped walnuts
1 cup raisins

Brought to us by Damayanti (who used to receive this cake every year on her birthday), this is a wonderful, rich treat. Cream the oil or butter with the honey. Add the remaining wet ingredients. Sift together the dry ingredients and add to the wet. Gently fold in your apples, nuts and raisins, being careful not to overbeat. Pour into a greased 9 x 13 in. pan, and bake at 325° for one hour.

A festive cake, this will satisfy fruit-lovers and cake-lovers at the same time. This is an excellent cake to send someone on Christmas or the holidays -- it actually gets better the longer it sits.

Yield: One 9 x 13 in. cake.

Honey Cake

½ cup melted butter
1 cup honey
½ cup yogurt
1 tsp. vanilla
2 cups whole wheat pastry flour
½ tsp. salt
2 tsp. baking powder
½ tsp. ginger
½ tsp. cinnamon
¼ cup water

Mix all the wet ingredients together; then mix all the dry ingredients together in a separate bowl. Sift the dry ingredients into the wet, stirring just enough to moisten them. Pour into an 8 in. greased cake pan and bake at 325° for 45 minutes.

This is a delightful variant on cake baking which will keep well if wrapped and refrigerated or sent in the mail as a gift. It's a very nice touch for the holidays.

Yield: One 8 in. cake.

Chitra's Orange Yogurt Cake

1 Tbs. grated orange rind
¾ cup melted butter
1 cup honey
1 tsp. vanilla
¼ cup orange juice
¾ cup yogurt or sour milk
3 cups whole wheat pastry flour
½ tsp. salt
1 Tbs. baking powder

Preheat your oven to 325°. Grate the orange rind, and combine the melted butter, honey and vanilla. Beat in the orange juice, orange rind and yogurt. Sift the dry ingredients into wet, and pour them into a greased 9 in. cake pan. Bake at 325° for 50-60 minutes. Serve topped with Sweet Lemon Sauce (see p. 216).

Yield: One 9 in. cake.

Icings, Glazes & Toppings

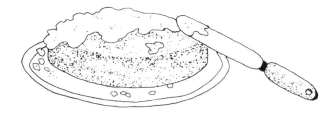

Icing. Who among us is so grown-up that they cannot recall visions of licking the icing bowl, or remember the one time intense longing for the corner piece of cake (the one with all the frosting)? Icing is *not* a thing of the past for the natural food lover; rather, the world of icings for cakes and cookies is a creative field for your pioneering. Given forthwith are our specialties; using these, let your imagination run wild and develop your own. Make extra for bowl lickers large and small (come on, you know you're one) and for generously icing your wonderful whole-grain cakes.

Carob Icing

1 cup milk
1½ cups honey
2 tsp. vanilla extract
¾ cup milk powder
¾ cup carob powder
½ cup butter

Blend all the ingredients in the above order. Heat over a medium flame for 3 minutes. Allow it to cool before using. Then ice your favorite cake or dessert specialty.

Yield: 4 cups.

Raw Carob-Almond

1 cup milk
¼ cup honey
2 tsp. vanilla
1/8 tsp. almond extract
¼ cup oil
1 cup carob powder
1 cup milk powder

Blend together the first six ingredients, then whisk in the milk powder to a smooth consistency. Chill before using.

Yield: 2¼ cups.

Orange Icing

4 cups yogurt cheese (see p. 168)
3 Tbs. orange juice concentrate (undiluted)
1½ tsp. fresh grated orange rind
6 Tbs. honey
1 tsp. vanilla
¼ tsp. nutmeg
¼ cup milk powder

Grate the orange rind. Place all the ingredients in your electric mixer, blend together for 4 to 5 minutes, and the icing is ready.

Yield: 3 cups.

Peanut Butter-Banana Icing

1½ cups mashed bananas
4 Tbs. honey
2 cups peanut butter

Mash the bananas and add the honey, blending in well. Then blend in the peanut butter, a little at a time. (Adding the peanut butter all at once or too quickly has a tendency to lump the mixture.) Make sure you blend this adequately. Also you might like to add a drop of vanilla flavoring. This icing combines an all-time favorite for many people -- peanut butter and bananas. Forget about cake -- your children may want it spread on their bread for lunchtime.

Yield: 3¾ cups.

Cream Cheese Icing

3 cups cream cheese
4 Tbs. honey
2 tsp. vanilla
¼ cup milk

Mix all the ingredients in an electric mixer or food processor, or in a mixing bowl using a wooden spoon and lots of elbow grease. This is an excellent topping for carrot cake, carob cream pie or gingerbread. For a variation, add 5 Tbs. peanut butter or carob.

Yield: 3 cups.

Whipped Tofu Cream

2 cups tofu
½ cup oil
⅓ cup + 2 Tbs. honey
1¼ tsp. vanilla
1 Tbs. + 1 tsp. lemon juice
3 Tbs. soymilk

Blend together all the ingredients, and chill for 1 hour before serving. This is an excellent non-dairy topping for cakes, pies and puddings.

Yield: 2 cups.

Sweet Nut Cream

1½ cups peanut, cashew, or almond butter
1 cup water
⅓-½ cup honey
¼ tsp. almond extract

Blend all the ingredients together, and serve as it is. For a variation, try *banana nut sauce:* add 1 ripe banana before blending the above. Delicious by itself, or over a fresh fruit salad.

Yield: 3 cups.

Sweet Lemon Sauce

⅓ tsp. lemon rind
1 cup orange or pineapple juice
1½ Tbs. arrowroot flour
2 Tbs. lemon juice
⅓ cup honey

Grate the lemon rind. Add the orange juice to the arrowroot with a whisk, and heat over a low flame. Add the lemon juice and honey, and cook until thickened. Add lemon rind and serve. Tastes especially good spooned over ginger cake!

Yield: 1 cup.

Creamy Citrus Sauce

⅓ cup sunflower seeds (pre-soaked overnight)
½ cup water
2 Tbs. honey
½ cup orange juice
2 tsp. grated orange rind
2 Tbs. lemon juice

Blend sunflower seeds with water until creamy. Add honey, orange peel and ¼ cup orange juice. Gradually blend in remaining fruit juices, blending until light. This "sauce" is wonderful over citrus or simply as a drink.

Yield: 1¼ cups.

Puddings

Creamy and thick, rich or custardy, these puddings can be served at breakfast or dessert. Made either from cow's milk, soy milk or juice, they're easy to make -- just add a drop of sweetener, a thickening agent and some heat and stir! Variations are as endless as the flavors you can think up (or arrive at haphazardly). The addition of fruit, nuts, raisin or bread pieces adds a nice touch and helps use up leftovers as well. We're fond of banana-date pudding as a hearty winter breakfast, while a light lemon pudding finds its way into tarts, pies and tasty desserts.

It's hard to fail at a pudding. If it doesn't thicken up, you can always call it a smoothie. If it's too thick, call it a gelatin dessert. A little lumpy? Toss it in the blender, then put it back on the heat and try again. We like to use arrowroot* as a thickening agent, though agar-agar** is also very effective. You can use either. If you happen to be using arrowroot, remember to first blend it with *cold* water or milk, then pour it slowly into the pudding while stirring rapidly. (Unless your blender is like ours -- all we do is whisper "lumpy pudding" around it and either a screw falls out or the wire shorts.) Some people have to spell out words around their children; we have to do it around our kitchen equipment. It's okay as long as you just sort of sneak up on it and dump the pudding in before it gets nervous. But never let the blender know you think you've failed. That'll be the end of it. (Sigh. The things we've learned as cooks . . .)

*Arrowroot is a powdered root of a tropical American plant. It's easily digested, high in minerals and is an excellent substitute for cornstarch and flour as a thickening agent.

**Agar-agar is a seaweed derivative. Also high in mineral content, when added to water and then cooked, it forms a gel much like that of gelatin.

Honey Carob Delight

4 cups milk or soymilk
⅓ cup arrowroot (½ cup for pie filling)
¾ cup honey
¼ cup butter
⅓ cup carob powder

Blend all the ingredients together, pour them into a medium-sized saucepan, and cook over a medium heat. Stir constantly until the mixture begins to boil and thicken. Simmer 5 more minutes, continuing to stir. Remove from the heat and cool.

Yield: 5 cups.

Old Fashioned Vanilla Pudding

4 cups milk or soymilk
¼ cup butter
⅓ cup arrowroot flour (½ cup for pie filling)
½ cup honey
2 tsp. vanilla

Blend together all the ingredients. Pour into a medium-sized saucepan. Over medium heat bring the mixture to a boil, stirring constantly. Simmer 5 more minutes, continuing to stir, and remove from heat and cool.

Yield: 5 cups.

Savory Bread Pudding

3 cups bread
1 tsp. lemon rind
½ cup raisins
Enough water to cover above ingredients in a saucepan

Vanilla Sauce:
4 cups milk
⅓ cup arrowroot
½ cup honey
1 tsp. vanilla
1 tsp. cinnamon
½ tsp. nutmeg
¼ tsp. cardamon

Prepare bread -- it should be dry, and cut into bite-sized chunks. Grate the lemon rind. Heat the raisins and lemon rind in enough water to cover them. Allow them to sit in heated water to get soft. Prepare the vanilla sauce -- stir the arrowroot into the milk and let it boil. Add the honey, vanilla and spices. Simmer for 10 minutes, stirring constantly, until the mixture thickens. Then mix the bread, soaked raisins, and half of the vanilla sauce and pour it into a 9 x 9 in. pan. Pour the remaining sauce over the top. Bake at 300° for 15 minutes. An excellent use for stale bread!

Yield: One 9 x 9 in. pan.

Raisin 'n Rice Pudding

½ cup rice
1 cup water
2 cups milk
½ cup raisins
¼ cup honey
1 tsp. vanilla
1/8 tsp. salt
1 tsp. cinnamon
¼ tsp. lemon juice

There's nothing like a good raisin and rice standby for that "I want something filling yet sweet" feeling. Bring the water to a boil and add in the rice. Simmer for 30 minutes and then add the milk and raisins. Bring back to a boil and then simmer for an additional 30 minutes. Stir in the honey, vanilla, salt, cinnamon and lemon juice. Serve hot or cold. An optional method is to bake the pudding in your oven (preferably over low heat for an hour or more). Top with a sweet sauce (see p. 216) or Whipped Soy Cream (see p. 185).

Yield: 2½ cups.

Cinnamon-Orange Pudding

1 Tbs. grated orange peel
⅓ cup melted butter
½ cup whole wheat pastry flour
½ cup orange juice concentrate
⅓ cup arrowroot
4 cups milk
5 Tbs. honey
1 tsp. cinnamon
½ Tbs. vanilla
1 cup water

Grate the orange peel. In a large saucepan, melt the butter, and stir in the flour. Add the orange juice concentrate and mix until smooth. Whisk arrowroot flour into milk until dissolved. Add this to the orange juice mixture, whisking it in to prevent lumping. If the mixture does lump at this point, pour into the blender and blend it until it's smooth. Pour it back into your saucepan and continue. Stir in the remaining ingredients. Cook over a medium heat, stirring constantly with a wooden spoon or wire whisk. The mixture will thicken as it comes to a boil. Cool and serve.

Yield: 6 cups.

Cardamom-Date Pudding

4 cups milk or soymilk
1¼ cups chopped dates
1 tsp. vanilla
½ tsp. cardamon
⅓ cup arrowroot

Blend all the ingredients. In a medium-sized saucepan, heat the mixture over a medium flame until it boils, stirring continually. Let it simmer for 5 minutes, continuing to stir. Chill and serve. If you haven't already made the acquaintance of the simple yet tasty cardamon pod, here's your chance! It has a wonderful taste and aroma.

Yield: 4 cups.

Lemon Pudding

1 Tbs. grated lemon rind
½ cup arrowroot
2½ cups water
1¼ cups honey
¾ cup lemon juice

Grate the lemon rind. Blend the arrowroot, water and honey. Pour into a medium-sized saucepan, adding the lemon juice and lemon rind. Stir over a medium flame until the mixture begins to boil. Continue stirring for 5 more minutes, then remove from the heat and cool. Be sure to cover while cooling, so a skin doesn't form on the top (unless you like it that way.)

Yield: 3 cups.

Squash Pudding

2¾ cups cooked squash or pumpkin
⅔ cup honey
1 cup cream
⅓ cup arrowroot
1 tsp. vanilla
½ tsp. cinnamon
½ tsp. nutmeg

An appetizing dish for the holidays, this is also very easy to make. Blend together all the ingredients. Cook over a medium heat, stirring constantly, until the mixture boils. Simmer for 5 minutes, cool and serve.

Yield: 4 cups.

Cookies

"Hira . . . don't forget to take the cookies out of the oven . . ."

"Okay, I'm on my way."

"By the way, what's the count on the peanut carob bars?"

"The last I counted there were about 170."

"170? But we baked off 200, didn't we?"

"Yeah, well that was early this morning. You know how it goes . . ."

"Yes, I know how it goes -- *quickly* is how it goes. I should have known. Okay, let's mix up some more dough now."

Round chewy drop cookies, crunchy, spicy spread cookies, sweet and decorated cut-out cookies. It's hard to tell which are the best. We love them all. Made with wholesome ingredients, they add nutrition as well as bulk to our diet. And special feelings . . . With their warm aromas wafting through the entire building, they bring a happy anticipation to all who come near . . . "Okay, folks -- here's some fresh-baked cookies."

Sunny Circles

1 cup melted butter
1 cup honey
2 cups coarsely ground sunflower seeds
1 tsp. vanilla
2½ cups whole wheat pastry flour

Whisk all the wet ingredients together. Stir in the dry ingredients. Roll dough into 1½ in. balls and flatten out onto a greased cookie sheet. To decorate the top, press one raisin in the center of each cookie or several sunny seeds or shredded coconut. Bake at 350° for 15 minutes.

Yield: 2½ dozen.

Peanut Butter Swirl Bars

⅔ cup butter
1¼ cups honey
1½ cups peanut butter
1 Tbs. + 1 tsp. vanilla
2½ cups whole wheat pastry flour
1 tsp. baking powder
Dash salt
½ cup yogurt

Carob Mixture:
½ cup dough from above mix
1½ Tbs. milk
½ tsp. honey
1 Tbs. carob powder
¼ tsp. cinnamon

Cream the butter and honey; then add the peanut butter, vanilla and yogurt. Sift together the flour, baking powder, and salt. Add to the creamed mixture. Spoon the mixture into a 9 x 11 in. cake pan. Prepare the carob mixture; it should be very thick. Swirl it into the other mixture. (A zig-zag pattern is very attractive.) Bake at 350° for 30-35 minutes and then slice into bars.

Yield: One 9 x 11 in. cake.

Oatmeal Cookies

¼ cup milk
1 cup honey
½ cup melted butter
1 tsp. vanilla
3 cups rolled oats
1½ cups whole wheat pastry flour
1 tsp. cinnamon
1 cup raisins
½ cup chopped walnuts
½ tsp. salt
1 tsp. baking powder

Combine the milk, honey, butter and vanilla. Sift the dry ingredients together and add to the wet ingredients. Add the raisins and walnuts and drop the dough in tablespoon portions onto a greased cookie sheet. Bake at 350° for 15 minutes.

Yield: 1½ dozen 2 in. cookies.

Banana Oatmeal Cookies

½ cup walnuts
¾ cup butter
1 cup honey
1½ cups mashed bananas
1½ cups whole wheat pastry flour
½ tsp. salt
½ tsp. baking soda
1 tsp. cinnamon
½ tsp. nutmeg
4 cups oatmeal
½ cup sunflower seeds
¾ cup raisins

Chop the walnuts. Cream the butter and honey and add mashed bananas. Sift the flour and other dry ingredients and add to the wet. Stir in oatmeal, seeds, raisins and walnuts. Allow the batter to sit for 10 minutes before placing it on your cookie sheet. Drop dough in two table-spoon portions and flatten with the bottom of a floured glass. Bake at 350° for approximately 20 minutes.

Yield: 20 large cookies.

Sesame Oat Surprises

3 cups whole wheat pastry flour
1 cup rolled oats
½ tsp. salt
1 tsp. baking powder
¼ cup butter
½ cup oil
2 Tbs. tahini (sesame seed meal)
¾ cup apple juice
1½ cups honey
2½ tsp. vanilla
2½ tsp. cinnamon
¾ cup sesame seeds

Sift the flours and combine all dry ingredients. Cream the butter, add oil, tahini and the remaining wet ingredients. Combine the wet and dry ingredients together plus the sesame seeds, and drop the cookies by the tablespoonful onto greased cookie sheets. Bake at 350° for 15-20 minutes.

Yield: Thirty 3 in. cookies.

Granola Cookies

¼ cup butter
1/8 cup milk
⅓ cup honey
½ tsp. vanilla
½ cup whole wheat pastry flour
¼ tsp. cinnamon
½ tsp. salt
1½ cups granola
½ tsp. baking powder

Cream the butter and honey and add in milk and vanilla. Stir in dry ingredients. Add granola. Drop by the tablespoonful onto a greased cookie sheet and bake at 350° for 15 minutes.

Yield: 1 dozen cookies.

Ginger Snaps

3 Tbs. orange or lemon rind
1¼ cup molasses
3 Tbs. oil
½ tsp. cardamon
2 tsp. cinnamon
½ tsp. ginger
3½ cups whole wheat pastry flour
1 Tbs. baking powder

These are "snappy" little cookies which you'll enjoy. Prepare the rind as needed. Heat the molasses and oil until liquid. Add the rind and spices to the molasses mixture. Sift the flour and baking powder and fold into molasses mixture also. Mix into a stiff dough. Drop by tablespoons onto an oiled cookie sheet and flatten the cookies with the bottom of a floured glass. Bake 10-12 minutes at 350°.

Yield: Twenty 3 in. cookies.

Spicy Vanilla Cookies

¾ cup honey
¼ cup melted butter
1 tsp. vanilla
2 cups whole wheat pastry flour
¼ tsp. salt
½ tsp. nutmeg
1½ tsp. cinnamon
½ tsp. cloves
1 tsp. baking powder

Cream the wet ingredients together. Sift together the dry ingredients, add to the wet and mix well. Make ½ in. balls and flatten onto a greased cookie sheet. Bake for 12-14 minutes at 350°.

Yield: One dozen 3 in. cookies.

Date Bars

Crust
4 cups rolled oats
1 cup shredded coconut
1 cup whole wheat pastry flour
½ cup oil
¾ cup honey
1 tsp. salt
Filling
4 cups dates
2 cups water
2 Tbs. lemon or orange rind

Prepare the date filling by stirring the filling ingredients together over a low flame and gradually bringing to a boil. Continue stirring over a low heat until the mixture thickens and the dates become soft. Allow it to cool while preparing crust.

Mix the crust ingredients together and press about ⅔ of the mixture into an oiled 8 x 12 in. baking pan. Spread the crust with the date filling. Spread the remaining ⅓ of the crumb mixture on top of the date filling. Bake in a 375° oven for 25 to 30 minutes. Cut into bars while still warm.

Yield: One 8 x 12 in. baking pan.

Holiday Cut-Outs

2¼ cups whole wheat pastry flour
1½ tsp. baking powder
¼ tsp. salt
½ cup butter
1/8-1/4 cup water
½ tsp. vanilla or almond extract
¾ cup honey

Sift together the flour, baking powder and salt; cream the butter and add water, honey, and the extract. To prepare the cookies, either of two methods can be used. 1. Shape the dough into a log 2 in. thick and chill one hour. Slice ¼ in. thick, round cookies. 2. Form the dough into a ball; chill one hour and then roll out 3/8 in. thick on floured board. With a cookie cutter, cut the cookies into desired shapes and bake on greased cookie sheets at 325° for 15 minutes. These are traditional Christmas cookies and can be dressed up with your favorite flavors and colors for the holiday season.

Yield: 4 dozen.

Carob Brownies

1 cup butter
1½ cups honey
½ cup milk
¾ cup yogurt
½ cup peanut butter
1 tsp. vanilla
2 cups whole wheat pastry flour
1¼ cups carob powder
2 tsp. cinnamon
2 tsp. baking powder
¼ tsp. salt
1 cup crushed walnuts

Cream the butter and honey. Beat in all the wet ingredients. Sift together all the dry ingredients and stir into the wet. Gently fold in the walnuts. Spread in an oiled 9 x 11 in. pan. Bake at 325° for 45 minutes to one hour. Store in a secret hideaway or they'll never last until dessert time.

Yield: 16 pieces.

Walnut-Raisin Cookies

1½ cups walnuts
1½ cups butter
3 cups honey
¾ cup milk
2 tsp. maple flavoring
2 tsp. walnut flavoring
6 cups whole wheat pastry flour
2 Tbs. baking powder
1 tsp. salt
1½ tsp. cinnamon
1 tsp. nutmeg
1 cup raisins or dates

We make these as wide-diameter cookies, and they're amazingly good. Try them for picnics or outings, or to spruce up an otherwise ordinary lunch box. Chop the walnuts into small pieces suitable for cookies. Cream the butter and honey. Add the milk and flavorings. Sift the dry ingredients and add them to the wet. Add dates or raisins and nuts. Spread into cookies about 4½ in. in diameter. (Use a spatula that is dipped frequently into hot water.) Bake at 325° for approximately 20 minutes, cool and serve.

Yield: Twenty-five 3 in. cookies.

Carob Macaroons

1 cup whole wheat pastry flour
6 Tbs. carob powder
1 tsp. baking powder
¼ tsp. salt
½ cup rolled oats
½ cup butter
10 Tbs. honey (½ cup + 2 Tbs.)
¼ cup yogurt
¼ tsp. almond extract
¾ cup shredded coconut

These are Parimala's favorite (along with soy ice cream, of course . . .) Sift together all the dry ingredients. Cream the butter and add all the wet ingredients, mixing well. Combine with the dry ingredients. Blend in the coconut with a spatula and then drop in one tablespoon mounds onto greased cookie sheet. Bake at 350° for 15-20 minutes.

Yield: Approximately 16 cookies.

Peanut Butter Cookies

2¼ cups peanut butter
2¼ cups butter
3½ cups honey
1 tsp. vanilla
3¼ cups whole wheat flour
2½ cups white flour
2 tsp. baking powder

Mix together the peanut butter, butter, honey and vanilla. Sift the flours and baking powder and add to the mixture (the batter will be quite wet, but it needs to bake that way.) Drop cookies onto the tray, using approximately 2 Tbs. of batter for each cookie. Spread each cookie out, then bake at 275° for 30 minutes. Cookies must be completely cooked before being removed or else they will fall apart. These cookies taste better fresh but will become even more moist after a few days in the refrigerator.

Yield: 22 cookies.

Pies & Pastries

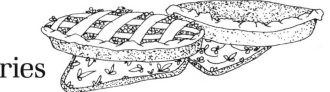

Making a delicious pie has always seemed to me to be the test of a good cook. Working with whole wheat flour and unrefined oils can make a light flaky crust a real challenge in the beginning. With a good recipe, however, your efforts will be almost foolproof. We've come up with some recipes that work every time and make eating a piece of pie a gourmet experience. Try mixing and matching crusts and fillings. An apple pie can nestle nicely into a traditional flaky crust or with equal appeal in a raw crust of finely ground nuts and dates. Served warm from the oven and topped with a luscious scoop of Soy Maple Walnut Ice Bean (see p. 184), it's really a treat.

When working with pies and pastries, the following hints will be of help:

1. Handle the dough as little as possible. It will become cardboardy if handled too much.
2. Chilling the dough before baking helps to give it a light, flaky consistency.
3. Make sure to poke some fork holes in the bottom of a pie crust before baking so that it doesn't bubble up. This applies only when baking crusts without the filling.
4. Use fresh flour, butter or oils. Chilled ingredients usually work best. We like using safflower oil for pastries. Soy and corn oil tend to predominate over the other ingredients, giving too strong a flavor.
5. Rolling the dough out between two sheets of waxed paper helps to cut back on the need for extra flour. Too much flour in the dough makes it chewy instead of flaky.
6. Because of their delicacy and thinness, pie crusts and pastries tend to burn quickly. Watch them carefully toward the end of the baking time. If the edges of the crust begin to darken before the pie is done, cover them with strips of aluminum foil and continue baking.

Pecan Pie

2 cups pecans
3 Tbs. arrowroot
¼ cup butter
1 cup honey
¾ cup milk
1 tsp. vanilla
½ tsp. salt
One 8 in. pie crust

Here is a true delicacy . . . Chop 1 cup of the pecans. Blend all the ingredients, leaving the remaining 1 cup of pecans aside. Turn into a pre-baked pie shell, then arrange the remaining pecans over the top. Bake at 325° for 40 minutes, and let it cool before slicing.

Yield: One 8 in. pie.

Honey Cheesecake

4 tsp. arrowroot
¼ cup water
1¼ lbs. cream cheese
⅔ cup honey
1 tsp. vanilla
1¼ tsp. lemon juice
Crust for 9 in. pie (see p. 230)

This is an extraordinarily simple, tasty cheesecake. In order to make, mix the arrowroot in water. Pour all the ingredients into your blender and blend until smooth. Pour into a 9 in. pie pan with a graham cracker or okara crust. Then bake at 350° for 25 minutes. Remove and chill overnight. Delicious!

Yield: One 9 in. pie.

Banana Cream Pie

1 recipe vanilla pudding
1 bottom pie crust
4 medium ripe bananas
⅓ cup coconut

Make one recipe vanilla pudding (See p. 218). Make 1 bottom pie crust (see p. 230). Bake at 350° for one half hour until lightly browned. Cool the pudding and the crust. Slice the bananas. In a pie shell, layer the bananas, pudding and coconut. Finish the top with an outside ring of banana slices and a sprinkle of coconut. Chill and serve this yummy dessert.

Yield: One 9 in. pie.

Yogurt Cheese Pie

3 cups cottage cheese
1¼ cups yogurt
¾ cup honey
1 tsp. vanilla
½ tsp. nutmeg
½ tsp. cardamon
 One 9 in. pie crust

Blend together all the ingredients. Pour into a pre-baked 9 in. pie crust. Chill and serve. This is a rich, creamy dessert, similar to cheesecake, yet lighter (and with fewer calories)!

Yield: One 9 in. pie.

Pie Crust

2½ cups whole wheat pastry flour
½ tsp. salt
⅔ cup + 1 tsp. oil
⅓ cup + 1 tsp. *cold* water

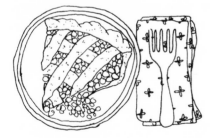

Sift together the flour and salt. Whip the oil and water together with a fork until they form an emulsion (become cloudy and non-separate). Pour the liquid over the flour, and mix with a fork until just mixed. Form 2 balls of dough, and roll each ball out between 2 sheets of waxed paper. Peel off the wax paper carefully, placing the dough in a pie pan. Save the second ball for another bottom crust or for the top crust. Chill in your freezer for 1 hour before filling and baking the pie.

If your recipe calls for a pre-baked pie shell, remember to make several fork holes in the bottom of the shell to prevent the bottom from bubbling up while baking.

A variation is to follow the same basic recipe, using 5/8 cup butter instead of oil. Cut the butter into the flour mixture until the flour is crumbly; slowly stir in water and proceed as above. Fill with your favorite filling; you'll have enough dough left over for strips across the top or for a few Cinnamon Swirls (see p. 232).

Yield: Two 9 in. pie crusts.

Chitra's Baklava

Phyllo pastry:
3 cups white flour or 1½ cups whole wheat flour and 1½ cups rice flour
½ tsp. salt
¾ cups cold water
3 Tbs. melted butter

Baklava:
1 cup honey
1 lb. crushed walnuts
1 cup melted butter
2 tsp. cinnamon
½ tsp. lemon juice

A Greek specialty -- outrageously wonderful! Phyllo pastry: Sift flour and salt together. Add 3 Tbs. butter -- mix with fingers until flour is crumbly. Add water. Form a smooth ball, and knead 5 minutes. The dough will be very dry, but will form a smooth ball if you just keep working it together and kneading it with your fingers. Refrigerate dough overnight. Next day -- let dough warm to room temperature. Roll out ¼ of the dough at a time until paper thin. With a pastry brush, brush the bottom of pan with butter. Cut a piece of pastry to fit the pan. Place in pan and brush with butter.

For Baklava: Mix walnuts and cinnamon together. Sprinkle walnuts on pastry. Add another sheet of pastry, brush with butter. Sprinkle on walnuts. Repeat until 2 pieces of pastry are left and all walnuts are used. Use last 2 pieces of pastry for the top, brushing butter between layers. Make diagonal cuts on top of baklava, reaching through to the bottom of the pan.

Heat remainder of the butter with lemon juice and honey. Pour over baklava. It will sink into the layers. Bake at 375° for 30-40 minutes. Let cool overnight before serving.

Traditionally, baklava is made with white flour so that it can be rolled paper thin. A combination of whole wheat and rice flour works well though. It is not as finely textured and crisp as the white flour phyllo, but just as yummy -- and much more nourishing.

Yield: One 9 x 9 in. pan.

Lemon Pie

1 recipe lemon pudding (see p. 220)
One 9 in. pie crust
2 cups Sweet Nut Cream (see p. 216)
Whipped cream

Besides the strawberry pie, this is one of Chitra's favorites. If she had her choice we'd eat only pies for dessert . . . nothing else.

Bake the pie crust for ½ hour until it's lightly browned. Let it cool. Make 1 recipe of lemon pudding. When the pudding is completely cold, pour it into a pie shell. Top with 2 cups Sweet Nut Cream. Chill the entire pie. Serve with a scoop of whipped cream (dairy or soy). This will bring you to pie-eater's Nirvana instantly.

Yield: One 9 in. pie.

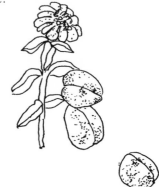

Cinnamon Swirls

Leftover unbaked pie crust dough
Cinnamon to sprinkle
Honey to drip and swirl
Butter to spread

This is a recipe written to use up all of those little pieces of pie crust dough that invariably wind up sitting on the counter after the pie has been formed and popped in the oven.

Form a ball of all the "scraps", and roll it out 1/8 in. thick. Spread it with butter, sprinkle with cinnamon, and drip and swirl honey over the entire surface. Roll up the dough into a log, and slice the log into 1 in. pieces. Place on a cookie sheet and bake at 350° until light brown -- about 40 minutes. Let cool and enjoy.

Making these little treats is the only way I've been able to keep fingers out of the pie until after dinner!

Squash Pie

2½ cups cooked squash
1 cup cream
⅓ cup arrowroot
½ cup honey
½ tsp. vanilla
½ tsp. cinnamon
¼ tsp. nutmeg
¼ tsp. ginger
1/8 tsp. cloves
One 9 in. pie crust

Blend all the ingredients together. Pour into an unbaked 9 in. pie crust, and bake at 350° for 45 minutes to 1 hour. Cool and serve.

This pie has a more delicate flavor than pumpkin pie, and fewer calories.

Yield: One 9 in. pie.

Strawberry Pie

5½ cups sliced strawberries
¾ cup honey
⅓ cup arrowroot
One 9 in. pie crust

Preheat your oven to 350°. Wash, hull and slice the strawberries. Blend together 1 cup of the strawberries, the honey and arrowroot. Stir this mixture into the remaining strawberries. Pour this into an awaiting pie crust. Gently place on the top crust, and pinch the edges of the bottom and top crusts together. Bake for 50 minutes at 350°. Let cool before slicing. This is a superb dessert for a summer day or any time you run into some plump fresh strawberries. Serve with Vanilla Ice Cream (see p. 170).

Yield: One 9 in. pie.

Apple Pie

6 medium apples
1 cup dates
1 cup water
1 tsp. cinnamon
One 9 in. pie crust

Core and thinly slice the apples. Cook the dates in ½ cup water for 10 minutes. Blend the date mixture with the remaining ½ cup water. Mix together the apples, cinnamon and date mixture. Pour into a pie crust, and top with another crust. Form edges of the crust, pressing with a fork around the entire edge to seal it. Make 4 sets of fork holes in the top to allow the air to escape. Bake at 350° for 1 hour. Cool and serve (preferably with some home-made ice cream on top; see pp. 169-170).

Yield: One 9 in. pie.

Carob-Peanut Pie

1 pie crust
4 cups carob pudding (see p. 218)
1 cup vanilla pudding (see p. 218)
1 cup roasted peanuts

Bake pie crust for ½ hour until it's lightly browned. Make 1 recipe of carob pudding and 1 cup of vanilla pudding. While the crust and puddings are cooling, crush 1 cup roasted peanuts. When the crust and puddings are completely cooled, pour ½ of the carob pudding into a pie shell and swirl in ½ of the vanilla pudding. Sprinkle ½ of the crushed peanuts onto the pudding. Add the second half of the carob pudding. Swirl in the remaining vanilla pudding, and top with remaining peanuts. Chill and serve.

Yield: One 9 in. pie.

Snacks & Treats

The following recipes are quick, easy, nutritious answers to the inevitable "what can we have for a snack?" question. They pack well in lunch boxes and store well for later in the afternoon grownup activities as well. Also fun to decorate and serve as party treats, these snacks are money savers, health boosters and savory treats. I've heard of many a school child who was coaxed into trading his peanut butter logs or "dream clouds" for some other child's store-bought candy. And the same goes for adults. Many of our residents found they needed to pack double just to get a bite at work before their colleagues devoured all their goodies. So as you try each recipe, plan to make a double batch. Or try several recipes at a time. They'll be gone in a jiffy.

Peanut Butter Balls

1½ cups peanut butter
½ cup honey
⅓ cup raisins
¼ cup chopped dates
4 Tbs. carob powder
1 tsp. cinnamon
2 cups coconut

In a mixing bowl, combine the peanut butter, honey, raisins and dates. Sift the carob powder and cinnamon into this mixture, and mix thoroughly. If your peanut butter is very moist, you may need to add 2 Tbs. dry milk powder to the mixture before forming balls. Wet your hands (each time) and pinch off enough "dough" for a 1 in. ball. Roll the balls in coconut, chill and serve.

Yield: Twenty-five 1 in. balls.

Peanut Butter Carob Bars

Peanut butter layer:
1 cup peanut butter
1 cup honey
¼ cup melted butter
1 tsp. vanilla
1 cup milk powder
Pinch salt

Frosting:
½ cup butter
4 Tbs. melted butter
½ cup honey
1 tsp. vanilla
1 cup carob powder
1 cup milk powder
Pinch salt
1½ tsp. cinnamon

Combine the ingredients for the peanut butter layer in a bowl. Mix to a uniform consistency, and press into the bottom of a 9 in. cake pan. Combine the ingredients for the frosting, mixing until smooth. Spread this over the peanut butter layer. Refrigerate, then cut into small pieces. This is a real kid pleaser -- for big and little kids alike.

Yield: One 9 in. pan.

Nut Logs

1 cup roasted almonds
¼ cup honey
1 Tbs. liquid lecithin
½ cup coconut
½ tsp. ginger powder
1 tsp. cinnamon

Crush the almonds very finely (with a blender, a rolling pin and cutting board, or a grinder on a coarse setting). Add all the ingredients in a bowl and mix thoroughly by hand. Wet your hands with water before making each log, rolling each piece 1½ in. long by 1 in. in diameter. Chill and serve.

Yield: 10 logs.

Herbed Tamari Popcorn

1 Tbs. oil
1 cup popcorn kernels
A generous pinch of each:
rosemary, parsley, thyme, oregano, basil
1 tsp. salt
1 tsp. tamari
1 Tbs. nutritional yeast

A marvelous spicy popcorn! Using a large saucepan or pot, generously cover the bottom of the pot with oil and stir in all the herbs. Heat over a medium-high flame until the oil almost smokes. Add the popcorn to cover the bottom of the pan. Cover and let it sit about a minute or until the kernels begin to pop. Then shake the covered pot over a medium-high flame periodically until all the kernels are popped. Remove from the heat and pour the popcorn into a large bowl. Sprinkle generously with tamari and dust with nutritional yeast for a cheesey flavor. Salt to taste and if preferred, melted butter may be drizzled over the popcorn before serving.

Yield: 4-5 cups.

Herbed Croutons

8 cups stale whole grain bread cut into cubes
¾ cup butter
1 cup nutritional yeast
1¾ Tbs. chili powder
1 tsp. salt
1 Tbs. parsley

These croutons are superb with salads or soups, and make a healthful, crunchy snack as well. To make, melt the butter, and add bread cubes. Allow the bread cubes to soak up the butter. Then add yeast and spices, and saute in a large frying pan. Then place on baking tray and toast at 350° until crunchy for 10-15 minutes.

Yield: 6 cups.

Dream Clouds

¼ cup chopped dates
¼ cup chopped walnuts
1 tsp. orange rind
1 cup cream cheese
½ cup shredded coconut
¼ cup honey
1 tsp. cardamon
½ cup coconut

We wouldn't call these dream clouds if they didn't carry you off in a revery at the very first bite . . .

Chop the dates and walnuts, and grate the orange rind. Mix all the ingredients together thoroughly in a medium-size bowl. Wet your hands and pinch off enough "dough" to make a 1 in. ball. Roll the balls in coconut; chill and serve.

For a variation, roll balls in crushed walnuts or toasted sesame seeds.

Yield: Twelve 1 in. balls.

Easter Eggs

Yolk:
¼ cup cream cheese
1½ tsp. carrot juice
1 Tbs. honey

Egg White:
1 cup peanut butter
⅓ cup dry milk powder
2 Tbs. honey
¼ cup coconut

Carob Topping:
¼ lb. butter
½ cup dry milk powder
½ cup carob powder
¼ cup arrowroot
1 cup honey
1 tsp. almond extract

Carob Topping: Melt the butter in a saucepan, and add the honey and almond extract. Sift in all dry ingredients. Stir constantly over medium flame or 15 minutes.

Yolk: With a spoon, cream the cream cheese, carrot juice and honey and form into 10 small balls. Egg White: Mix the peanut butter, dry milk powder, honey and coconut together. Form into 10 portions. Shape around yolks, making an egg shape. Dip eggs in carob topping. Refrigorate on waxed paper to harden, and *hide (but not too well)* on Easter morning for family and friends to find!

Yield: 10 eggs.

Italian Ice

Choice of:
Frozen orange or grape juice
Frozen lemonade; or
Frozen sasparilla or sassafrass tea (honey-sweetened)

Choose your favorite frozen juice drink . . . or try some of your own combinations. A great idea would be to try one of our smoothie drinks (pp. 197-202) or some blended fruit combination, and then freeze it. Prior to serving, take out the frozen juice or drink, break it into chunks and blend it in your blender with a small amount of water (½ to 1 cup). This is cool and refreshing! P.S. Sasparilla or sassafrass tea make good root-beer tasting ices!

Mataji's Chevado

1 tsp. oil
2 cups rice flakes
¼ cup cashews
¼ cup pumpkin seeds
1 Tbs. sesame seeds
¼ cup raisins
½ Tbs. salt
¾ Tbs. honey
1 tsp. oil
2 chili peppers
1 tsp. ajvan (an Indian spice)
4 crushed cloves
1 tsp. chili powder
Pinch asafetida
½ tsp. turmeric

This is one of Mataji's spicy Indian snacks which we enjoy at the Retreat. It can be made in two ways: either mild or spicy. Try both ways -- you'll love it! The rice flakes may be purchased in an Indian store; or try the health food store varieties. Also, if you'd like to try the spicier versions, the ajfan and asafetida are available in Indian shops or gourmet spice shops. Pumpkin seeds and cashews are optional but lend flavor to this snack food.

To prepare in a wok or deep fry pan, heat 1½ cups oil, fill a strainer with some rice flakes, and deep fry them in the hot oil until they puff. This usually happens very quickly. Finish frying the rice flakes, a little at a time. Place the flakes in a bowl; now roast the peanuts. Let them roast for a while, then add the cashews to the mixture. When they're almost done, add the pumpkin seeds and then the sesame seeds. After roasting, add the nuts to flakes; for mild chevado, add raisins, salt, honey, turmeric and chili powder to the nut mixture. For hot spicy Indian chevado, add all ingredients as above, and in addition, heat the teaspoon of oil. When hot, add chili pepper, ajvan, cloves, asafetida and turmeric. When spices have cooked with the chili pepper one or two minutes, add them to the nutty mixture, stir and mix together well. Serve while still warm, if you like, for a spicy, crunchy snack treat.

Yield: 3 cups.

Candied Apples

2 cups honey
1 cup molasses
½ cup milk powder
18 whole ripe apples
18 popsicle sticks
2 cups crushed peanuts (optional)

Sift the milk powder into the honey and molasses. Mix in well and heat the mixture to boiling. Turn down the flame and simmer for 15 minutes. Cool the mixture in your freezer for 10 minutes. While the mixture is cooling, place some waxed paper on 1 or 2 large trays and place popsicle sticks in the apples. When the mixture is cool enough to work with, but not stiffened, dip the apples, coating them completely, and place them on the waxed paper. Place the apples in your refrigerator for 5 minutes to cool. You can then roll the coated apples in crushed nuts if you wish. They look very attractive this way, and are less messy to eat. If you don't want 18 candied apples sitting in your refrigerator to distract your children (or you), you can dip only a few apples at a time, saving the rest of the candy mixture in the refrigerator. Heat the mixture to a consistency which can be used for dipping as you want more candied apples.

Yield: 18 apples.

Sesame Granola Bars

⅓ cup dates
⅔ cup butter
1 cup honey
2 cups rolled oats
¾ cup coconut
1½ cups sesame seeds
½ cup + 1 Tbs. whole wheat pastry flour
⅓ cup raisins

Preheat your oven to 325°. Chop the dates. Heat the butter and honey in a large saucepan until bubbly. Add the dry ingredients with a whisk and cook until thick like taffy. Add the raisins and dates. Oil your pan and spread your batter evenly. As the batter is very dry, it helps to use a dowel-type rolling pin to smooth and spread it evenly. Do not spread too thick as it will not bake properly. Bake for 15 minutes, until the edges are brown. The bars will harden as they cool. If undercooked they will be too moist. If overcooked, too crumbly. The bars are intended to be chewy.

Yield: One 12 x 16 in. tray.

Natural Cracker Jacks Popcorn

1 cup honey
½ cup molasses
5 quarts popcorn
2 cups roasted peanuts
2 cups pumpkin seeds or other nuts (optional)

Cook the honey and molasses til boiling. Simmer 10 minutes, stirring occasionally. Watch carefully, as this mixture tends to boil over easily. Pour over the mixture of popcorn and peanuts (and anything else you might like to try), and mix until the popcorn is well-coated. Allow it to cool. This can be left as a loose mix, or formed into balls while the mixture is still warm, but cooled enough to work with. Wet your hands under cold water each time before making each ball.

Yield: 22 cups.

Date Prasad

2 cups dates
¼ cup almonds
¼ cup cashews
¼ cup butter
½ cup honey
¾ cups milk powder

"Prasad" is food which has been blessed by the guru, or spiritual teacher, and is a blessing to those who partake of it. To make this prasad, chop the dates, almonds, and cashews. Then melt the butter in a large cast-iron frying pan or a large saucepan. Add the honey and dates, and cook to a mushy consistency. Sift in the milk powder. Stir this in well. Add the nuts and stir them in well. Press this mixture into an 8 x 8 in. cake pan, and slice into squares. Cool it in your refrigerator for 2 hours, then remove from the pan and serve. If the candy won't come out, place the pan in a hot oven for 1 to 2 minutes. For a variation, sprinkle the top of the candy with coconut before slicing, pressing it into the mixture so that it sticks.

Yield: One 8 x 8 in. pan.

Orange Almond Turkish Delight

1½ cups fresh orange juice
⅔ cup crushed almonds
½ cup honey
½ cup cold water
6 Tbs. arrowroot flour
1 tsp. arrowroot flour

Line the bottom and sides of an 8 x 8 in. cake pan with waxed paper. Sprinkle the bottom with arrowroot flour. Squeeze the orange juice. Place it in a saucepan and add the almonds and honey. Mix cold water with the arrowroot. Heat the orange juice mixture and slowly stir in the arrowroot. Stirring constantly, heat the mixture over a low to medium flame until it's *very* thick. Spoon the mixture into a pan. Smooth the top and sprinkle lightly with the remaining arrowroot flour. Refrigerate for at least 2 hours. Slice it into pieces and serve; it's a delicious and unusual treat for a change of pace dessert.

Yield: One 8 x 8 in. pan.

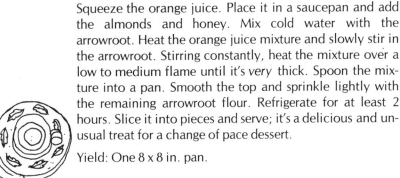

Peanut Clusters

3 Tbs. hot water
¼ cup molasses
½ cup honey
2 Tbs. lecithin
3 Tbs. peanut butter
⅔ cup milk powder
½ cup carob powder
1/8 tsp. salt
1½ cups roasted peanuts
⅔ cup raisins

Preheat your oven to 300°. Mix the first eight ingredients in a bowl, working them until smooth and stiff. Work in the peanuts and raisins. Spoon into 12 clusters and place on a lightly greased cookie sheet. Bake for 15 to 20 minutes. Allow to cool, and serve.

Yield: 12 clusters.

21·
Sprouting
and
Live Foods

Consider for a moment the tiny seed which holds in itself the potential to develop into a plant -- or a tree, or a melon ripening on a vine. All that is needed for life to germinate is within that seed, and when we allow the seed to sprout, and then eat it, its life-giving properties become ours. Likewise, when we grow and consume fragrant wheatgrass, renowned for its healing, restorative qualities, we join with nature in the exciting process of not only healthy eating but also the creation of a wholesome source of nutrition. Above all, growing our own food (indoors) is fun!

At the Retreat we grow trays upon trays of delicate sprouts -- mung beans, lentils, alfalfas -- and buckets of tiny sunflower seeds. We use different techniques according to the season of the year, creating an indoor "hothouse" effect with sunlight, several 60 watt bulbs, and the use of trays diagonally placed, facing the sun. Green wheatgrass trays can be seen in the windows of different residents' rooms, waiting to be cropped, and in the summertime many people contribute time and energy to cultivate outdoor wheatgrass plots.

Speaking of sprouts, you can experiment with different methods of sprouting and try sprouts in your salads, soups, sandwiches -- even desserts. Wheatgrass, on the other hand, is such a potent and con-centrated source of nourishment that you'll find it best taken alone once juiced. Many of our residents eschew coffee but take a daily 4-ounce wheatgrass juice "awakener", and that may be all they need for an energetic breakfast. Some wash it down with a rejuvelac "chaser" -- another enzyme food you'll have a chance to get acquainted with in this chapter. Enjoy this opportunity to make your home a garden, and with simple, standard equipment (jars, trays, etc.) convert ordinary seeds into living delectable sources of nourishment for you and your family! An additional word: although we present you with several different techniques for sprouting, growing wheatgrass and preparing rejuvelac, none of these live foods require a cumbersome time-consuming process. Once you've got the basic sprouting idea, it takes very little of your time and energy; just a vigilant eye and an occasional watering once or twice a day. That's a small price to pay when you consider the reward -- a live-foods harvest (with a ratio of 4:1 -- you get four times as many sprouts for the seeds you begin with) and a full regimen of protein, vitamins and minerals -- yours for the preparing. Now think about that on a cold winter's day when you're tired of canned goods and the market has nothing cheery in the produce department. Sprouts can be your fresh, growing greens -- year-round!

The most perfect "living" food available, sprouts are high in protein, vitamins and minerals, are easily digestible, and can be served in a wide variety of ways. In the sprouting process, complex starches are changed into simple sugars, which make the sprouts easier to digest. At the same time, sprouting improves the nutritional value of the seed by increasing the vitamin content from four to ten times!

"Researchers at the Universities of Pennsylvania, Minnesota, Yale and McGill have found that sprouts retain the B-complex vitamins present in the original seed and show a big jump in Vitamin A and an almost unbelievable amount of Vitamin C over that present in unsprouted seeds . . . the figures are impressive: an average 300 percent increase in Vitamin A and a 500 to 600 percent increase in Vitamin C. As a result, *one half cup of almost any sprouted seed provides as much Vitamin C as six glasses of orange juice . . . .*"[1] (italics ours).

Almost any natural seed will sprout. Generally the resultant sprout has a hint of the mother plant in its flavor. Radish sprouts are "radishy" and hot; sunflower sprouts taste nutty; soybean sprouts have a "beany" twang. You can experiment with whatever suits your fancy -- peanuts, lentils, mung beans, oats, rye, corn, fenugreek, red clover. Our perennial favorites and the year-round best bets in terms of good sprouting crops are alfalfa, mung bean and lentil sprouts.

When you begin sprouting, you'll need to be particular about what seeds you use. Seeds for sprouting must be of good quality, unbroken, free from insects, and, not treated by harmful chemicals (of extreme importance). *Never buy seed intended for agricultural use.* Heat-treated seeds, such as toasted sunflower seeds, will not sprout. Be sure to remove any bruised, broken or hulled seeds from your sprouting mixture.

Once your sprouts are completely sprouted, they can be stored in your refrigerator, just like any other fresh vegetable. They'll keep for several days to a week if properly covered. Use them in soups, salads, sandwiches and to enhance the flavor of cereals, blended drinks or salad dressings.

How to Sprout Seeds

Here are three sprouting methods which can be used:

JAR METHOD

1. Use a wide mouth jar which can be securely covered by a wire screen or a piece of cheesecloth. Secure to jar top with a strong rubber band.

2. Soak the seeds overnight in water (3 Tbs. alfalfa seeds to a quart jar).

3. Drain the water from the jar through a screen, cheesecloth or stocking, and rinse the seeds well.

4. Turn the jar upside down in a bowl and put in a dark, warm place.

5. Rinse the seeds two to four times a day. Keep the jar inverted and shake the seeds to evenly distribute them over the walls of the jar.

6. Most sprouts are ready to use when they are between ¼ and ½ inch long, although alfalfa sprouts are best when allowed to grow to about 1½ inches. After two days, put the sprouts in the sun to develop a bright green color and increase their Vitamin A and chlorophyll content.

PAN METHOD

1. Soak the seeds overnight.

2. Drain the seeds, rinsing them well, and spread them thinly and evenly on the bottom of a glass pan.

3. Sprinkle the seeds generously with water two or three times a day, covering them with a wet cheesecloth and keeping the pan in a warm, dark place.

4. In four to five days, your seeds will have sprouted and will be ready for eating.

STRAINER METHOD

1. Soak the seeds overnight.

2. Line a colander or wire strainer with cheesecloth.

3. Put the soaked seeds in the colander or strainer, cover with a cloth and put them in a warm, dark place.

4. Run cold water over the seeds two or three times a day until they have sprouted.

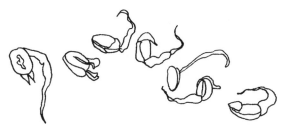

Sprouting Tips

1. Do not soak the seeds more than one time. Large seeds may be soaked up to twenty hours, but small seeds need to be soaked only 3 or 4 hours. Be sure to use plenty of water when soaking seeds.

2. Use high quality seeds. Seeds which are broken or bruised will not germinate.

3. If sprouts are damaged in handling, they will become rotten.

4. If poorly drained, sprouts may become waterlogged and rotten.

5. Be sure to rinse the seeds 2 to 4 times a day. If the seeds are not rinsed, they will become dehydrated and die.

6. Keep sprouting containers in a warm, dark spot during sprouting. If sprouting seeds are kept in an overly warm area they may rot.

Grow Your Own Wheatgrass

A true wonder food, wheatgrass is reputed to have therapeutic effects upon the body. Many digestive enzymes, killed by the ingestion of unnatural foods or poor food combinations, as well as by chemicals in our foods, can be rebuilt by juice made from wheatgrass. Full of chlorophyll, wheatgrass juice is a neutralizing agent which corrects the acid-alkaline balance of the body, helps enhance the body's healing powers and works in a cleansing, rejuvenating manner within the body. A poultice of wheatgrass helps a cut or burn heal more quickly, helps skin sores, relieves the pain of bee stings and the itch of bug bites. Wheatgrass pulp has an absorbent property; it is reputed to withdraw toxic material from the body's tissues. Wheatgrass juice makes an excellent gargle for a sore throat and relieves indigestion, sluggishness and respiratory ailments as well. Daily users of wheatgrass constantly discover new healing properties of this wonder food.

Wheatgrass can easily be grown in your own home; you'll need wheat seeds, trays, soil and plastic bags. Using shallow trays or pans, spread one inch of good quality earth over the bottom of each tray. Soak the wheat seeds for 12-16 hours, then rinse and thoroughly drain them. Let them stand for a day in the soaking jar, as you would if you were growing sprouts. Then evenly spread soaked wheat seeds over the soil, one or two layers deep. Place the tray in a plastic bag to achieve a greenhouse effect, keeping one end of the bag open so that air may circulate over the seeds, to avoid mildew. Sprinkle daily with plain water (or water mixed with a tablespoon of kelp for added nutrition). Remove the plastic bag after the grass is 2 inches long, and place the tray in a window that gets only a moderate amount of sunlight. In 7 to 14 days, your grass will be 5-8 inches long and ready for harvest. When harvesting wheatgrass, cut only what you can use immediately, as the vitamins in wheatgrass are destroyed by prolonged exposure to oxygen. The top 2 inches of the grass are the most nutritious.

If the seeds have been soaked too long or if the soil is too wet, the seeds may fail to sprout properly. If there is insufficient circulation of air, mold may grow on your soil and on the wheatgrass itself. Grass which is yellow or poor in color needs more light, and you may want to add a 40-watt light bulb in your wheatgrass area if it is too cold.

How to Use Wheatgrass

There are several ways in which you can extract the vitamins, minerals and enzymes from the wheatgrass once it is ready to be harvested (5-8 in. tall).

You can make a vitalizing, high-nutrition wheatgrass juice using a simple kitchen blender and your wheatgrass. Cut a handful of grass, cutting close to the plant roots, and simply blend with about a cup of water. Strain the pulp, drink the juice, and hear your cells clapping for joy.

Wheatgrass juice contains so much chlorophyll and other nutrients that it is not advisable to drink more than a cup at a time, or you may feel "buzzy" afterwards. Using the blender method, some of the nutrients are lost through oxidation; however, this is still an effective way to derive the health-giving properties of wheatgrass in a refreshing drink. The pulp has many healing qualities and has been proven an effective healer in minor skin conditions, cuts, sores and other minor topical ailments.

THE WHEATGRASS JUICER

Once you are a wheatgrass afficionado, you may wish to invest in a commercial wheatgrass juicer. A hand-powered tool for extracting the juices from wheatgrass, the juicer yields a much higher proportion of nutrients in the grass, as nothing is lost through oxidation, as it is with the blender method. The juice extracted is pure and undiluted; take only a *very* small amount, say ¼ cup per juicing, to avoid too strong an effect on the body and nerves. You will find your natural limits as you experiment with the juice. To obtain a wheatgrass juicer check with your local health food store; be sure you specify a wheatgrass juicer and not simply a commercial vegetable juicer.

The "grazing" method is the old fashioned way -- very good for the jaw muscles, gums and teeth -- and otherwise known as chewing. Simply cut a small bunch and chew it until the flavor's gone. The wheatgrass juices will be taken directly into your system.

For best results you should drink wheatgrass juice daily, preferably on an empty stomach. It's often helpful to follow it with rejuvelac or a glass of water. Some people have found it easier to accustom themselves to the taste of the juice by diluting it with water. Once you become accustomed to the taste you will find it delicious and amazingly sweet. Consult Ann Wigmore's *Be Your Own Doctor* for further information and understanding of the healthful benefits of wheatgrass juice.

Rejuvelac

An easy to prepare, high quality enzyme drink, rejuvelac is helpful in stimulating digestion and helping to maintain healthy intestinal flora. Through the presence of various enzymes, as well as pre-digested proteins, rejuvelac helps activate digestion and promotes the growth of healthful as opposed to harmful bacteria. Another "wonder" food, rejuvelac is high in Vitamins E and K and most of the B-vitamins, and supplies a plentiful source of pre-digested sugars, amino acids and other minerals and enzymes. We use rejuvelac as our starter for seed cheese, and it can also be substituted for water in most of our fruit drinks or smoothies.

To make rejuvelac, soak 1 cup of wheatberries in 4-5 cups of water for 16-24 hours. Pour off the water and drink it. Rinse the berries, refill your jar with water and repeat the next day. You can use the same berries for 4 days before composting. Drink the rejuvelac several times a day to increase your digestive powers and add healthful enzymes to your system. Try some rejuvelac or leftover sprout soak water on ailing plants -- they'll love it too!

Sumneytown Seed Cheese

Starter batch:
1¼ cups sunflower seeds
½ cup sesame seeds
2 cups rejuvelac

Regular batch:
4 cups sunflower seeds
(or combined sun and sesame)
½ cup nutritional yeast

3/8 cup tamari
3 cups water
2 Tbs. seed cheese starter

This is an excellent recipe for a raw, non-dairy "cheese", pioneered by our fellow cooks Narendra and Parmananda from our Sumneytown family. Seed cheese is a power-packed nutritional food, with lots of protein, B-vitamins, minerals and enzymes, easy to digest and tasty as well. Very simple to make, seed cheese is similar to any enzymatic food preparation where you must ferment a particular culture (such as yogurt, kefir, sourdough, etc.). Once you have a starter, you keep adding portions of it to further recipes of the seed cheese, remembering to replenish the starter from time to time, and to watch for freshness.

In the starter batch, simply blend together the various seeds with rejuvelac water. Place the mixture in a covered bowl and leave it in a warm place for 18-20 hours. The longer the mixture ferments, the "cheesier" it becomes in flavor. (The top may be somewhat darker, due to the oxidation process. No need to worry, just blend it into the rest of the seed cheese.) After 18-20 hours, strain off the water and save some of the cheese for your next starter batch. Then for the second batch -- or any batch to follow, blend the sunflower seeds with your starter batch, yeast, tamari, and water. Or use different variants -- sunflower seeds tend to make the cheese sweeter in flavor, sesame makes it more bitter. You might try 3 parts sunflower seeds to 1 part sesame seeds.

After you've gotten a very thick, rich blend (the yeast helps thicken it a lot) place the mixture in a piece of cheesecloth and hang it up where it can lazily drip away (12-15 hours in a very warm place, 18-20 hours if it is a bit cooler.) Naturally you'll place a pan or bowl underneath to catch the drippings. These are wonderful to add to your soup, stock or Saturday night stew. Then at the end you'll have a nice lumpy cheese -- and lo and behold -- made without using milk. This is a very healthful, nutritious snack or meal in itself. Try it also with other dips, crackers and raw vegetables. You can store it refrigerated for 5-7 days; it will become more pronounced in flavor, or "cheesier", as time goes by.

Yield: 4 cups.

Sprouting Chart

	Seeds used	Sprout yield	Desired length	# Rinses per day	Sprouting Time	Comments
Alfalfa & clover seeds	1 cup	1½ gal.	1-2 in.	2-3	5 days	If exposed to light *before* the final stage, they tend to go limp. Can grow one or two inches covered, then mist them, cover with saran wrap on flat trays and expose to indirect sunlight for one day.
Chick peas (soy & other legumes)	1 cup	3 cups	½-¾ in.	4x or more	3 days	Rinse frequently or they may mold or spoil.
Lentils	1 cup	6 cups	¾ in.	2-3x	3-4 days	Very hardy and easy to grow.
Mung Beans	1 cup	4 cups	2	3-4x	3-4 days	Very perishable in warm weather. Rinse often. Short mung sprouts are sweeter than long ones.
Peas	1 cup	2 cups	¼-½ in.	2-3x	3-4 days	Like their legume friends, they require frequent rinses to avoid molding.
Sunflower seeds	1 cup	3 cups	¼-½ in.	2-3x	24-30 hrs.	In warm weather, rinse frequently to prevent spoilage. Superb nutty flavor.
Wheat & Rye Berries	1 cup	4 cups	¼-½ in	2-3x	3-4 days	Inexpensive high-yield chewy sprouts.

22·
Holiday and Ethnic Cuisine

At Kripalu Retreat, every season gives us cause for celebration. We honor both Judeo-Christian traditions as well as Indian observances, thus doubling and tripling our times of joy. Our calendar year is chock full of surprises: in December we celebrate Christ's birth and the Jewish Festival of Lights, Chanukah, in late February, Shivaratri, or the celebration honoring Shiva, the Hindu deity. Passover . . . Easter . . . July 4th . . . and in August, the birthday of Krishna -- all are feted with happy observance. For us, the highlight of the year comes in July on Guru Purnima, the highly revered Indian pilgrimage day, in which disciples traditionally come to honor their teachers, bringing all manner of gifts and flowers in an offering of loving homage and thankfulness.

With such a full calendar, we celebrate and bring alive many occasions in true ecumenical spirit. Along with observance, tradition and sharing, holidays call for many culinary celebrations. Some of our most creative, tasty menus have sprung up during holiday seasons. Now they're included here for you to sample.

Food is deeply woven into the fabric of many holiday experiences. What would Passover be without matzoh, or Christmas without cut-out iced cookies? As vegetarians, we artfully play with traditional foods and have found pleasing substitutes for the old inseparables: Thanksgiving and turkey, July 4th and barbecue, Easter and Easter chocolate eggs. Try our Barbecued Tofu, Hot Cross Buns, or millet stuffing listed on our holiday menu.

We've also included a host of international festive meals with which you can experiment, provided of course, that you go all out for the occasion! We enjoy making our meal into a work of art. At a Chinese meal, for instance, we adorned our tables with cut paper lanterns, chopsticks and tiny bowls of rice, playing delicate Zen koto music in the background. A French dinner featured kitchen guest staff "chefs" with gourmet hats and silk scarves, gallantly cooking crepes on inverted wrought-iron pans and serving them up with flamboyance and French accents -- and saucey French sauces besides. So come celebrate with us on these final pages and let every meal be your holiday and "cause celebre". Listed below are a series of menu ideas for the various holidays, as well as ethnic cuisine suggestions. All recipes are found in our cookbook. Joyeux Noel! Jai Sri Krishna! Jai Bhagwan!*

*Jai Bhagwan: Indian expression meaning, "I bow to God within you"; used as a greeting at Kripalu Retreat.

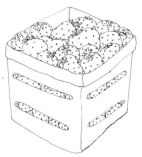

Holiday Fare

See index for page number of each recipe.

Children's Halloween Party
Hot apple cider
Squash pie
Natural Cracker Jacks Popcorn
Peanut Butter Swirl Bars

Thanksgiving Dinner
Millet Stuffing
Tofu Marinade
Mashed Potatoes with Country Style Gravy
Carrot-raisin Salad
Pecan Pie
Blue Mt. Herb Tea

Chanukah Dinner
Hot Beet Borscht
Tofu Spread (a la Chicken liver . . .)
Potato Latkes and sour cream
Cider Beans
Holiday Apple Cake
Soy Coffee with
Soy Whipped Cream

Easter Breakfast
Hot Cross Buns
Choice of:
Apple Butter
Creamy Date and Nut Spread
Nisha's Fruited Jello
Chamomile Tea

Christmas Dinner
Yam Casserole
Chickpea Patties with Tahini Sauce
Sunny Bean Casserole
Soy Mocha Ice Bean
Assorted Cookies
Nut Logs
Christmas Tea

New Year's Buffet
Choice of Dips:
Mala Bean Dip
Seed Cheese and Olive Slices
Pleasing Peas-Tomato Dip
Sesame Crackers and Bali's Rye toasted
Narendra's Knockout Pizza
Salad with Carrotbeet Dressing
At 12 Midnight:
Yog Nog and Crumbly Coffee Cake

Ethnic Feasts

See Index for page number of each recipe.

Fourth of July Picnic
Barbecued Tofu and Barbecue Sauce
Raisin Sun Slaw
Tater Salad
Marinated Rice and Bean Salad
Banana Cheese Cake
(with blueberries and strawberries
for the Red, White and Blue)
Iced Spearmint Tea

Oriental
Sweet n' Sour Cabbage
Chinese Egg Rolls
Feast of Wok Veggies
Szechuan Eggplant and Tofu
Ginger Tea and Fortune Cookies

Mexican
Baked Mexicali Casserole
Tacos and Refried Beans
Tapas Taco Sauce
Guacamole
Sparkling Perrier Water with a twist of lemon

French
Crepes with Sauteed Tofu
Ratatouille
Green Beans Vinaigrette
Cafe Au Lait

Middle East
Hummus with chopped mint leaves
Veggie Shish-Kabob
with Pita Bread
Marinated 3-Bean Salad
Spearmint Tea with honey

Italian
Ziti (Italian Noodles)
with Jashoda's Spaghetti Sauce
Spinach Salad
Italian Broccoli Dressing
Zucchini sauteed in Herb Butter
Italian Ice

Spanish
Sunseed Gazpacho
Spanish Rice
Golden Breaded Carrots
Herbed bread and butter
Heated Vanilla Pudding
(To make it like "flan", a traditional Spanish
custard, add lots of cinnamon and honey
and heat up)

Indian (Krishna's Birthday Feast)
Rice Pulau
Red Lentil Dahl
Curried Cauliflower
Cucumber Raita
Carrot Chutney
Chai Tea

Indian (Guru Purnima Dinner)
Horish
Beet Raita
Curried Celery and Carrots
Chappatis
Lassi Drink

Greek
Spanakopita
Greek Salad
Chick Pea Delight
Dates, figs and almonds
Baklava
Grain Coffee

Suggested
Reading

Airola, Paavo. *Are You Confused?* Health Plus Publications, Arizona, 1971.

Brown, Edward. *The Tassajara Bread Book*. Shambhala Publications, Colorado, 1970.

Cottrell, Edith Young. *The Peas, Beans & Barley Cookbook*. Woodbridge Press, California, 1974.

Duffy, William. *Sugar Blues*. Warner Press, New York, 1975.

Fredericks, Carlton. *High Fiber Way to Total Health*. Pocket Books, New York, 1976.

Gibbons, Euell. *Stalking the Healthful Herbs*. David McKay Co., New York, 1966.

Goldbeck, Nikki and David. *The Supermarket Handbook*. Signet Books, New York, 1976.

Heriteau, Jacqueline. *Grow It and Cook It* , Ballantine Books, New York, 1970.

Hurd, Frank and Rosalie. *Ten Talents Cookbook*. The College Press, Minnesota, 1968.

Jones, Dorothea Van Gurdy. *The Soybean Cookbook*. Arc. Books Inc., New York, 1971.

Lappe, Frances Moore. *Diet For A Small Planet*. Ballantine Books, New York, 1971.

Ohsawa, Georges. *Zen Macrobiotics*. Ohsawa Foundation, California, 1965.

Robertson, L., Flinders, C., and Godfrey, B. *Laurel's Kitchen*. Nilgiri Press, California, 1976.

Rodale, Robert, Ed. *The Basic Book of Organic Gardening*. Rodale Press, Ballantine Books, N.Y., 1971.

The Self-Health Guide: A Personal Program of Holistic Living. Kripalu Center for Holistic Health. Pennsylvania, 1980.

Shurtleff, W. and Aoyagi, A. *The Book of Tofu*. Autumn Press, 1975.

Smith, Frederick. *Journal of a Fast*. Schocken Books, New York, 1972.

Index

Bibliography

Airola, Paavo. *Are You Confused?* Health Plus Publications, Arizona, 1971.

Ballentine, Rudolph, M.D. *Diet and Nutrition.* Himalayan Institute, Honesdale, Pennslyvania, 1978.

Cochrane, William. *The World Food Problem.* Thomas Y. Crowell, Inc., New York, 1969.

Hunter, Beatrice. *The Natural Foods Primer.* Simon and Schuster, New York, 1972.

Jones, Dorothea Van Gurdy. *The Soybean Cookbook.* Arc Books, Inc., New York, 1971.

Krischmann, John, Ed. *Nutrition Almanac.* McGraw Hill, New York, 1979.

Lappe, Frances M. *Diet for a Small Planet.* Ballantine Books, New York, 1971.

Leonard, J., Hofer, J., and Pritikin, N. *Live Longer Now.* Grosset and Dunlap, Canada, 1974.

Monroe, Esther. *Sprouts to Grow and Eat.* The Stephen Green Press, Brattleboro, Vermont, 1974.

Null, Gary and Null, Steve. *How to Get Rid of the Poisons in Your Body.* Arco Publishing, New York, 1977.

Pfeiffer, Carl, M.D. *Mental and Elemental Nutrients.* Keats Publishing Co., Connecticut, 1975.

Rodale, J.I. et al. *The Complete Book of Food and Nutrition.* Rodale Books, Emmaus, Pennsylvania, 1971.

Shelton, Herbert. *Fasting Can Save Your Life.* Natural Hygiene Press, Chicago, 1978.

Shurtleff, W. and Aoyagi, A. *The Book of Tofu.* Autumn Press, 1975.

Walker, N.W. *Fresh Vegetables and Fruit Juices.* Norwalk Press, Arizona, 1978.

Whitney, E. and Hamilton, E. *Understanding Nutrition.* West Publishing Co., New York, 1977.

Wigmore, Ann. *Be Your Own Doctor.*

Notes

Chapter Three

1. Frances M. Lappe, *Diet for a Small Planet,* pp. 10-11.

2. William Shurtleff & Akiko Aoyagi, *The Book of Tofu,* p. 15.

3. *Ibid,* p. 16.

4. Leonard Pritikin, et al, *Live Longer Now,* p.24. Many studies now back these conclusions. A 4-year study involving 3,182 men in San Francisco showed that men whose cholesterol and fat levels were high had 5 times as great a chance of suffering a heart attack as men who had low levels of both fats and cholesterol.

5. Rudolph Ballentine, *Diet and Nutrition,* p. 119.

6. *Ibid,* p. 117.

Chapter Four

1. Expeller pressed oils: oils extracted from the product with pressure and a minimum of heat. The oils are pressed, settled and bottled with no other processing or chemical additives.

2. Tempeh: a cultured soy product, used in much the same way as tofu, it has the additional benefit of high quality enzymes and B-vitamins, due to the culturing process.

3. Wheatgrass, rejuvelac: live enzymes foods; see Chapter 22 for further explanation.

Chapter Eight

1. A.A. Milne, *The House at Pooh Corner,* p.32.

Chapter 15

1. John Fogg, "Milk: Moo Glue" *East-West Journal* , July 1978, p. 32.

Chapter 19

1. N.W. Walker, *Fresh Vegetables and Fruit Juices.*

Chapter Twenty

A.A. Milne, *Winnie the Pooh,* p.26.

Chapter Twenty One

1. Munroe, Esther, *Sprouts to Grow and Eat.*

About Kripalu Center

Located among the Berkshire mountains of western Massachusetts, Kripalu Center offers a variety of health holidays, educational programs and individual health services throughout the year. Our 200-member residential staff provides a setting which is uniquely supportive for bringing body, mind and spirit into the balance that is true health.

The basis of our approach is the ancient tradition of yoga and its principle that physical health is the foundation for emotional and spiritual development. Our programs and services combine time-tested yoga practices with more recently developed techniques in holistic health. They each provide experiential learning and first-hand knowledge of vibrant, comprehensive well-being along with practical methods for living a health-enhancing lifestyle at home.

Weekend, week-long and four-week programs focus on self-development through yoga, stress management, fitness, bodywork training and spiritual attunement. Our programs are excellent both for health professionals who want to expand the scope of their services and for individuals who, no matter what their background or occupation, want to derive more satisfaction and joy from their lives. Our guests can also individualize their visit, choosing from a wide range of classes, activities and facilities such as sauna, whirlpool, flotation tank and lakefront swimming.

From left to right: Chitra, Parimala, and Sukanya.

About The Authors

JoAnn Levitt (Parimala) came to Kripalu Retreat in 1974 from her work as a Registered Nurse, Spanish translator, and footloose traveler to experience yogic living. Her perceptive and caring energies have expressed themselves in her Retreat work as a women's counselor, Programs Director and skillful holistic health teacher. (Parimala's "de-stressing recipe": 1 part detached self-observation, 2 parts one-pointed activity, and 3 parts deep breathing in the form of belly laughter.) When not concocting culinary offerings in the kitchen, she provides a range of health services and counseling to our guests.

Linda Smith (Chitra) came to Kripalu Retreat in 1976 from her work as a yoga instructor and teacher of pre-schoolers. Moving from woodshop apprentice to staff coordinator, Chitra landed in Kripalu Kitchen, where her natural affinity for healthful cooking and serving others came into full play. Eventually coordinating a full-time staff of 8, Chitra's skills as nutritional consultant, teacher, staff coordinator and gentle "mom" -- caring for each and everyone -- blossomed fully. Chitra also currently teaches nutrition and health seminars and works with Resident Life Programs at Kripalu Retreat.

Lover of the outdoors and the spontaneous and artful in life, Christine Warren (Sukanya) brings to Kripalu Retreat a sensitive awareness that mark her as resident artist. Since 1974 she has contributed to the Retreat community -- gardening, counseling, and teaching, and serving as graphic designer and writer. At present, Sukanya teaches Outreach Seminars in Self-Development across the U.S., demonstrating the same love of life and artistry in her teaching as in the illustrations which grace this book.

*Work
is love
made visible.
Keep working with love.*